Feeding Istanbul

Studies in Critical Social Sciences

Series Editor

David Fasenfest

(*Wayne State University*)

VOLUME 186

New Scholarship in Political Economy

Series Editors

David Fasenfest
(*Wayne State University*)
Alfredo Saad-Filho
(*King's College London*)

Editorial Board

VOLUME 5

The titles published in this series are listed at *brill.com/nspe*

Feeding Istanbul

The Political Economy of Urban Provisioning

By

Candan Turkkan

BRILL

LEIDEN | BOSTON

Cover illustration: Bust of Karl Marx, 1939, by S.D. Merkurov, at the Fallen Monument Park (Muzeon Park of Arts) in Moscow, Russia. Photo courtesy of Alfredo Saad-Filho.

Library of Congress Cataloging-in-Publication Data

Names: Turkkan, Candan, author.
Title: Feeding Istanbul : the political economy of urban provisioning / by Candan Turkkan.
Description: Leiden ; Boston : Brill, 2021. | Series: Studies in critical social sciences, 2666-2205;
    volume 186 | Includes bibliographical references and index.
Identifiers: LCCN 2021006234 (print) | LCCN 2021006235 (ebook) | ISBN 9789004424517 (hardback) |
    ISBN 9789004424500 (ebook)
Subjects: LCSH: Food supply–Turkey–Istanbul–History–19th century. |
    Istanbul (Turkey)–Economic conditions–19th century. |
    Istanbul (Turkey)–Politics and government–19th century.
Classification: LCC HD9016.T93 I888 2021 (print) | LCC HD9016.T93 (ebook) |
    DDC 338.1/94961809034–dc23
LC record available at https://lccn.loc.gov/2021006234
LC ebook record available at https://lccn.loc.gov/2021006235

Typeface for the Latin, Greek, and Cyrillic scripts: "Brill". See and download: brill.com/brill-typeface.

ISSN 2666-2205
ISBN 978-90-04-42451-7 (hardback)
ISBN 978-90-04-42450-0 (e-book)

Contents

Acknowledgements

There are many people I would like to thank and acknowledge here; and though I am the author, I feel that they have contributed as much, if not more.

At the top of this long list of people, is Samarjit Ghosh. Not only did he read my copious chapters several times, he also copyedited them. He listened to my ideas, and my frequent rants about the state of contemporary politics and economy, wherever we and our families and friends happen to be. I know that without his unwavering support, this book would not have been possible. I have much to thank him for, and this book is definitely high on that list (his patience with me is a very close second).

Next are my two incredible research assistants: Elif Birbiri and Alperen Buğra Yılmaz. They read the chapters, checked for citations, compiled the index – and they did all the work necessary for me to be able to include the photographs spread liberally all over the book. This was no small or easy task: They went through quite a few public libraries and some private ones (!) and persuaded many stubborn copyright holders for rights. I cannot believe how lucky I am to have worked with them.

Following is my incredible librarian, Neslihan Yalav at Istanbul Kitaplığı. She was such a tremendous help during the research process that at this point, frankly, I cannot imagine working on any project without her. She gave me access to an incredible collection of books on Istanbul, and put me in touch with key informants, whose insights enabled me to get a comprehensive look at the city's contemporary provisioning apparatus.

On that note, I am thankful to all the informants who were kind enough to talk to me about how Istanbul is provisioned. In particular, I should mention Serdar Manioğlu. Thanks to Serdar Bey, I was able to find key informants, who filled me in on the critical gaps in the city's contemporary food supply chain; the kinds of gaps that do not meet the eyes or ears of the general public – the dirty secrets, the cut corners, and the backdoors. I am thankful for their candor as well as their trust in me.

Lastly, I would like to thank my family. I know it has been a long, bumpy road. But without Grandma Müşerref's obsession with storing food in the freezer, my sister's consistent questions, my father's love of good food, and my mom's relentless efforts to figure out what it is that I have been working on for so long, I know I would not have held out as long as I have been able to. You all have made me stronger. Thank you for helping me make all of this happen. This book is for you.

Of the family, and deserving his very own special paragraph, is Mr. ShiroKuro; who has, irrespective of the circumstances, steadfastly reminded me that 7 PM is feeding time, and that even if the world is burning, food needs to be had. No matter how widely I read about hunger, famines, malnourishment, as well as gastronomy, food culture, and history, my insights on food never seem to even come close to his simple yet deep connection to food. One has to merely see him eat chicken, his all-time favorite, with such pure joy and concentration, to be mesmerized with and intellectually intrigued by food and eating. I thank him for teaching me and for awakening me to the sharp and intimate separation between the hunger for and the pleasure of food.

Benjamin Nolan and Shai Gortler read and gave me extensive comments on earlier versions of Chapter 1. Duygu Beykal İz and Murat Bayramoğlu read the whole manuscript and gave me comments and ideas. Nilhan Aras and Özge Samancı have given me ample space and opportunity to explore and articulate my thoughts and findings on the subject in much shorter pieces for *MetroGastro* and *Yemek ve Kültür*, respectively.

Errors remain mine, and mine alone.

Figures and Tables

Figures

Tables

Introduction

> Capitalism was born when market imperatives seized hold of food production, the provision of life's most irreducible necessity. (...) We should not take for granted that extensive commerce even in the most basic necessities always carries with it the imperatives of competitive production, profit-maximization, and the relentless development of the productive forces.[1]
>
> ELLEN MEIKSINS WOOD

∴

I come from a family of bread eaters. My family won't admit it – since it is now accepted wisdom that the increased consumption of sugars and carbohydrates is not the best for the body – but my parents, my sister, and my Grandma, all love to eat bread, as much as they can, in every meal of the day; and sometimes in-between the meals as well, as an accessory to whatever sweet or savory item they are snacking on. Bread is a fundamental component of their diet. For Grandma, bread is more than fundamental; it is existential. My sister and my parents will not have bread when there are other major starches around (rice or pasta, for example), but my Grandma will. She will happily devour slices of bread even when she is eating her beloved *erişte*. Regardless of how hard it is, how stale it has become, brown or white, multigrain or plain or nutty – so long as there is no mold on it, Grandma will consume every single morsel of bread she can get her hands on.

If you were to pester her about why she eats bread with everything or how she can tolerate the taste of stale bread, she will berate you with stories from her childhood – stories of scarcity and the adjoining pain of hunger. "You didn't see it," she would say in her usual solemn voice, "my mother would beg the soldiers for their share of bread. If she could get any, she wouldn't eat it herself. She would give it to us". Even before the "Great War", as she calls World

---

1 Meiksins Wood, Ellen. 2017. *The Origin of Capitalism: A Longer View.* New York, NY: Verso, 81.

War II, my Grandma saw her younger sister die soon after she was born, simply
because there wasn't enough food to go around:

> We didn't have much to eat then. My father paid the penalty and didn't let
> me go to school so that I could work in the fields. I was in the 3rd grade.
> When there was scarcity, my parents would go through the horse dung
> to find undigested kernels of barley. You don't know what hunger is like.
> May *Allah* never show us those days again. May *Allah* protect us all.

Now at the age of 85, her fear of hunger and scarcity is still so strong that she
stocks the freezer with bread. The household may run out of other foods, but
so long as my Grandma is around, it will never run out of bread.

Turkey did not fight in the "Great War". By the time the country officially
signed up on the side of the Allied Powers, the war was on its way out. Still,
with almost all its neighbors invaded and in disarray, it spent four hard years
directing its meager resources to fund the war effort, in addition to deploying
most of its young adult men. In a country still mostly rural, this meant a significant reduction in agricultural labor power, which in turn, meant reduced
yields for consecutive years. While scarcity was not elevated to famine, it
was still widespread and prominent enough to leave its mark. Unfortunately,
importing food was also not an option. The war had disrupted production patterns and blocked shipment routes all around. Plus, in a context of spiraling
exchange rates, the barely accumulated financial reserves were allocated to
supply the needs of the military. In fact, to generate more revenue, the government imposed higher taxes across the board – which forced the rural populations to stretch further their already insufficient means, and hit the urban
populations with price increases on whatever commodities were still available
in the market. In other words, between the tax hikes that left the countryside
depleted and the rations that left the city folk hungry and wanting, people suffered through a "Great War" that the country did not even fight in.

My Grandma's experiences are neither unique, nor are they recorded in the
annals of history, never to be repeated. We know that food scarcity and hunger
has kept our species company for most of our time on the planet. Even today,
behind the façade of abundance our local supermarkets put up, there lies a
fragile apparatus. Actors with conflicting interests, located in various parts of
the world, subject to diverse macroeconomic dynamics, and utilizing different tools and practices, need to work together seamlessly to deliver food to us.
Moreover, they need to do this more and more efficiently, as the world population continues to increase. For those of us who live in dense, crowded cities,
the fragile apparatus they constitute is also our lifeline. While stocked shelves,

a diversity of products, and frozen, canned, and ready-to-eat conveniences reassure us of the resilience of our food system, it does not take much to make the precarity of the whole apparatus blatantly obvious. A delayed delivery[2], a particularly brutal hurricane[3] or even a steep rise in oil prices can easily prove to us that my Grandma's stories are not relics of the past.

This is not a book about scarcity, however. It is not meant to tell you what to do in the event of scarcity or how to prepare for an expected spell of scarcity or even how to read for signs of scarcity coming your way. Rather, it is a book about how food scarcity – particularly urban food scarcity – is avoided and why that matters. It explains how different food regimes dealt with food scarcity, and in doing so, the kinds of tensions and conflicts they had to wrestle with and the sorts of practices, mechanisms, and tools they established and maintained to do so. It also traces the transformation of food scarcity from an everyday, public concern to a discussion on social policy that targets only low-income households. Indeed, just a few centuries ago, fears over looming hunger – signaled by rising prices and empty stores – could easily topple rulers. For example, a prince unable to secure provisions for his city was likely to face a mutiny, or see his city fall to his enemies; whereas, as Machiavelli reminds us, cities that "ensure[d] that their public storehouses contain enough food, drink and fuel to last for a year" (Machiavelli 2016, 38) could maintain their independence from sneaky neighbors and powerful emperors alike. How did this change come to pass? What happened to the princes, sultans, emperors – rulers – who ensured that public storehouses were full? How about the *public* storehouses themselves – where did they go? More importantly, how do our cities and towns remain so quiet today, given that segments of our populations consistently battle food scarcity? When did the act of ensuring that we have enough to eat become solely our responsibility as individuals? These are the primary questions this book is going to answer.

For Turkey, the answers partially lie in the long 19th century. On the one hand, the Ottoman Empire liberalized its economy, through a series of trade agreements with major and minor European states: customs taxes were decreased or removed altogether; price controls were eliminated; exports and imports increased significantly; and farming communities near port cities and railway lines shifted, from producing for sustenance and domestic consumption to producing for export. As a result, a two-tier system began to emerge: those regions and classes of people who produced for foreign markets and were

---

2   See, for example, the recent KFC crisis in the UK (Waever 2018).
3   Damage caused by Hurricane Maria (2017) in Puerto Rico and the Caribbean at large is a clear example.

much more integrated with the Europe-dominated world economy, and those who produced for the domestic market and were more sheltered from the creeping shift to the capitalist mode of production. The difference between the two groups, however, did not lay solely in their target customers. They were also distinguished from each other by the socio-cultural norms they abided by, ideals they were influenced by, and the discourses they utilized, as much as they were by disparities in wealth and purchasing power. In other words, as a result of this two-tier economic system, it was almost as if two socio-culturally distinct populations resided in the Empire. On the other hand, the peripheries – the regions that fed the Empire for all this time – were in disarray. Peoples in the Balkans, the Caucasus, the Middle East, and North Africa, were either seceding and/or were being colonized by European imperial forces. Those running away from the turmoil were headed to territories still under Ottoman sovereignty; while others, worried about rising ethno-nationalist tensions within the Empire, were fleeing the very same territories. Regional wars, armed conflicts, and rebellions were pervasive; and agricultural production was faltering.

It was under these conditions that 'public storehouses', as Machiavelli calls them, started disappearing. The dismantling of price controls effectively meant that prices would fluctuate based on global market rates, and accessibility of foods came to depend solely on the purchasing power of households. Yet the availability of food in the market itself was also an issue. While imports could – in theory – make up for the deficiency in the aggregate customarily procured from the seceding, or seized, peripheries, reliance on them was not sustainable: wars disrupted trade routes; local conflicts interrupted production patterns; the rapid devaluation of the Ottoman currency made imports too expensive; and most importantly, such reliance gave the traders an unwieldy power over the Ottoman sultans that went right through the subjects' stomachs. Though cities and towns were not quiet in the face of this new sense of subjection to the market, rising voices did not necessarily prioritize food scarcity. The Empire was falling apart; and maintaining sovereignty over the territories took precedence. Making sure that the peoples living in those territories could continue to live – that is, have enough food to survive – was, bizarrely, not a priority.

My Grandma's childhood memories from World War II are glimpses into a time when these series of transformations left the population stuck with a seriously flawed food regime; and hunger and scarcity were its consequences. Today, the situation is not as dire for as many people. Nevertheless, for certain populations, scarcity, even in the midst of abundance, continues to be chronic.

To better understand how we got here, and why the changes in the long 19th century were particularly acute, it is necessary to go back to the 1500s,

FIGURE 1   During WWII, the Turkish Red Crescent was one of the main organizations that
            did extensive provisioning and rationing work, in Istanbul and beyond
            PHOTO COURTESY OF THE CENGIZ KAHRAMAN ARCHIVE

when the proto-capitalist market economy began forming in Europe and its
colonies, and began destabilizing the Empire. Though I will make comparisons
from that history along the way, my focus will remain primarily on Istanbul
and Istanbul's provisioning apparatus. This is not an arbitrary choice: Istanbul
was the capital of an empire which, like the mighty Roman Empire, spawned
over the Balkans, the Eastern Mediterranean, North Africa and the Levant[4];
and it served as a major hub that connected these vast territories and their
peoples. On a larger scale, it was a port city that delivered to Europe the luxuries of the Spice and Silk Routes, and as such, functioned as a bridge between
world empires. A major trading post for the pre-capitalist long distance trade,
the city of Istanbul witnessed – first-hand – the shift of trade routes from the
Mediterranean to the Atlantic, and the accompanying changes in modes of
production and relations of exchange. Finally, like any city that contains the
seat of power of a sovereign entity, it was subject to certain specific dynamics

4   This correlation with Rome is not incidental. Ottoman sultans were known to profess their
    descent from the mighty Roman Empire (which even Foucault mentions (2003, 75)), and
    adorned themselves with the title *Kayser-i Rum,* or Caesar of Rome.

that border towns and hinterland cities were not. For example, it housed large numbers of "politically active constituents" (Uzun 2006, 1; author's translation) – i.e. high-level bureaucrats, the royal family and their extensive staff, foreign officials, military officials, and the Janissary Army itself, among others. If not provisioned, these populations had the resources to unsettle the Empire. Regular residents of the city, though by no means as active (or impactful), were not entirely powerless either. In fact, their sheer proximity to the sultan and his family gave them a similar capability to destabilize the Empire – a capability their counterparts in distant border towns, hinterland cities, and peripheries, effectively lacked. In the event of prolonged, city-wide hunger, for example, who these resident-subjects were going to align with, and whether they would join in on a mutiny or maintain their loyalty, could determine if the reigning sultan would keep his head on his shoulders.

These dynamics were and are not unique to Istanbul. Other cities which contained seats of power were susceptible to them as well, to varying degrees. As such, the conclusions derived from the analyses offered in the book are applicable across a range of contexts – particularly for the first food regime I will be discussing. Capital cities like London, Paris, Lisbon, Madrid, Machiavelli's principalities, as well as regional capitals that formerly housed Ottoman governors – such as Baghdad, Cairo, Edirne (Adrianopolis), Manastır (Bitola), Crete, Beirut, Aleppo – were and are subject to similar political-economic dynamics. Still, as generalizable as my conclusions are, I would caution against their uncritical application to any city. Trajectories diverge quite radically, particularly once we move closer to the contemporary era. Istanbul, for example, lost its privileged position when the seat of power moved to Ankara (soon after the establishment of the Republic in 1923), and the city's provisioning apparatus began to reflect a different set of macroeconomic dynamics.

1   Three Food Regimes

As I will be discussing in the chapters that follow, in the last 500 years of its history, three distinct ways of conducting, organizing, managing – in short, governing – Istanbul's provisioning have emerged. The oldest among these was the dominant food regime from roughly the mid-15th century until the 19th century, when the Ottomans liberalized trade. I call it the *urban food provisioning* food regime. The primary aim of this food regime was to ensure that the city was fed, and scarcity and famine were kept at bay. To do so, the Ottoman central authority – the sultan and the high bureaucracy, or what is known as the Sublime Porte (*Bab-ı Ali*) – made significant interventions into the provisioning process, documenting, registering, measuring the quality and the quantities of foods produced, sometimes even arranging shipping routes and enforcing storage and distribution in the city through various networks, practices, and mechanisms. It also inspected the quality of the foodstuffs coming into the city and enforced compliance with its storage, sale, and pricing regulations. If conditions were particularly dire and food scarcity seemed possible, the Ottoman central authority set prices. Aimed at making food accessible to the residents of the city, these practices implied cuts in the profits for merchants, shopkeepers, and artisans – who regularly looked for ways to go around the enforcement mechanisms. Thus, bribery and corruption, hoarding, redirecting the produce to the black market, or selling it off to foreign buyers who were willing to pay more, were chronic problems. Most importantly, the apparatus was not always successful in provisioning the city. Albeit irregularly, Istanbul did suffer from hunger and scarcity – like any other city of its time. The Ottoman central authority's direct involvement in the provisioning of the city, however, inadvertently drew attention to this apparatus. Recognizing that impairing the capital's provisioning apparatus was an easy and direct way to unsettle the Empire (and get the sultan's and the Sublime Porte's attention), frustrated bureaucrats, disappointed military officials, revolutionaries, sectarians, and puritans, aired their discontent by blockading trade routes and disrupting shipments of provisions to the city throughout the Ottoman period.

Interestingly, none of these structural weaknesses led to the dismantling of the food regime, though they most certainly rattled the provisioning apparatus – and by extension, the Empire – at times. What led to the demise of the *urban food provisioning* food regime was the trade treaties the Ottoman central authority signed with the United Kingdom in 1838, and with other European states in its aftermath. The liberalization of trade removed price fixing, altered customs and transportation costs, and rerouted where the city was getting its food from. In the absence of regulation, and with merchants and shopkeepers keen to make as much profit as possible in supplying the city, food increasingly became inaccessible for certain segments of Istanbul's population (as much as it became abundant for others). In addition, the interventions of the central authority became event-specific. In instances like national and/or international wars, for example, the Ottoman central authority – and later, the Republican central authority – instituted fixed prices, allocated storage facilities and transportation routes, and regulated distribution practices. During all other times, however, merchants, shopkeepers, and later corporations – motivated to make as much profit as possible – were left in charge of feeding the city. As such, I call this (second) food regime *codependent provisioning*.

Prevalent during the war years (1912–1945) and up until the market liberalization reforms in the 1980s, *codependent provisioning* remained, in essence,
a transitory food regime. It shared similarities with both the food regime that
came before (*urban food provisioning*) and the one that followed after (*urban
food supply chain*). For example, the regulation of prices, documentation of
production and shipment, and meticulous inspection, continued on from
the *urban food provisioning* food regime. At the same time, the previous food
regime's most important aspect – making sure that the residents are fed, or
that they received adequate provisions to at least subsist – disappeared.
Relying on private actors to produce, distribute, and exchange food in the city,
the central authority instead began to ensure only that food production in the
aggregate was sufficient to feed the country's population. In other words, the
focus of the food regime shifted from urban provisioning to agriculture and
related industries. The central authority intervened to provision the city only
when there were major problems or crises, such as wars and particularly severe
droughts, bad harvests, and so forth. The central authority instead channeled
its resources to support private actors – directly (with tax breaks and subsidies,
for example) and indirectly (by undertaking infrastructural investments, giving sales rights on certain goods, for example) – so that they could accumulate
enough capital as they supplied the city.

What is critical for this (second) food regime is the two interconnected
shifts that occurred in the way the central authority approached urban provisioning. The first shift had to do with the site of intervention. In *codependent
provisioning*, the central authority was no longer focused on Istanbul – unless,
of course, a major tragedy like an earthquake or an epidemic unsettled the
city. Rather, it was focused on Turkey as a whole. The entire country became
its site of intervention. As it regulated prices in Istanbul, for example, it would
do the same in Burdur or Trabzon or Hakkari. It would monitor, control, pro-
hibit, or incentivize certain trade routes over others in the western part of the
country, as it would in the northern, southern, or eastern. Concomitantly, its
primary focus shifted, from whether Istanbul was adequately provisioned, to
whether Turkey, as a whole, had enough to eat: were there enough legumes,
pulses, grains, fresh fruits, and vegetables? Was there enough meat? How efficient were the dairy farms? Could the existing production supply the country? Was the country self-sufficient or did it need to import? These, however,
were questions of scale, not of (re)distribution. In other words, they focused
on the amount of food the country produced and consumed in the aggregate, without considering whether individual subject-citizens had access to
them, logistically and/or financially. Put differently, in this food regime, the
central authority prioritized production and consumption in the aggregate,

as questions of economics and as issues of scale, and de-prioritized the sub-sistence of individual subject-citizens. In conjunction, the central authority's governance of actors, mechanisms, and practices, shifted away from interven-tions that ensured that Istanbul was provisioned to interventions to rebuild agriculture as a capital-generating sector that could spearhead the country's economic development.

As my Grandma's memories solemnly remind us, the *codependent provision-ing* food regime was not able to fully prevent hunger and scarcity. The insur-mountable bottlenecks did not occur during the war years, however. Rather, it was frequent and irrepressible currency exchange crises in the 1970s that shook the food regime to its core. It became clear that the capital generated through agriculture was insufficient to spearhead the desired development, let alone achieve self-sufficiency. Food scarcity and high inflation became everyday experiences for many, particularly in the cities.

To fix these problems, suggested solutions included the liberalization of capital and commodities markets, greater integration of domestic financial institutions with global ones, privatization of public assets, and the shift to a fluctuating currency exchange rate, i.e. structural adjustments. The new food regime that emerged was also defined by these policies. Populations and subject-citizens were rebranded as customers with different socio-economic statuses, and the provisioning actors adjusted to satisfy their differentiated demands in the most cost-effective way possible. Today, private actors run most, if not all, supply operations; and depending on the fluctuations of the market, there could be several suppliers, hence giving the supply chain a frag-mented form (as in the case of lettuce, for example); or, there could be few, making the supply chain more integrated and oligopolistic (as in the case of asparagus, for example). Either way, this new food regime is built on the coop-eration of private provisioning actors, whose sole aim is to accumulate capital through the provisioning apparatus.

This cooperation is the most critical characteristic of this (third) food regime, which I call the *urban food supply chain*. It makes the whole regime work, particularly since, unlike the *urban food provisioning* food regime, there is no reigning sultan who oversees the entire operation and ensures that the city is provisioned adequately. The present central authority is almost com-pletely displaced from its position of governing the provisioning actors. When it intervenes, it is mostly indirectly, by increasing or decreasing the import and export quotas on certain food items, changing the regulations on quality stan-dards, or through macroeconomic policies on inflation, unemployment, and credit rates, for example. As such, scarcity is avoided not as a result of gov-ernance, but as a result of vertical cooperation between private provisioning actors along the supply chain. And this is done in the most cost-effective way possible; that is, through initiating horizontal competition between provisioning actors who operate in the same node of the food supply chain.

To be more precise, in the *urban food supply chain* food regime, scarcity is not avoided. It is contained to certain segments of the population: the poor, or those who cannot afford to buy the provisions available in the market; the unemployed and the precarious, who only have irregular access to food; and depending on the context, those who are sick, elderly, and those who live in food deserts because they cannot afford to live elsewhere. While scarcity could be a chronic condition for these populations, it is not experienced *en masse*, as was the case in the *codependent provisioning* and *urban food provisioning* food regimes. This is a critical shift, one that runs through the heart of every current political community – not just in Turkey, but across the world, where similar political-economic transformations have crowned global capitalism (in its neoliberal variety) as the dominant mode of production. Understanding how this shift happened and how it hollows out the political community, are concerns that invigorate this book.

I should note that the brief descriptions of food regimes I am providing here are models. In the following chapters, it will become clear that the reality was and is messier: practices, mechanisms, and institutions, are regularly carried over from one food regime to another, until specific measures were and are taken to unmake them. Similarly, when a food regime begins or ends remains relatively nebulous. However, such lack of precision – if it can be so called – does not undercut these models. Rather, the continuities and discontinuities thus manifested, illuminate each food regime's pressure points; and expose the various ways in which mechanisms, forces, and tensions, that constitute one food regime, can be rearticulated to serve different purposes in another.

2   So, What Are Food Regimes?

A key argument this book puts forward is that how the *body politic* – the political community – is fed, is political. The argument itself is not radical – from Marion Nestle to Amartya Sen to E. P. Thompson, a wide range of scholars, activists, and thinkers, have underlined the inherently political nature of the food question. Here, I want to push this point a little further, and treat how the *body politic* is fed (and all the ways it is *not* fed) as a representation of the relationship between the sovereign and the subjects that constitute the *body politic*. That is, how food is produced, which foods are produced, how they are transported from their locations of production to locations of consumption, where and how they are sold and bought, and who processes and consumes them – all these are political questions. And as political questions, they are indicative of how the *body politic* is constituted, and the nature of the relationship between the sovereign and the subjects – who governs whom and how, and what that governance entails.

My emphasis on the *body politic* here is intentional. I am not employing this conceptualization just because there is a well-established tradition within political theory to describe political communities as such[5], but because I find it relevant to the arguments I make in this book. After all, thinking about the political community as a body inherently implies thinking about food – because if our political communities are indeed bodies, then as bodies, they need to be fed. They can be nourished, replenished, refreshed, and even healed at times, only if and so long as (though not exclusively) they are fed. Conversely, if they are not fed, they will be depleted, extinguished, starved, and as such, destroyed. Feeding enables the *body politic* to maintain itself; whereas the lack of food – that is, scarcity, hunger, and/or famine (and we can perhaps also add malnutrition here) – leads to its dissolution. As such, anti-scarcity measures and provisioning apparatuses are vital for the survival of the *body politic*; they can make or break the political community[6]. Concomitantly, the arrangement of these anti-scarcity measures and provisioning apparatuses, the codes of conduct governing the participating actors, and the overall success of the provisioning apparatus in feeding the *body politic*, all make the constitutive dynamics of the political community explicit.

As we move closer to the contemporary food regime (*urban food supply chain*) , for example, a transition becomes explicit – from provisioning being an obligation of the sovereign to a responsibility of the subject. In each stage of this transition, the relationship between the subjects and the sovereign is reconstructed on different principles and priorities. Moreover, this relationship is not a binary that positions subjects in opposition to a sovereign. The sovereign may side with certain subject populations; or s/he may refrain from arbitrating directly between different subject populations altogether. Alternatively,

---

5   One of the oldest, and by far the most interesting iteration of the political community as a body, goes back to a fable, titled "The Belly and the Members," attributed to Aesop. For a historical discussion of the fable and the metaphors it contains, see the chapter titled "Aesop and Others" in Harvey (2007).

6   Perhaps Polybius's Book 6 of *The Histories*, where he details the cycle of revolution political communities undergo, should be reconsidered from the point of view of food. Degeneration as well as regeneration from one form to another may have to do with whether (and how) the *body politic* is fed, as much as the institutionalization and propagation of civic virtues.

the sovereign's objectives and the *mentalité*[7] of government may change. In the *codependent provisioning* food regime, for example, there was more emphasis on development, and agricultural activity and provisioning were organized around the sovereign's specific understanding and projection of development. In comparison, the *urban food supply chain* food regime is geared toward boosting the comparative advantage of the subjects' (who are conceptualized as 'entrepreneurs'). Agriculture is thus conceived as yet another sector for capital accumulation, which, if insufficient, may well be restructured to serve or support other sectors; it can even be minimized or eliminated. As such, there isn't much emphasis on the provisioning of subject-citizens. In either case, however, the provisioning apparatuses and anti-scarcity measures make visible these divergent priorities, objectives, and mentalities of government. Through them, we can understand what makes the political community work.

Yet, as Marx said, understanding is not enough; we should also look for ways to change those structures, relations, codes of conduct, and mentalities of government, that systematically disenfranchise certain populations and leave them to deal with hunger and scarcity on their own. Change, however, can only come if we consider provisioning (or the lack thereof) as a component of sovereignty, as a factor in the relationship between the sovereign and the subject. In other words, it is not enough to claim that food (and the production, distribution, exchange, and consumption thereof) is inherently political. We must treat the entire food system as foundational to the *body politic*. Only then would we be able to work against practices that disenfranchise populations, undo structures that pit citizens against each other for supposed competitive advantage, and, demand a *right to subsistence* that would include, among others, a right to healthy, balanced, socio-culturally acceptable, tasty, and nutritious food.

A food regime, then, refers to a specific construction, ordering, and/or arrangement of the relationship between the sovereign and the subjects-citizens that are embedded in a food system[8]. A food system, in turn, refers to

---

7   Following Wendy Brown's discussion of Foucault, I use *mentalité* to mean a political rationality that "posit(s) ontological qualities and relations of citizens, laws, rights, economy, society, and states – qualities and relations inhering in order of reason (...) which may combine awkwardly, but nonetheless all become salient parts of that by which worlds are ordered, humans act, and governments rule" (Brown 2015, 116).

8   My use of the term 'food regime' here differs significantly from how Friedmann and McMichael (1989) use it. While they use the concept to indicate different eras of global interconnectedness in food provisioning, I use it to explore how such interconnectedness has framed, ordered, and shaped the relations between subjects-citizens and their central authority in a political community. While Friedmann and McMichael's discussion has been critical in bringing together the socio-historical analyses of the political economy of

a specific way of producing (mode of production), distributing (circulating), exchanging (transacting, or buying and selling), and consuming food. It is, to a large extent, impossible to talk about food regimes without talking about food systems; however, as I show in the book, it is also, to a large extent, meaningless to talk about food systems, without talking about food regimes. At every instance, food systems need to be recognized as thoroughly political entities, and to be reformulated as foundational to the *body politic*. Concomitantly, the critiques of the food regimes I offer here should be taken as critiques of their political communities. In parallel, we must think of fixing food systems comprehensively; that is, as ways of fixing the structural, political, and economic problems of the *body politic*.

3   Success vs. Failure: Scarcity, Hunger, Malnutrition, and Famine

It is difficult to assess the success of a food system. After all, there is no clear method of determining whether a population is well-fed or not. Measuring caloric intake per individual, for example, excludes the nutritional composition of the diet, and as such, may not necessarily indicate if a person or a population is well-fed. Focusing solely on nutritional composition, in turn, may ignore political-economic forces and socio-cultural rules that shape diets. Plus, there may be – and there almost always are – groups within political communities with significant variations between their diets, although they rely on the same food system for their provisions. The failure of a food system, in contrast, is easier to discern. The effects of chronic malnourishment are medically diagnosable. Scarcity may be visible in the form of empty shelves and long lines in front of stores; restaurants and food stalls might be closed; mobile vendors might disappear from the streets; and incidents of violence and mobbing may occur, particularly in sites where food enters the city (wholesale markets, for example). Like my great-grandma, people can beg for food; they can dumpster-dive, or hunt and forage. If they have the means, they can try to procure some of the food, which disappeared from shops, through the black market. Because scarcity does not happen overnight, it is probable that the provisioning agents along the food supply chain saw it coming and perhaps even contributed to it by hoarding. Yet even these behaviors are not necessarily indicative of

---

agriculture, urban provisioning, and food consumption, all under the same conceptual banner (for a good summary of these discussions, see Dixon and Campbell 2009; Magnan 2012), scholars of food regimes have been somewhat slow to engage with the political-theoretical implications of their analyses. I aim to address those implications in this book.

failure – after all, the expectation that there will always be food enough to feed everyone, come rain or shine, is too high a threshold for success. When we are talking about feeding populations or urban provisioning, there will always be contingencies: scarcity, hunger, malnourishment, and even famine, remain possibilities. Nevertheless, what makes a food system fail is the frequency of these instances, or, by the same token, how pervasive they become for certain populations within the political community.

There are, then, 2 types of indicators of a food system's failure: Type 1 – the frequency of cases of *en masse* malnourishment, hunger, and scarcity, which we commonly see during wars, for example, or during epidemics; and Type 2 – the rate of malnourishment or the experience of hunger and scarcity, which we see almost as a standard of living, for certain populations, usually lower-income households and marginalized groups. While Type 1 and Type 2 failures are not necessarily mutually exclusive, they are products of different food systems and different problems within food systems. For example, a food system prone to Type 1 failures has periods of function and periods of malfunction. A crisis might be brewing during periods of function, with systemic problems contributing to an aggregate outcome of *en masse* malnourishment, hunger, scarcity, even escalating to famine. The transition between periods of function and malfunction may be relatively smooth, and signs of crisis might be muted – until the crisis becomes full-blown. As a result, identifying systemic problems and fixing them are difficult. In contrast, Type 2 failures indicate a system that seems to work just fine for some and leaves others chronically malnourished and/or exposed to hunger and scarcity. Episodic crises are unlikely, though certainly possible, especially if macroeconomic parameters take a turn for the worse. Food will be available; but it will be inaccessible (either physically or economically or both) to certain populations. The reasons for this lack of access, to food that is technically available on store shelves, will vary, and because they might be related to other political or economic problems, they will be hard to fix. In fact, depending on the political culture and the structure of government in place, Type 2 failures may not even be considered as failures of the food system, and thus, may not make it to the government's or the central authority's agenda.

It is important to note that for both indicators, an exact measurement is difficult to devise. How frequently do cases of *en masse* malnourishment, hunger and/or scarcity need to occur, to qualify as failure? What percentage of the population should be unable to access food regularly, for us to mark a failure? (In other words, how big is '*en masse*' supposed to be?) These are hard questions – not because coming up with a convincing measurement is arduous, but because, in the final analysis, the answers and indeed the questions themselves, are political. To put it somewhat bluntly, the difference between 5% and 35% of a population is not only a matter of numbers. It is also a matter of a tacit decision, made by the political community, about the amount of misery it is willing to tolerate in its midst, and exactly who will have to endure such suffering. Alternatively, if famine-like conditions occur every 10 or 20 years, the issue is not the frequency of the crises, but the web of crises-inducing practices, interests, and relations, that implicate the members of the political community. Each case indicates a preference for certain relations, interests, segments of the population – certain *lives* – over others, and as such, offers us a glimpse (through the stomach!) into the constitutive principles, mores, ideas, and bonds (the heart?) of the *body politic*. We can certainly judge these decisions as morally right or wrong; we can unearth the various ways in which such preferences get articulated through racism, sexism, ethno-nationalism, and so forth; and through such exposition and analysis, we can work to change them. We have to reckon, however, that politically, none of these decisions are exceptional, and that every political community makes such decisions. What is exceptional is the shift, as we move closer to the current food regime, from episodic (Type 1) failures to chronic (Type 2) failures.

Why this shift? Part of the reason has to do with how the relationship between economy and sovereignty is structured in each food regime. If the decisions vis-à-vis the production, circulation, and consumption of food, are more centralized, episodic failures are more common. In other words, for example, if the sovereign dictates to the farmers what, how much, where, and how they should produce, and at what prices to sell – and to consumers what and how much they should consume – then it is more likely that the food system will fail ever so often. Perhaps enforced prices will be too low for the farmers or too high for the consumers; perhaps the demand for food will exceed the planned supply, or perhaps, given the prices, the intermediaries will not shoulder the costs of transporting the food from their locations of production to the locations of consumption, choosing instead to hoard it and then to sell it for much higher prices through the black market. The sovereign can use a variety of measures to ensure conformity with its dictates; but there will always be some who will take the risk and go around them. Thus, food will either physically disappear from the markets or its price will increase. In either case, impending scarcity will affect most of the population; and unless measures to make food accessible are implemented, scarcity will escalate into famine.

In contrast, if the decisions are less centralized, hunger, scarcity, and malnourishment will be more chronic for certain populations. In the absence of the sovereign's dictates, profit will become the dominant motive to produce and to sell food. Farmers will decide on what to produce based on how much profit they can make; intermediaries will shoulder the costs of transporting foods from their locations of production to locations of consumption only if they think they can make a handsome profit. Aggregate demand and supply will certainly be essential for determining the prices of food items; however, whether these food items will be available locally or not will impact the scale of crisis. Consumers, in turn, will be stranded, with their appetites on the one hand, and with their budgets on the other. They can certainly choose what to eat (assuming that different foodstuffs are locally available); they can switch between different items depending on their preferences and prices; but at one point, they will have to eat *something*. A crisis due to lack of accessibility occurs when the consumers' purchasing power, incomes, or wages, are not sufficient to afford the market prices. At some point, a balance might be achieved between the price that producers want to sell at and the price that consumers are able or willing to pay. However, this will be a balance achieved on the average – meaning, for some, market prices will be below what they are willing to pay (thus, if they want, they can benefit from the market's diversity and abundance), whereas for others, prices will be above what they are *able to* pay. And for this latter group, hunger, scarcity, and malnourishment, will be chronic.

If you are following contemporary (political-)economic discussions on neoliberalism, what I am describing here might sound eerily familiar. On the one hand, you have centrally planned systems in which the sovereign (the central authority) directly intervenes into the economy and makes decisions on supply, prices, storage facilities, inventory management practices, and even transportation routes. As classical and neoclassical economists point out, however, such central management can be highly inefficient, prone to corruption, and is usually incapable or unwilling to integrate input from the subjects it governs; thus, such systems can easily clog, leading to episodic crises ever so often. On the other hand, you have highly privatized, highly competitive, and highly decentralized, profit-driven food systems, where the sovereign – if it were to intervene – does so only to regulate competition and to protect private property. Yet, these systems are equally fragile and prone to corruption: Not only because concentration of capital tends to curb competition, but also because macroeconomic parameters (foreign exchange rate, inflation, unemployment, national income, and so forth) have a direct impact on what people can/not eat. In other words, their instability can easily destabilize these food systems.

What, then, is a 'good' food system? I will come back to this question in more detail toward the end, but for now, suffice it to say that this too is a political question – and a decision. For those who can afford it, the contemporary food system is indeed 'good': food is abundant and diverse; out-of-season fruits and vegetables are available year around; trained chefs, ethnic food restaurants, and specialty stores, bring ingredients and flavors from across the world to our tables. Competition between the bazaars, the supermarkets, and the greengrocers, generates low prices; and environmental movements have been pushing for sustainable production practices, which have given rise to a vibrant market for organic, sustainably produced foods and rising trends for healthier lifestyles and food consumption habits. What's not to like? And why change it? Is a fail-safe food system even possible? For those who cannot afford what the contemporary food system has to offer, however, none of these supposed advantages provide any relief. Struggle for survival is the *modus operandi*; and hunger, scarcity, and malnourishment, are daily experiences.

That brings me to the other part of the reason for the shift from systems prone to Type 1 failures to those prone to Type 2 ones. As I mentioned before, at some point, we, as the *body politic*, seem to have made a choice: rather than most of us suffering occasionally, we decided that it is better (or at least, acceptable) for some of us to suffer constantly. Keeping scarcity thus contained, we might have thought we could avert tragedy *en masse*. Yet today, regardless of that collective decision, we assume that if people are unable to feed themselves, it must be their fault; that if they are obese or if they are battling any of the myriad food-related diseases – chronic or acute – it is because they do not know better or have decided not to do or be better. What is worse, perhaps, is that when we are trying to come up with solutions to fix these problems, we do not consider food and eating – access to a healthy, balanced, socio-culturally acceptable, tasty, and nutritious diet – a fundamental, inalienable right that every one of us, as members of the *body politic*, should have. Instead, we continue to assume food provisioning to be a competitive, profit-driven, private enterprise that can be improved for the benefit of more – but not all – simply with better practices (for the producers) and better choices (for the consumers). With such an approach, it is no surprise that the contemporary food system, which is prone to Type 2 failures, persists.

It is up to the reader to decide whether they want to live in a *body politic* in which some of the members live in conditions of chronic hunger, malnutrition, and/or scarcity. Regardless of that personal decision, however, today's political communities must take ownership of the collective decisions that led to the shift in their food systems, and as their authors, they must deal with that decision's consequences. Practically, this may involve a variety of policies that can alleviate the conditions for those in need, for example, and/or private-public joint efforts to make food accessible, and/or perhaps, encouragement of certain urban food production practices that lower-income and marginalized groups can use to feed themselves. In addition, and I think more importantly, taking ownership of that decision must come with a sense of empowerment, a realization that we, as the *body politic*, have the power to constitute a different food regime that feeds us via a more just, egalitarian, sustainable food system. What is at stake, then, is not only feeding our hungry and fixing our food system, but also regaining a sense of ourselves – as constituents of our political community – as the actual decision-makers and the unconditional sovereigns.

4   The Political Economy of Urban Provisioning

So far, I have suggested that the shift from Type 1 to Type 2 failures seems to be a choice (tacit or explicit) we made as a *body politic*: We shifted to a different food system so that rather than all of us experiencing food scarcity, hunger, malnutrition, and so forth, ever so often, food system failures remain chronic yet contained to specific populations within our political communities. Yet it is possible to explain this shift also as a side effect – one among many perhaps – of a greater political-economic transformation; that is, the move to the capitalist mode of production and to the free market economy. After all, as Ellen Meiksins Wood points out, "until the production of the means of survival and self-reproduction is market-dependent, there is no capitalist mode of production" (Meiksins Wood 2017, 140–141). So, the shift to a food system that provisions the city principally and exclusively through the market, while eliminating all other networks, practices, and *mentalité* of provisioning, and generates dependencies for producers to produce for the market and consumers to provision themselves through the market, seems inherently related to the rise of capitalism. And indeed, it is. But there is more to it as well: It also demonstrates the subjugation of the power of the sovereign to the power of the economy. That is, the subjugation of the right to life and death (which becomes the right to make live and to let die (Foucault 2003, 241)) to the imperatives of the market.

How does this work? Well, what differentiates capitalism from other modes of production is neither the prevalence of markets, nor the desire for profit. Markets have existed since (at least, we might add) the beginning of history (Meiksins Wood 2016, 118); and traders and others did try to make as much profit as they could through the various market opportunities that were available to them. In other words, neither markets nor the profit motive is unique to capitalism. What is unique is the preeminence of "the imperatives of competition, accumulation, and profit-maximization, and hence a constant systemic need to develop productive forces" (Meiksins Wood 2017, 97). It is these imperatives that, in turn, made the pre-capitalistic political rights of the landlords – which enabled them to squeeze and appropriate the surplus labor of the direct producers – unnecessary. Direct producers, once expropriated from their means of production, had to already consent to 'forego' their surplus labor to the landlords so that they could access the means of production (Meiksins Wood 2016, 29). Thus, not only did the appropriation of surplus labor become an inherent component of the relations of production as well as the production process, but also, the appropriators (i.e. the landlords) no longer required extra-economic coercions (i.e. political rights) to appropriate the direct producers' surplus labor. Direct producers, now having nothing but their labor to sell, indeed sold it in return for wages, to access the means of production, produced whatever they could (which wholly belonged to the landlord), and with the wages so earned, bought whatever they needed (Meiksins Wood 2016, 109). All these contributed to an exclusionary understanding of private property, with market opportunities (turned market imperatives) pushing producers to produce for the market, an increasing availability of and a reliance on commodity exchange through the market to satisfy life's necessities, and freedom of the laborers from pre-capitalist relations of bondage (ibid, 28–31).

Because capitalism enabled the extraction and appropriation of surplus labor through purely economic means, the sovereign, who monopolizes extra-economic state power, was put in an ambiguous position: On the one hand, the laws as well as the violent and the non-violent means to enforce the laws were still necessary to maintain the relations of production; on the other hand, because political rights were no longer necessary for the owners of the means of production to appropriate the surplus labor from direct producers, there wasn't much need to sustain a political entity that monopolized the distribution of such rights or to kept the rights exclusive to the appropriators (Meiksins Wood 2005, 14–22). In the long run, this ambiguity generated the possibility of universal suffrage and triggered the transitions to the sovereignty of the people, both results of long and bloody struggles. And though these are significant gains on their own, as Meiksins Wood points out, they came at the cost of the/ a "*devaluation* of the political sphere" (Meiksins Wood 2016, 211; emphasis in the original). That is, the delinking of the civic status and the class position: As "socio-economic position [no longer] determine[s] the right to citizenship (...), civic equality [no longer] directly affect[s] or significantly modif[ies] class inequality" (ibid, 213).

With capitalism, then, sovereign power and economic power become differentiated. Economic power – inherently related to class (appropriators vs. direct producers), though it "rests firmly on the political" (Meiksins Wood 2016, 30–33) – is subject to the imperatives of the market and has its own dynamics and power relations. It is private, in the sense of exclusively belonging to specific subject-citizens (i.e. appropriators), as also in its sphere of exercise. Sovereign power, in contrast, is public, and following universal suffrage, belongs to everyone. It is premised on civic equality – that is, the political equality of socially unequal individuals; and as such, it is (or at least, is supposed to be) neutral and impersonal (ibid, 43). Problematizing this differentiation, Meiksins Wood asks, very fittingly, "what would it take to recover democracy from the formal separation of the 'political' and the 'economic', when political privilege has been replaced by economic coercion, exerted not just by capitalist property directly but also through the medium of the market?" (ibid, 237).

This differentiation, however, is not a retreat. Sovereign power does not disappear nor is it reduced to the negligible.[9] Rather, it is subjugated to the imperatives of the market. That is, the political rights that legitimize the use of extra-economic means of coercion are used, instead, to support and to sustain the market. Karl Polanyi highlights this when he underlines the role of the government in establishing and protecting the free market through "repealing restrictive regulations" (Polanyi 2001, 145) and "increase[ing] the administrative functions of the state" (ibid). Most of these functions, Polanyi suggests, quoting Bentham, have to do with the " 'minister of the police' " (ibid): "Of the three things needed for economic success – inclination, knowledge, and power – the private person possessed only inclination. Knowledge and power, Bentham taught, can be administered much cheaper by government than by private persons. It was the task of the executive to collect statistics and information, to foster science and experiment, as well as to supply the innumerable instruments of final realization in the field of government" (ibid, 145–146).

As I explore in the chapters that follow, the transformations – both in the provisioning apparatus feeding the city and in the food systems – show that these administrative functions also involve distinguishing between *friends* and *enemies* (Schmitt 1976) – between those who get fed (*friends*) and those who

---

9 Meiksins Wood does not tell us all that much about how exactly state power sustains and supports economic power, nor about the different ways those functions might be (and arguably, are) performed, nor how different ways of performing those functions might lead to different amalgamations between economic and political power. Rather, "the unique development of capitalism", according to Meiksins Wood, rests on "property and class relations, as well as the functions of surplus appropriation and distribution, so to speak liberat[ing] themselves from – and yet are served by – the coercive institutions that constitute the state and develop autonomously" (Meiksins Wood 2016, 33). Even various divergences in the development of capitalism "have to do with the nature and sequence of relations between public power and private appropriation" (ibid). State power, thus, with its myriad functions, is not really in the picture.

do not (*enemies*). And in conjunction, the purposefulness of not feeding some by way of "deliberate refraining or withdrawal from action – not simply the inertia of non-action, but a strategically conceived retreat, a leaving alone or an abandonment" (Hill and Montag, 2015, 263–264), as well as actively pooling and directing resources to selected others to make sure that they have access to provisions. The criteria for distinguishing between these two populations changes from one food regime to another, but the *mentalité* of government that assigns the sovereign the right to decide life and death as such, does not.

Though capitalism *compels* laborers to access the means of production as well as "the most basic commodities and the implements of daily subsistence" (which prominently includes food), it does not mean that the laborers will have the *ability* (Meiksins Wood 2017, 138) to acquire them. The power of the sovereign becomes critical precisely at this point as well. Transformed from the "right to take life or let live" to the "right to make live and to let die" (Foucault 2003, 241) and subjugated to the power of the economy, the power of the sovereign is exercised to normalize an economy of death and decay, by limiting which populations – which members of the political community – can engage in the productive and reproductive labor necessary for subsistence. The aim is to keep in check the reserve army of labor, and/or to discipline (*a la* Foucault) workers to the strict regimen of the capitalist work ethic, and/or to support and to sustain the free market. But more critically, it is to subjugate the processes of life and death to the imperatives of the market. In other words, it isn't that "power no longer recognizes death" or that it "literally ignores death" (ibid, 248); rather, sovereign power makes the possibility of death, embodied in hunger, famine, scarcity, and malnourishment – or simply, in the malfunctioning of the food system – subservient to capitalism. In short, *necroeconomics* (Montag, 2005) becomes a tool of government; as sovereign power serves economic power, *necroeconomics* serves *necropolitics* (Mbembe 2003).

Taking such a *longue durée* view of these transformations, it does not seem like there was ever a clear moment of choice: That is, there was not one specific event or instance where we – as a *body politic* – collectively changed our minds about the kind of food regime we should be living under. It seems more the case that, with the rise of capitalism, and the accompanying separation of sovereign power and economic power, this economy of death and decay – serving and sustaining a politics of letting die and sometimes even making die – has just come to be. But if Foucault is right, in that if "power comes from below; that is, there is no binary and all-encompassing opposition between rulers and ruled at the root of power relations" (Foucault 1990, 94) and if "where there is power, there is resistance" (ibid, 95), then there has to be not one, but many moments, instances, events, decisions, acceptances, tacit consents, active participations – as well as protests, rejections, confrontations – along the way, that led us to the present moment. And in the chapters that follow, it is these many moments that I hope to trace, leaving it to the reader to decide where (or even if) we go from here.

5   Notes on Terms, Periodization, and Methodology

I have already discussed some of the terms I use in the text. Food regimes, for example, denote specific constructions, orderings, and/or arrangements, of the relationship between a sovereign and his/her (but in this case, really mostly 'his') subjects/citizens that are embedded in a food system. Food systems, in turn, are specific ways of producing (mode of production), distributing (circulating), exchanging (transacting, or buying and selling) and consuming food. There are, however, a few terms that remain unexplained. What, for example, is a 'provisioning apparatus' – and how does it differ from a food system? What is the difference between 'people' and 'population'? What do I mean when I say 'central authority' (and why don't I use 'the state' and/or 'the government' instead)? While the discussions in the following chapters will make clear the meaning and the history behind these terms and concepts, I think it is best to define – at least in a preliminary way – what I mean when I use certain terms, before proceeding further.

To begin with, a *provisioning apparatus*[10] refers to a network of actors who may use different mechanisms, practices, and codes of conduct to bring, distribute, and sell foodstuffs in the city. Producers (farmers and small- and large-scale companies that produce a variety of processed foods – anything

---

10   In the text, I use *apparatus* to refer to *dispositif*, and not to *appareil*, which can also be translated as such. *Appareil* indicates tools, mechanisms, strategies, relations, and/or institutions the state in the Middle Ages deployed

on the basis of a multiplicity of prior powers, and to a certain extent in opposition to them: dense, entangled, conflicting powers, powers tied to the direct or indirect dominion over land, to the possession of arms, to serfdom, to bonds of suzerainty and vassalage (...) [which] were able to gain acceptance (...) [because] they presented themselves as agencies of regulation, arbitration, and demarcation, as a way of introducing order in the midst of these powers, of establishing a principle that would temper them and distribute them according to boundaries and a fixed hierarchy (Foucault 1990, 86–87).

As such, as Bussolini notes, it is "more circumscribed and is affiliated with State mechanisms of power" (2010, 93). *Dispositif*, in relation, refers to "a wider and more diffuse, yet also more effective, form of power (...) which includes the said and the non-said, institutions, structures, decisions, etc." (ibid, 94).

from tomato paste to candy bars to olive oil) are external to this network, so long as they remain exclusively producers. However, one of the interesting changes we can see, as we move from the *urban food provisioning* food regime to the *urban food supply chain* food regime, is that large-scale producers are beginning to enter the apparatus. Either they accumulate enough capital and expand into other nodes (usually into the logistics sector[11]), or they are taken over by another actor who is already in the apparatus (through contract farming, for example, supermarkets have ended up integrating farmers directly into the apparatus). As I will discuss in Chapters 5 and 6, such expansions have made the provisioning apparatuses more versatile: able to supply widely different demands far more quickly; to be more flexible, and to respond nimbly to changing economic and climate conditions. At the same time, these expansions have made the provisioning apparatuses much more vulnerable: if a major actor in the network goes under (for whatever reason), the whole apparatus suffers; hazardous vectors can spread more easily along integrated supply chains; financial problems of one may more quickly spillover to others, and so forth. The important point here is that provisioning apparatuses are constantly changing networks. The food supply chains feeding Istanbul today are not like the ones from the 1500s or the long 19th century. However, that does not mean that there are no similarities and continuities. As I will discuss in Chapter 3, for example, the provisioning apparatus feeding Istanbul after the Treaty of 1838 was as global as the supply chains feeding the city today.

The key characteristic of the 'provisioning apparatuses' is that they are networks. How these networks are constituted, however, is shaped by the food regime. In the contemporary food regime, for example, the primary aim of the provisioning actors is capital accumulation and profit generation (and how that came to be is one of the questions that animates this book!). This presumes, in turn, that the production and consumption of food is, to a large extent, disengaged from one another, that provisioning is a relatively linear process (production-> transportation -> exchange -> consumption); and our current food system, which is a 'supply chain', reflects this assumption. Go back, however, to my Grandma's generation, and you would see that provisioning is not such a linear process; everybody – particularly the women – is a producer, transporter, and consumer, all at the same time. As I will discuss in Chapter 6, the producer-consumers of contemporary alternative food networks, who are resisting the current food system (with the existing tools of the food regime!)

---

11   This is easier especially if the foodstuffs they are producing already require refrigeration. They usually just move into the cold chain logistics.

are indeed reinvigorating the practices of my Grandma's generation. How successful they will be, however, remains to be seen.

Another term I use very often is *central authority*. I prefer 'central authority' to 'the state' or 'the government' because when food regimes and/or food systems – or for that matter, provisioning apparatuses – are in question, it is difficult to maintain a difference between 'the state' and 'the government'. For example, were the 24 January Decisions (in Turkey in 1980) made by 'the government' or by 'the state'? It is a government that passed the Decisions, but it is difficult to argue that either the Decisions or the waves of liberalization and financialization that followed the Decisions were purely the government's doing. In fact, arguably, the primary impact of the Decisions was to alter the *mentalité* of government (how, what, and when to govern, and to what intent); as such, it is difficult to claim that 'the state' had nothing to do with them. The problem is even more palpable in the Ottoman period, when the relations between 'the state' and 'the government' were a lot more personal and fluid. Thus, rather than using 'the state' and/or 'the government' interchangeably, I use 'central authority' to indicate both. It is not that there isn't a difference, nor that the difference is unimportant; it is that maintaining the difference between the two does not contribute much to the analysis this book offers.

Plus, as will become clear in Chapter 3, during the war years (roughly from 1908 to 1923), both 'the state' and 'the government' changed; and these changes were so powerful that it is difficult to impose a neat separation between those changes that affected only the state, those that affected only the government, and those that affected both. To make matters even more complicated, the one-party rule until the end of World War II further consolidated these already fluid relations and spillovers between the Republican state and the Republican government(s). Using 'central authority' to indicate both thus enables me to underline these continuities, without disregarding the discontinues, as they shape the *codependent provisioning* food regime.

My choice of a hyphenated *subject-citizen* arises from a similar consideration. While using 'subject' to indicate peoples of the Empire may be appropriate for the Ottoman era, marking a switch to 'citizens' is difficult. Should we take, for example, the First Constitutional Era (*1. Meşrutiyet*), 1876–1878, as the key moment, when there was some representation of the peoples through the Chamber of Deputies (Zürcher 1997), but nothing like the general elections we have today? Or should we mark the Tanzimat Era, particularly the Edict of Gülhane (1839), when the Ottoman subjects' lives, honor, and property were recognized as solely theirs and were bestowed protection upon (ibid)? Or, perhaps, we should save the term 'citizen' for the early Republican era: a time when there were general elections, and in the words of Atatürk, the founder of the Republic, sovereignty lay with the people – albeit with frequent party closures and more than 2 decades of one-party rule (ibid)? Again, while these discussions are significant for scholars and students of Ottoman-Turkish political history, they do not contribute much to my analysis here. Thus, by using a hyphenated 'subject-citizen', I hope to convey to readers, that I recognize the significance of these discussions and that I will mention them only so far as they are critical for my analysis. Equally importantly, as in the case of 'central authority', using 'subject-citizen' enables me to mark a certain level of continuity between eras, without foregoing the discontinuities.

Two terms I use interchangeably are the *political community* and the *body politic*. As I have explained above, this is an intentional choice. By using the two terms interchangeably, I intend to convey, first and foremost, the long tradition in political theory of describing political communities as bodies – and political bodies at that. Further, the reference to the body enables me to make the case that food is fundamental for the survival of the political community, and as such, food systems (that is, specific ways of producing (mode of production), distributing (circulating), exchanging (transacting, or buying and selling) and consuming food) are one of their critical constituents. With this intentional choice, I also implicitly recognize that political communities can be otherwise constituted; that is, they need not be bodies and/or political bodies. They can be thought of as a sum total of their individual members[12]; or as institutions, made up of, yet different from, their members, with perhaps a spirit of their own[13]; or as networks, with members connected to each other through various forms of division of labor. While each of these have value (and merit their own book-length study), they are not useful frames for what my analysis aims to offer. Correlating 'political community' with '*body politic*' and using the terms interchangeably, in contrast, allows me to bring food and provisioning, and concepts like sovereignty, the sovereign's right to life and death, right to subsistence, and biopolitics, to the forefront of my analysis.

The *right to subsistence* is the other significant concept that will underlie particularly the discussions on sovereignty in the following chapters. The right to subsistence refers to an individual subject-citizen's right to maintain his/her life in a dignified manner. What 'maintaining life in a dignified manner' specifically entails, however, is less clear. For example, it may seem acceptable that healthy, balanced, socio-culturally acceptable, tasty, and nutritious food is necessary for everyone to maintain their lives, and as such, a *right to food*

---

12   See, for example, the distinction between 'Will of All' and the 'General Will' in Rousseau's *The Social Contract* (1972).

13   Hobbes' *Leviathan* (1996) can be considered an example.

should be covered under the right to subsistence. Yet it is as possible today, as it was in Adam Smith's time (on this, see Hill and Montag 2015, 235–342), to claim (as some do) that one does not need healthy, balanced, socio-culturally acceptable, tasty, and nutritious food to live; rather, one just needs food to live – and if one cannot afford a healthy, balanced, socio-culturally acceptable, tasty, and nutritious diet, well, so be it! They will have to live with whatever they can get. They may even go to bed hungry. So long as they are not dying of hunger, their right to subsistence is not violated.

The right to food aside, the right to subsistence may also cover the right to shelter (or housing – and there is a difference!), right to sanitary living conditions, right to safety, and right to medical treatment. While we can expand the list here, it is worth noting that there are debates yet unfolding about what exactly to include in each, who is covered, how such rights should be enforced, and who should pay for the expenses of enforcing them; and reading Polanyi on the Speenhamland Laws of 1795 in *The Great Transformation* (2001, 81–89), we can see that these discussions have been going on for a while, with no end in sight. Plus, there is no consistency across countries either, with definitions, coverage, and enforcement varying according to the country's legal tradition. For example, some, like India and South Africa, have enshrined a few of these rights in their constitutions as fundamental rights for their citizens. Others have covered these under human rights more broadly, and/or as economic, social, and cultural rights, more specifically, and though they might accept them as general principles, how they enforce them as rights show significant variation. This rich diversity is not an inconvenience, however. On the contrary, these different conceptualizations and practices prove that political communities all over the world are taking these issues seriously and are trying to do what they can within their own social, historical, economic, and political constraints.[14] Thus, in the text, I use the right to subsistence to indicate as broad and as general a meaning of the 'right to maintain life in a dignified manner' as possible.

Regardless of how they are defined, the enforcement of rights always requires some sort of authority. Usually this authority is what we call *the sovereign*; and in parallel, we define *sovereignty* as "supreme authority within a territory"

---

14   An important distinction here: the right to subsistence is different from the right to life. The right to life, usually raised in debates on abortion and capital punishment, is a moral principle that argues for a human being's right to live. The right to subsistence, in contrast, is a political-economic right that is concerned with maintaining a human being's life. Moreover, the right to life is concerned with when life begins and ends (how we mark when a cell, an organism, or a 'body' is alive or dead); whereas the right to subsistence is concerned with what is necessary for life to continue.

(Philpott 2016). In other words, the sovereign is someone who has authorship over whatever is going on in the territory they are ruling over. What this means, following Thomas Hobbes – one of the major thinkers on sovereignty – is that they have "the right of doing any action" (Hobbes 1996, xx) over that territory. Because defining sovereignty as such also implies that the sovereign has dominion over their territory (i.e. what Hobbes calls "right of possession" (ibid.)), with whom sovereignty lies has been a hotly contested issue across history and has shaped conversations over a range of issues – from inheritance rights to taxation to administration of justice. Yet, this definition, by keeping the spotlight on the sovereign (and on the one with sovereignty), leaves the subjects(-citizens) in relative darkness: Who are the subjects(-citizens)? Or rather, who is included in the category of subjects(-citizens)? Are criminals and immigrants included, for example? How are the markers of inclusion and exclusion determined – and by whom? Moreover, how much power do the subjects(-citizens) have relative to the sovereign?[15] Is the source of this power some sort of foundational right, that comes from their role as the constituents of the political community, or is it bestowed on the subjects(-citizens) with specific limits, by the sovereign? While political theorists continue to debate these questions (see the highly informative chapter on *'the people'* by Margaret Canovan (2006), for example), I operationalize sovereignty in this analysis as a relation between a ruler (the sovereign) and the ruled (subjects, citizens). In other words, when I talk about sovereignty, I look at the consequences of "the right of doing any action" (Hobbes 1996, xx) over a territory, both for the sovereign (the ruler) and the subjects, and later, citizens (the ruled).

The final distinction I want to emphasize is between the terms 'people' and 'population'. *People* here refers to the sum total of all the members of the political community; *population*, in contrast, is, following Foucault, a unit of operation for particular forms of government. Foucault argues in *Security, Territory, Population* that in the 16th century, the object of government shifted from the individual (who needed to be protected, guided, shepherded) to the population, which was a compilation of individuals identified by certain markers that are common to them all (Foucault 2007). The markers so identified depend on what the sovereign power wants to intervene upon – what it wants to govern. These could be mortality rates, ethnicity, sex, age of pregnancy, rate of vaccination, rate of homelessness, frequency of certain contagious diseases, and so forth. Once the marker is determined and the information generated,

---

15   See for example, the discussions on the 'right to self-preservation' *a la* Hobbes' *Leviathan* (Schrock 1991; Steinberger 2002; Warrender 1957; Zarka 2004; Dyzenhaus 2001; Nagan and Haddad 2012; Sheridan 2011; Pitkin 1964a; 1964b).

a population can be modified through direct and/or indirect interventions ('security') until some sort of desired normal is achieved ('normalization'). As Foucault indicates in *The Birth of Biopolitics*, the form of government that works on the individual and molds the individuals into specific types of subjects ('normation') has not disappeared (Foucault 2008); rather, with the rise of statistics and other forms of scientific knowledge – that enable counting, measuring, analyzing, identifying certain common denominators, and grouping individuals into populations – new forms of government became possible in tandem with already existing forms of governing (though perhaps they were changed in substantial ways!). In other words, as technologies of power changed, so did the unit of intervention and the *mentalité* of intervention.

Population will feature as an important concept in the chapters following (and including) Chapter 3, when there is a shift in the *mentalité*. For example, after the rough war years, the central authority of the young Republic begins to think about self-sustenance: whether it is possible to feed the country with its own resources and the kind of work, planning, and inputs that would entail. This requires the central authority to focus not only on agriculture and related industries, but more importantly, on feeding the country rather than simply provisioning cities. Residents of Istanbul, thus, become a 'population' – one of the markers that identify them is indeed being residents of the old capital. Even if they are faced with scarcity, the central authority does not intervene directly, so long as there is enough food to feed the country in the aggregate. Yet, a closer look at who among the subject-citizens experiences scarcity, reveals that such seeming non-intervention is a form of government in itself – one that leaves some populations (those it considers *enemies*) to live in constant scarcity, while intervening to protect others (those it considers *friends*) against even the possibility of scarcity. Of course, which population gets what treatment was – and is – an inherently political decision.

In the chapters that follow, I cover roughly 5 centuries. However, it is not my objective to provide a chronology of the provisioning apparatuses in each century. Rather, the chapters each focus on the provisioning apparatus of a specific food system, followed by an in-depth discussion of the relation between the sovereign (the central authority) and the subjects(-citizens) that was implied in each food system. Thus, the chapters first delineate how the city was fed, who the provisioning actors were, who was/not fed, what the mode of production was (particularly in agriculture), the assumptions (social, cultural, juridical, philosophical) that mode of production entailed, and the kinds of consumption practices, and discourses it necessitated/brought about; then, they explain the political-economic implications that follow from those factors. As such, while the chapters provide abundant historical detail on the provisioning of Istanbul, they do not offer a history of urban provisioning. Instead, they keep the spotlight on how food systems as a whole mal/function and the sorts of food regimes thus generated.

This approach brings up few important methodological questions: How do we mark the beginning and end of a food system and a food regime, for example – and as such, of their provisioning apparatus(es)? How do we identify the causes for change of and change in a food system and a food regime? How do specific provisioning apparatuses come to belong to specific food systems and food regimes? Can different provisioning apparatuses coexist, or does one need to expire for another to emerge? Can different modes of production coexist? What kind(s) of tensions would that produce within food systems and within food regimes?

First, it is not possible to mark an exact beginning or an end of a food system – and thus, a food regime. This is primarily because food systems are amalgamations of practices, mechanisms, codes of conduct, discourses, and mentalities, and each of these individual components can be found in many different food systems. What distinguishes a food system from another is not the specificity of the practices, mechanisms, and discourses, but the specific way in which these components come together to form the food system. That said, there can certainly be practices, codes of conduct, and discourses, that are either specific to a food system, or are more likely to be found in one food system than another. For example, the food systems of the *urban food provisioning* and the *urban food supply chain* food regimes contain more distinctive practices, codes of conduct, and discourses, that are less likely to be found in each other; whereas, the *codependent provisioning* food regime shows similarities with both, and contains practices, discourses, and mechanisms, that can be found in either.

Second, food systems are very dynamic. Not only do their components change (i.e. the mode of production, the technologies of distribution, the mechanisms, and the codes of conduct for exchange, the discourses and the practices of consumption), but also the specific way(s) these components may come together. It is difficult to discern which change in which component brought about the overall change from one food system to another, or where, when, and how exactly, one food system began to unravel and another one began to emerge.

Third, the unraveling of one food system and the emergence of another one may be due to multiple changes. Even within a specific food system, it is extremely difficult to argue for a linear and unidirectional causal relation between two things. Therefore, we must assume that the change of or change within a food system has multiple causes and triggers. For example, towards the end of the 19th century and especially early in the 20th century, the fresh fruits and vegetables (FFVs) that came to Istanbul from the Marmara region – Yalova, Bursa, Sakarya, Silivri, Tekirdağ, etc. – began to increase. This is partly because the population of the city increased – due to increasing commercial activity following the Treaty of 1838, as also to increasing migrations as a result of regional conflicts. In parallel, again following the Treaty of 1838, the life-styles of particularly the Ottoman elites began to change. For example, the royal family relocated, from their traditional residence at the Topkapı Palace, to the Dolmabahçe Palace; the elites moved out of the city's old quarters and dispersed to the city's immediate hinterlands; and both took up commuting. This, in turn, required street planning to be readjusted to fit horse-drawn car-riages, and later on, cars and street cars. With increasing construction also in older residential areas, to accommodate the city's growing population, urban planning and land ownership ordinances changed – which in turn led to a slow takeover of urban neighborhood gardens (*bostan*s). These *bostan*s, however, were key in-city production locations that had historically supplied the local residents with FFVs. Yet they get taken over by the city's first, modern, con-struction spree; in the long run, the decrease in their numbers led to a decrease in the local (in this case, in-city) production, further exacerbated by a growing population, such that the city began to rely more on the provisions that came from the Marmara region. As this example shows, identifying, documenting, and analyzing all the events, processes, and/or mechanisms that (may) have contributed to and/or triggered a change of or change within a food system is a gargantuan – if not impossible – task, and one perhaps better suited to a historian of urban provisioning. In the book, I explore these processes, to the extent that they are useful for my analysis; that is, so long as they contribute to the understanding of how food systems function and the kinds of food regimes they generate.

In conjunction, what constitutes change is an important ontological ques-tion in and of itself. In the analysis, I conceptualize 'change' as either a quan-titative or a qualitative (and in some cases, both) shift in a food system, that had manifest consequences for the provisioning apparatus: such as an increase or decrease in population, land area cultivated, land-to-labor ratio, etc., geo-graphic shifts in sourcing (local to peripheral, peripheral to peripheral, periph-eral to global, etc.), and/or type of foodstuffs consumed (FFVs to processed FFV products, for example). Most of the time, such movements become visible because one set or subset of actors are adversely affected, while others ben-efit. For example, during the Ottoman period, following a shift in the trade routes to the Atlantic, we see that the merchants and artisans in the central Anatolian cities – who were making money from the caravan trade – gradually lose their incomes and their political-economic influence; whereas the merchants and the artisans in the eastern Mediterranean port cities gain in both. For the provisioning apparatus, these changes bring in concomitant changes in the *mentalité* of agricultural production on the one hand (increasing focus and pressure on some farmers to produce for the global rather than the domestic market), and a tendency to think of urban provisioning within a framework of imports and exports on the other (rather than securing the subsistence of the subjects). These changes, then, trigger yet other changes, which have major political-economic implications for the food regime: the emergence and expansion of the capitalist mode of production in the port cities, accompanied by private property-oriented relations of production (also juridically recognized with Tanzimat), and globally influenced culture(s) of consumption that are only possible with increasing imports into the Empire.

Because the analysis here aims to unravel the differences between *what was* and *what is*, in order to understand why we now provision our cities the way we do, it focuses on the ruptures that gradually got us here. Thus, methodologically, it first delineates certain consequences that make up the *what is* (low agricultural yields, low labor-to-land ratio, scarcity-fueled unrest, ration lines, naval and/or land blockades, devaluation, and currency exchange crises) and then working backwards, it identifies events, forces, tendencies, processes, and mechanisms (Jelali Revolts and the *Büyük Kaçgun*, the Treaty of 1838, World Wars, 24 January Decisions) that led to those consequences.

And finally, periodization: In traditional approaches to the study of food, agriculture, and provisioning, analyses are usually limited to the lifetime, or period within a lifetime, of a state. This is primarily because of the state-centrism that, intentionally or unintentionally, assigns a certain agency to the state and attributes credit or blame to it for the changes explored in those studies. States are certainly powerful, and there indeed are connections between states and (changes in) the mode of production or certain production and consumption practices (the Turkish tea consumption 'habit', for example, is a product of early Republican tea initiatives,) or different mentalities of government, or the generation of new subjects and methods of subject formation. While such an approach can be valuable, it is not inherently useful for tracing continuities and identifying discontinuities that go beyond the state that establishes the frame of reference for these studies. Taking a *longue dureé* approach instead can help overcome these weaknesses, in addition to helping identify the formation of certain relations, mechanisms, and structures, which may themselves change during the process. Equally importantly, a *longue dureé* approach makes identifying periods with common political-economic characteristics possible – even when those characteristics may be outcomes of different processes, events, and discourses. This provides us with new pathways to map, while also pushing us to explore and understand how connections, structures, and decisions that may seem unrelated, can lead to similar consequences.

With these considerations in mind, in the analysis I offer here, I do not follow the state-centric and the relatively rigid division between the Ottoman Empire and the Republic of Turkey. Instead, I have given priority to the food systems and divided the analysis according to the changes in the food regimes. Moreover, I have not fixed when food systems and food regimes begin and end. Rather, I have marked specific, important events that have triggered changes in the food systems and put the food regimes on the wane and/or rise. Thus, the *urban food provisioning* food regime, for example, can go further back than the 15th century, though I have started the analysis with Istanbul's takeover in the 15th century. Its wane, in contrast, can be more clearly marked with the Treaty of 1838. Yet, *codependent provisioning* – the next food regime – does not exactly start with the same agreement. What follows, rather, is an amalgamation of practices, mechanisms, and relations, that eventually became *codependent provisioning*. While this transition happens, however, governments change aplenty, as does the state (from the Empire to the Republic), and the political regime (from a parliamentary monarchy, to an interim parliament, to a constituent assembly, to a parliamentary republic), and as can be expected, there is a lot of going back and forth, a lot of indecision, and a lot of making and changing of minds. Just when the political scene seems to calm down, the Great Depression hits, changing global political-economic conditions entirely, which provides the conditions for the *codependent provisioning* food regime to ripen, though arguably it had started 'brewing' much earlier, as early as 1838 perhaps. Yet, if the analysis were to follow a state-centric periodization, identifying these continuities and discontinuities would have been more challenging, and ultimately, may not have been as productive.

6   Chapter Outlines

In the next chapter, *The Hungry Capital*, I start with a discussion of how Istanbul was provisioned during the Ottoman period. Using a range of primary sources and historical, anthropological, and geographic works on Ottoman Istanbul's provisioning, I mark the characteristics of the food system, identify its pressure points, and trace its dissolution in the 19th century. This historical discussion of the provisioning apparatus is followed by an analysis of the food regime. I argue that in the *urban food provisioning* food regime, the provisioning of the city was considered the sovereign's obligation. The Ottoman central authority had to make sure that Istanbul was well provisioned, not only for practical reasons (to prevent hunger-triggered instability, for example), but also because food transported from the peripheries to the capital represented the reigning sultan's *kudret*[16]: that is, by making fruits of distant lands present in the city, this functioning provisioning apparatus made Ottoman sovereignty viscerally present (or *re-presented*) over those territories and peoples.

Chapters 3 and 4 focus on the *codependent provisioning* food regime. Chapter 3, *Unruly Transitions*, begins the discussion in the early 20th century, emphasizing how some of the mechanisms, measures, practices, relations, and codes of conduct of the previous food system were utilized, as also when the emerging food system was faced with various types of pressure. Following its consolidation, however – as I discuss in Chapter 4, *Planned Scarcities* – concerns, goals, and codes of conduct stemming from the state-led development begin to govern the food system. While the sovereign – in this case, the Republican central authority – was no longer obliged to provision the city, it continued to intervene whenever crises hit Istanbul and/or whenever private actors were simply insufficient and/or unable to provision the city. Rather than ensuring that Istanbul was fed, however, such interventions were directed at the aggregate food supply and demand. They involved the redirection of state resources to support certain private provisioning actors, for example, to build infrastructure to reduce costs, to assign exclusive rights to trade, to provide subsidies and/or to institute certain limits to encourage capital accumulation among the provisioning actors. Of course, not everyone benefitted equally. Distinguishing between *friends* and *enemies*, the state directed its resources and provided support to some (*friends*) and left others on their own (*enemies*) – to deal with the instabilities of the market on the one hand, and hunger, scarcity, and malnutrition, on the other. As such, for both producers and consumers alike, being and remaining within the category of *friends* became literally vital – though how that category was constituted was nebulous and was subject to frequent change. Indeed, for certain ethnic and religious minorities, being or remaining *friends* proved to be too difficult, to put it mildly.

Chapter 5, *Feeding Global Istanbul*, focuses on the contemporary food system and its food regime, which I call, the *urban food supply chain*. Beginning with the crises in the 1970s, which led to the structural adjustment policies and the liberalization of the economy in the 1980s, the chapter explores a set of

---

16   'Kudret', in Turkish, implies health, power (as physical force), and wealth. It can also be used to imply sexual prowess. For more on the term, see Chapter 2, *The Hungry Capital*.

economic transformations that defined, roughly, each decade: the 1980s was the time of the 24 January Decisions, which brought in trade liberalization, and the coup, which enforced the Decisions; the 1990s entailed the liberalization of the capital markets, and subsequently, the increasing preeminence of the finance sector over other sectors; and the 2000s involved further integration with foreign markets and vociferous debates over globalization. At the macro level, these processes (trade liberalization, financialization, globalization) led to a redefinition of economic demands on the one hand (fair wages, job security, unemployment benefits, and so forth), and increasing precarity of both the provisioning agents who supplied the city and the residents of Istanbul who needed to be fed, on the other. In contradistinction from the previous food regime, what governed the classification of people into populations of *friends* and *enemies* (those who have access to food and/or were receiving public resources to access food, as against those who do not) was not just the dominant discourses of the day that defined and redefined *friends* and *enemies*, but also the projected capability of each population and each subject-citizen to become and remain competitive economic agents. I should note that Chapter 5 is significantly longer than other chapters. This is because the liberalization, financialization, and globalization that the Decisions initiated, fundamentally transformed the provisioning apparatus and the food system. In addition, this chapter documents Istanbul's current provisioning apparatus and explains in detail the food supply chains most provisioning agents now use. I take up this opportunity in the section, 'The Contemporary Provisioning Apparatus', and relying on photographs and interview data, I offer a glimpse of how contemporary Istanbulites are provisioned on a daily basis.

Next, in Chapter 6, *Diverging Paths*, I explore the counter-movements that are promising both a different food system and a different food regime to contemporary Istanbulites. The chapter begins by clarifying some of the tensions that have started to widen the cracks within the *urban food supply chain* food system and goes on to discuss how some (particularly affluent) Istanbulites, using those tensions and cracks, are working to actively change the city's contemporary provisioning apparatus. Yet, these changes are not merely practical; they also carry theoretical implications for the food regime – which I discuss in the section, 'Of the Sovereignty, Political Community, and the Central Authority'. Like Chapter 5, most of the data for this chapter comes from interviews with informants, as well as participant observation conducted at relevant sites. The chapter concludes with an assessment of the generalizability of both the *urban food supply chain* food system and the new food system and the food regime the counter-movements are trying to institute.

The conclusion underlines some of the major underlying themes that tie the chapters together, and brings the discussion back to an aspect I highlighted in this introductory chapter: The separation between political and economic forms of coercion, and the dependence on the market and the commodity form to access what one needs to survive and to self-reproduce. Given that these were such key factors in the rise of capitalism (Meiksins Wood, 2017) and have been so critical in the formulation and evolution of sovereign-subject relations in each food regime, the conclusion asks whether it is possible to re-make them in such a way as to make sure that democracy can be recovered, that the right to food and the right to subsistence can be brought back to the foreground of political demands, and that food regimes are organized such that no one in the political community goes hungry. The answer (spoiler alert!) is complicated. However, there is, I think, a clear starting point, and even clearer dos and don'ts, for the way ahead.

CHAPTER 2

The Hungry Capital

The Provisioning of Ottoman Istanbul

> The cities of Germany are completely independent, have little rural
> territory, and obey the Emperor only when they want to. They do
> not fear him or any other neighboring power. (...) For they all pos-
> sess strong walls and adequate moats, and sufficient artillery; and
> they always ensure that their public storehouses contain enough
> food, drink and fuel to last for a year.
>
> NICCOLÒ MACHIAVELLI[1]

∴

From a provisioning perspective, city walls constitute a dilemma: on the one
hand, they protect those residing within from violent intruders and provide
control over what goes in and comes out. On the other hand, they can help
the enemy sequester residents in their own homes. Once shipment routes are
blocked and the wells are poisoned, urban dwellers are on their own. If they
have well-stocked public storehouses, as Machiavelli advises that they should,
they can last longer (perhaps longer than the army setting siege to the city,
who would also be relatively food-insecure); but eventually, they will have to
relent to their stomachs and surrender the city. Exposing the enemy to hunger is perhaps one of the oldest biological weapons; and it is a relatively easy
one to use. There is no need for advanced technology or expensive equipment.
Good planning, intelligence on shipment routes, and strict control over who
and what goes in and comes out, are all that are necessary.

Yet even when they are not under siege, cities may not be the most food-
secure places. If their immediate hinterlands do not produce enough to sustain
them, they will have to rely on producers further out for their provisioning
needs. As such, the location of the city is a key factor – if it has to rely primarily

---

1   Machiavelli, Niccolò. 2016. *The Prince*. Quentin Skinner and Russell Price (eds.) Russell Price
    (trans.) 29th ed. Cambridge: Cambridge University Press, 38.

on its hinterland, then the local production capacity will put a limit on the city's growth; in contrast, the more accessible the city is by water or by land routes, the easier it is for food to be transported, which will, in turn, attract more commercial activity and thus, more people. However, this is not necessarily an advantage. Wealth and crowds are hard to sustain, and they make the city a prize target for looters, invaders, and jealous neighbors. Plus, once the population grows to such an extent that the immediate hinterland cannot meet the food demand, the city will have to expand into a widening periphery to supply its needs. This means, in the long run, it will have to engage in some level of imperial expedition to colonize other cities and divert their resources for its own provisioning needs.

Following Istanbul's conquest by the Ottomans in the mid-15th century, the city's provisioning apparatus reflects these dynamics. When Istanbul was taken, the Ottoman state was on the way to becoming a strong sea-faring empire. Large territories had already been conquered in the Balkans, Anatolia, and around the Mediterranean and Aegean seas, thus making the Ottomans a strong presence in southeastern Europe. The conquest of Constantinople enabled the Ottomans to reinforce their position even more, by closing a byzantine gap between their lands, both east and west of the city. Indeed, after the conquest, for the next 300 years or so, the Empire kept on expanding: into the Balkans in the west, the Levant in the east, and North Africa in the south. Concomitantly, all these newly acquired regions of the Empire began to supply its new capital. Moreover, Istanbul's population, which was diminishing before the conquest, continued to rise well into the 18th century. This population increase, in turn, required expansion in and of the city's older quarters and the integration of peripheral areas into the city proper. In parallel, the demand for food also rose. Although Istanbulites continued to grow some of the fresh fruits and vegetables (FFVs) they consumed (all the way into the 20th century), the rising demand for food pushed provisioning actors to draw from a wider range of producers, thus expanding supply networks. Following the changes in the world economy in the 19th century, such provisioning became a global endeavor.

This chapter explores these dynamics in detail. The next section, 'The Provisioning Apparatuses: Routes, Ports, and Actors', lays out the provisioning actors, their transportation routes, the ports they utilized, their storage and distribution practices, and the various rules and regulations and other forces that governed their operation. The primary focus of this section is the provisions that came from the peripheries of the Empire. In contrast, the section that follows, 'Shared Provisioning Apparatuses', focuses on local supply lines which provided the city with FFVs grown in the city proper and the immediate hinterlands. The changes that led to the dismantling of this food regime were particularly destructive for these local supply apparatuses, because they effectively transformed the cityscape. This section analyzes those dynamics as well. The next section, 'Sovereignty and *Kudret*', shows how the operation of different provisioning apparatuses was indicative of the state of the Empire. The Ottoman central authority had to make sure that Istanbul was well provisioned, not only for practical reasons (to prevent hunger-triggered instability, for example), but also because food transported from the peripheries to the capital represented the reigning sultan's *kudret*. The two sections that follow, 'Timelines and Macro Processes' and 'Transitions: Global Wheat, Local Plum', discuss macro processes that governed Istanbul's provisioning, various problems, tensions, and weaknesses that undercut the smooth functioning of the provisioning apparatus, and finally, key developments that led to its breakdown and the emergence of a new apparatus with different players and dynamics. The final section of the chapter, 'The *Urban Food Provisioning* Food Regime', unpacks the food regime that was constructed by this new apparatus – the actors, practices, and mechanisms – that provisioned the capital.

1   The Provisioning Apparatuses: Routes, Ports, and Actors

Even though trade routes and codes of conduct were changing, the procedures involving the transportation of food into the city and its distribution to various domestic agents remained relatively stable until the 19th century. Given the high number of items – food and other commodities – coming into Istanbul every day, the authorities had to allocate different ports of the city to specific items (Tabakoğlu 2014). For example, Unkapanı (Wheat Port) served as an entrance for wheat, while dried and fresh fruits were received into the city from *Yemiş İskelesi* (Fruit Docks); Bahçekapı İskelesi (Pier of Garden Gate) was used to unload items exclusively destined for the Palace, whereas various food items for the consumption of commoners entered the city from Balat Kapısı İskelesi (Pier of Balat Port) (Kauffer 1996). Each cargo ship had to dock at the correct port, get its cargo inspected, its papers checked, and the quality and quantity of its cargo registered with the Ottoman authorities.

   Until the trade agreements of the 19th century, prices would be determined by a negotiation process between the trader and the guild (*lonca*) (İnalcık 1994). The guild master would suggest a price to the trader, in line with estimated transportation costs, taxes, and wages (ibid). Traders did not necessarily have to accept the suggested price immediately; however, unless an agreement was reached between the trader and the guild on the price, cargo was not allowed to be unloaded at the docks – which put pressure on both the traders (to minimize costs) and the guilds (to not cause scarcity in the city) to agree on a price as quickly as possible (ibid). Furthermore, Ottoman officials facilitated the negotiations to make sure neither side suffered losses in the process (ibid). In times of crisis, however, the Sublime Porte sent officials to the production locations and bought the produce in bulk from the traders for fixed prices (*narh*).[2]

The Ottoman authorities were aware that if *narh* was applied in normal times, the produce might disappear entirely from the markets (Güran 2004, 322; Pamuk 2014, 103–122), or traders might work to undercut the *narh* (İnalcık 1994; Pamuk 2014, 21–22). Traders could, for example, register whatever they were bringing into the city as low-quality and then sell the better-quality produce illegally for higher prices; or declare their cargo as less in weight, and then sell the remaining cargo on the side – again, illegally (Murphey 1987; Sakaoğlu and Akbayar 2000). Some traders would hoard the produce and push the prices up by causing shortages in the city (Sakaoğlu ve Akbayar 2000; Tabakoğlu 2014). Since inspections were stricter at the ports in Istanbul, they would strike deals with producers and hoard the produce close to its location of production (İnalcık 1994, 118; Murphey 1987; Sakaoğlu ve Akbayar 2000; Tabakoğlu 2014). This was especially common during winter months, when the sea traffic in the Black Sea slowed down and/or stopped, due to the weather and sea conditions (Güran 2004, 322; Murphey 1987). In response, the central authority would send out ships to locations of production and enforce *narh* locally; however, this time, the traders would sell the produce to higher paying foreign traders. Over the years, Ottoman authorities even closed off certain sea routes to foreign ships and assigned sales rights to specific traders, to maintain control over especially the meat and the wheat trade (Güran 2004, 322; Murphey 1987). In addition, they made some of these activities punishable by death, particularly those involving hoarding and speculating, and causing shortages and famine in the city, (Güran 2004, 322; Murphey 1987). Still, the illegal trade outside the Bosporus coastline flourished (Güran 2004, 322; Murphey 1987).[3]

---

2   I should note that *narh* was primarily practiced for the provisioning of the capitals (Istanbul, and before that, Bursa and Edirne) (Pamuk 2014, 49). This selectivity tells us: first, the significance of the capital's provisioning for the Empire; and second, the limited power of the Ottoman central authorities, preventing them from enforcing *narh* everywhere across their territories.

3   *Narh* practice continued until 1865 (Toprak 1994a, 221). After the establishment of the municipality in Beyoğlu district, called *Altıncı Daire-i Belediye*, setting prices and enforcing the use of correct measurements became the municipality's duty (ibid.). However, in 1865, it was decided that the municipality would enforce *narh* only for bread (ibid). Given that most

FIGURE 2   Itinerant garlic seller, late Ottoman era
             PHOTO COURTESY OF THE ENGIN ÖZENDES COLLECTION

The tug of war between the Ottoman authorities and the traders in the
earlier periods foreshadowed the tensions of the 19th century. However, the

members of the municipality council were traders, and the *narh* practice often worked
against them, the abolition of *narh* shows the power the trader class gained within Ottoman
administrative structures in the 19th century (ibid, 222). Note that to be elected to the municipality council, candidates were required to own at least 100,000 *kuruş* worth of private property in the district (Toprak 1994a, 220).

involvement of the Ottoman authorities in the provisioning of the city, the punishment of illegal trade activities, and their relationship to the provisioning actors, was much more interventionist in this earlier period. The imperial court, *Divan-ı Hümayun*, was the ultimate judge for all sorts of disagreements that could arise between actors. It attended to cases of hoarding and speculation and prosecuted illegal trading activities (Uzun 2006; İnalcık 1994). In addition, it decided whether to open more bakeries or expand the available ones based on the proposals of the Qadi (*kadı*), and the minimum and maximum profit[4] each shop could make per type of commodity sold (Güran 2004; İnalcık 1994). Primarily, however, the Qadi was the official responsible for overseeing the provisioning system (Güran 2004; Uzun 2006; İnalcık 1994; Samancı 2009; İstanbul 1993d). Most importantly, he decided when *narh* was necessary and recorded the prices in price notebooks (*narh defterleri*) (Samancı 2009). In the docks, the customs officials and the custodians (*emin*) supported him (İnalcık 1994, 117–118).[5] Appointed by the sultan, these customs officials and custodians inspected, recorded, and taxed each cargo ship, and made sure that the shops received their allocated shares (ibid). If the shopkeepers had any problems or if they wanted to change their delivery days, for example, they would have to talk to the customs officials and the custodians (ibid, 117). For legal matters, *emin*s consulted with appointed *naib*s (ibid, 118). Finally, *muhtesib*, or the constabularies, checked on the shopkeepers, making sure that the shops were clean, the scales were not tampered with, and the profit margins declared by the imperial court were respected (ibid). Each of these actors worked under and in cooperation with the Qadi.

Even though there were attempts to mediate it, corruption was still very common in this convoluted provisioning network, especially among officials. As Inalcik notes, complaints from the traders often made all the way up to the *Divan-ı Hümayun* (İnalcık 1994, 118). In those cases, the imperial court tended to side with the traders; however, it deferred to the Qadi on the regulatory and preventive measures to be taken, and how they would

---

4   According to Inalcik, prices for wheat, meat, and other staples would be determined seasonally, for 3 months, by the Qadi (1994, 118). Groceries were usually allowed a 10% profit margin; and for other goods that required more labor, a 12% profit margin was deemed acceptable (ibid.).

5   Once expensive commodities and spices were cleared by the customs, they would be taken right to the Spice Bazaar – which is located close to the dock area. The head of the custodians (known as '*Emin*') also resided close to the docks, making sure that the cargo under custody was closely inspected and recorded, and that there were no thefts while the cargo was under custody. This customs-dock area is still known as *Eminönü*.

FIGURE 3   Men carrying fat from the Oil Port, late 19th century
PHOTO COURTESY OF THE CENGIZ KAHRAMAN ARCHIVE

be enforced (ibid).[6] The success of the Qadis in preventing and punishing corruption is unclear. Nonetheless, beginning in the 18th century, but more so in the 19th century, even after the position of the Qadi weakened and the *narh* practice was stopped, there is no indication that the problem(s) of corruption went away. The newly established ministries and their subcommittees, which overtook the Qadi's power and responsibilities, seemed to have maintained relations and practices that tolerated, if not encouraged, corruption.

The strict controls at the Istanbul ports continued during the storage and the distribution of the cargo. Immediately after it was unloaded, the produce was stored at the ports, and then promptly moved to the distribution locations

---

6   On a more interesting note, it is known that some sultans would dress up as commoners and
    visit shops and marketplaces. While in disguise, if the sultan were to catch any of the shop-
    keepers overcharging for goods or operating with tampered scales, those shopkeepers would
    be executed. Messing with the poor man's bread was considered particularly deserving of
    punishment. Even in contemporary Turkish, "*ekmekle oynamak*" (playing with [someone's]
    bread) is an epithet frequently used to portray someone as greedy and/or cruel, or wishing ill
    upon others.

managed by the guilds (İnalcık 1994). In the case of wheat, these distribution locations were the guild-registered bakeries around town; for meat, they were the slaughterhouses, butchers, etc. How much each shop received as well as how big each shop was, depended on the population of the neighborhood the shop operated in (Güran 2004, 323).[7] Moreover, the neighborhoods were established along ethnic and religious lines; thus, each neighborhood had its own butcher, baker, greengrocer, etc. which were, in turn, regulated according to their own, specific religious ordinances.[8] Although some ethnic and religious groups tended to specialize in specific jobs, the Sublime Porte meticulously regulated who could shop from where, who could employ whom and who could become a member of the guild network (Göktaş 2010; İnalcık 1994).

I should note that the Ottomans considered sheep's meat and wheat (or rather, bread) as the primary staples and the measures to ensure that the city was always well-provisioned mainly focused on these two items.[9] This is not to say that the provisioning of other foods were neglected. Coffee, for example, even though initially prohibited, was regularly supplied to the city, after it gained public and royal acceptance. Similarly, the insatiable sweet tooth of the Ottomans kept the demand for honey and sugar high; and the city was well provisioned with sweets throughout its history. The famous Spice Market (*Mısır Çarşısı*) drew spices from as far as the traders were willing to travel to; and although preferences changed over the centuries, the demand for spices did not. As much as the staples, the availability and accessibility of these other food items in the city provided a clear sign of the Empire's – and the reigning sultan's – *kudret*.[10]

---

7   Bakeries often had animal-powered mills attached, where wheat was turned into flour (Güran 2004, 323). Expanding the shop here means essentially expanding the mill (ibid). Güran states that by the 18th century, most bakeries were owned by state-funded charities, or waqf (*vakıf* in Turkish) (323); and according to İnalcık, most other food shops were owned by high-ranking officials (*paşa*), members of the Janissary Army, legal and religious scholars (*ulema*), and rich peasants from the countryside (*bey*; *ağa*) (118).

8   Jews, Muslims, and Christians also had different butchers (İnalcık 1994, 118; Sakaoğlu 1994a). For example, most of the chicken shops were owned by non-Muslims (ibid.); and until 1861, non-Muslims were not allowed to own or run grocery shops (*bakkals*) (Göktaş 2010, 361).

9   For studies on Istanbul's meat provisioning, see Uzun (2006); Greenwood (1988).

10 '*Kudret*', in Turkish, implies health, power (as physical force), and wealth. It can also be used to imply sexual prowess. *Kudret helvası*, for example, is a type of sweet paste that is made up of honey or simple syrup or grape or mulberry molasses (and sometimes a combination of these) mixed in with nuts, seeds, grains, and spices. It is believed to provide men (and only men) with sexual prowess. Later in the chapter, I will discuss how a functioning provisioning apparatus indicated the sultan's *kudret*.

2   Shared Provisioning Apparatuses

There were also locally produced foods. These were mostly perishables (such as FFVs, fish, and dairy products) which are generally more difficult and costly to deal with in the absence of refrigeration, pasteurization, and air-tight packaging. Their production-consumption cycle tends to be short since they needed to be bought and consumed as fresh as possible. Their perishability thus necessitates a different – more local – provisioning apparatus. In the case of Istanbul, we know, for example, that most of the fish (and sea food) that the residents of the city consumed came from the three seas surrounding the city.[11] While salted, dried, and smoked fish were also available, these were imported and as such, they followed procedures similar to other foods coming into the city.[12] Fresh fish was caught daily, and the harvest was sold close to the docks, under the control of the fishermen's guild. Most of the regularly consumed dairy products were also locally sourced. Due to the population density of the old quarters, the villages in the immediate hinterlands of the city and along the Bosporus supplied Istanbul with milk, butter, yoghurt, cheese, and cream daily. Animals were also kept in the more sparsely populated neighborhoods, close to the northwestern and the northeastern walls of the city. There are plenty of records, land registries, and maps also showing the *bostan*s in these areas. It wouldn't be a stretch of the imagination to assume that among their other uses, animals were also kept for ploughing and fertilizing these in-city fields.

Fresh fruits and vegetables had a similar shared provisioning apparatus. As I mentioned before, *Yemiş İskelesi* (Fruit Docks) was the primary port through which dried and fresh fruits arrived into the city. It also functioned as a wholesale location for the neighborhood greengrocers, mobile vendors, large households, charities (waqf; *vakıf*), and other institutions that preferred to buy the produce in bulk (Göktaş 2010, 360–361; Ünsal 2010). However, there were also plenty of FFVs produced in and around Istanbul. Traditional Ottoman houses fancied a front and a back garden and sometimes also a courtyard (*avlu*), where various vegetables and fruit trees were

---

11   The Marmara and Black Seas are inland seas, connected to the Mediterranean via the Aegean Sea. Each of these seas have different salinity and water temperatures. Consequently, they harbor different types of fish in different seasons.

12   However, I don't think it would be wrong to assume that there was some salted, dried, and smoked fish production in the city. Tracing the production and consumption patterns of *lakerda* (pickled bonito) historically, for example, may give us an idea about this aspect.

FIGURE 4   A *bostan* (vegetable garden) along the Edirnekapı Walls, 19th century
PHOTO COURTESY OF THE CENGIZ KAHRAMAN ARCHIVE

cultivated alongside flowers. Plus, charities, schools, hospitals, religious institutions, and military barracks had gardens and fields for vegetable, fruit, and
medicinal herb production. Finally, patches of gardens (*bahçe*s), orchards
(*bağ*s), and fields (*tarla*s; *bostan*s) in almost every neighborhood supplied
the residents of the capital with fresh produce. Depending on their property
status, these local production sites were worked on by different groups of
people: *Bostancı Ocağı* (Bostancı Guild), immigrants (who usually worked on
the *bostan*s in the old quarters), rich families who had slaves and/or who
could hire seasonal laborers, or villagers along the coasts of Bosporus were
contracted out to cultivate these lands. Unfortunately, clear records of how
much was produced and consumed by these local supply lines do not exist.
However, based on existing sources, it is possible to deduce that Istanbul had
enough gardens, orchards, and fields, and concomitantly, enough production,
to counter the stereotypical portrayal of urban areas as non-agricultural. On
the contrary, Ottoman Istanbul was a green city with many gardens, fields,
and orchards.[13]

---

13   Please see Appendix 1 for a note on some early sources on Ottoman Istanbul's *bağ, bahçe,*
and *bostan.*

3   Sovereignty and *Kudret*

Before it lost its prominence, the *urban food provisioning* food regime served
a few important purposes: it delivered food to the residents of the capital; it
tied Istanbul to the rest of the Empire (and vice-versa) spatially and gastronomically; and it represented the *kudret* of the sultan. What I mean by *kudret*
here goes beyond the ritualistic displays of the sultan's good character, which
were considered reflections of Allah's glory in his persona. As Suraiya Faroqhi
diligently details in *Another Mirror for Princes*, the sultans regularly gave alms,
built charities, funded wakfs, and held lengthy festivities (weddings, circum-
cision celebrations, religious holidays – *bayram* – and ascension parades) in
which they fed commoners alongside the officials of the Imperial Court and the
Janissary Army (Faroqhi 2009, 7–34). These acts communicated to the subjects
that their sultan was modest, open-handed, just, compassionate, and as hum-
ble as they were (ibid). In comparison to these more traditional displays, the
provisioning of the city represented the sultan's glory at a completely different
level: a well-provisioned city and a smooth-functioning provisioning apparatus communicated to the subjects that their sultan was capable of controlling
resources, that he could dominate different peoples spread over large territories, that he was skilled in directing, managing, organizing – in short, *governing* – what they produced and what Istanbulites consumed, that he could command and maintain influence – coercively and otherwise – over the merchants
who frequently tried to outwit his laws, rules and regulations. Finally, a well-
provisioned city and a smooth-functioning provisioning apparatus showed
that the sultan's sovereignty was absolute, his authority was supreme, and
that he was the judge over rebellious subjects, law-breaking merchants and
artisans, and scheming foreigners who would take away Istanbulites' food by
paying more to the greedy traders ever on the lookout to make more profit. In
other words, the provisioning apparatus put on display the sultan's tact in overcoming problems and threats directed at the political community, and as such,
his prowess in governing the peoples and the territories under his authority.

However, it would be a mistake to perceive this representation of the sultan's capability and control as unidirectional and unidimensional. In showing
the extent of his reach, the force of his law, and the degree of his involvement
in the organization and the management of the actors, the city's provisioning also represented the limits of his reach, force, and control.[14] As far as the

---

14   Perhaps one of the most explicit articulations of this limit was packed into a commonly
        used idiom that is still in currency: "*Ferman padişahınsa, dağlar bizimdir*" (roughly trans-
        lates to: If the *ferman* [word, law, command, decision] belongs to the sultan, the mountains

sultan could reach, he could not reach further; each corrupt administrative official and each scheming merchant offered a challenge to the force of his law; and every war, every incident of bad weather and/or drought, every interruption of production patterns and transportation routes dispelled the illusion of his – and the Empire's – *kudret*. Indeed, the peasant rebellions that went on for almost a century (mid-16th to mid-17th centuries) and upset production patterns in mainland Anatolia at the height of Ottoman power, were clear indications of these limits, as was every concession government officials were willing to make to traders, Europeans, and regional elites. Finally, tacit, and explicit recognition of the disruptive potential of a hungry populace set the ultimate limit to the sultan's force and control. What was at stake was not only the violence that the residents of the city could conjure, but more importantly, the disillusionment that followed on two fronts: one, the vulnerability of the sultan, and two, through the sultan, the vulnerability of the Empire.

With vulnerability, I mean the imminence of death; the shifting of the limits of one's mortality and endurance, due to external or internal infringements; and the breaking down of one's bodily order, harmony, constitution, and/or balance. Note that this conceptualization casts vulnerability as a bodily as well as a social characteristic. It recognizes that the corporeal aspects of vulnerability are reflected, shaped by, and shape its social aspects. As such, awareness of one's vulnerability creates, on the one hand, a sense of existential insecurity, being under threat, or being in risk of bodily harm; and on the other hand, a sense of social insecurity, being constantly on the verge of losing various communal attachments. The political community is understood to be founded on this sense of bodily and social vulnerability, with the aim of *governing* – managing, containing, protecting, concealing – members' vulnerabilities so that they do not lead to the members' death and/or to the dissolution of the *body*

---

belong to us). Similarly, *dağa çıkmak* (ascending a mountain) was (and is) used to imply taking up arms against the central authority. The practice and the idiom make clear the significance of distance in the relationship between the sultan (the ruler, the sovereign, the central authority) and the subjects: whereas the sultan could take his time responding to the grievances of his subjects in the countryside (although dragging the conflict out could leave the situation open to interference by third parties), his response had to be immediate for Istanbulites. Indeed, as opposed to the provincial folks who ascended and (re)claimed the mountains, Istanbulites 'lift cauldrons' (*kazan kaldırmak*) to make themselves heard. This idiom comes from the Janissary Army's practice of lifting the cauldrons (which were used for cooking) and placing them in front of their barracks or parading them to air their grievances or to show their frustration or discontent. Depending on the climate in the city, these disgruntled, cauldron-carrying Janissaries could find support from Istanbulites – which would lead the protest to morph into a rebellion that could unsettle the Empire.

politic. The urban provisioning apparatus is one of many apparatuses the political community uses, to manage the members' and the community's vulnerabilities, both at the individual and collective levels.

Then, when the capital could not be fed, trouble was to be expected from the subjects. If scarcity took a turn for the worse, the sultan and the officials of the Imperial Court would suffer, much like the residents of the city; but more importantly, they would become targets of hunger-motivated violence that the subjects could and would conjure. Therefore, for their own sake, as much as the subjects', the Ottoman central authority had a stake in making sure that the capital (and primarily the capital) was well-provisioned. A failure of the food system exposed vulnerabilities – to subjects, that the sultan was incapable; to the central authority, that the provisioning agents were making light of its rules, regulations, and mechanisms of enforcement; and thus to enemies, inside and outside, that the central authority had weakened. Critically, the failure to feed the capital exposed the corporeality and the mortality of the central authority and the reigning sultan. Scarcity and hunger gripping the city reminded its residents that the sultan and the officials of the Imperial Court were 'mere bodies', just like them – eating, drinking, sleeping, excreting, etc.; and, as bodies, they could be starved, mutilated, and killed. Such violence, in turn, signaled to everyone that the Empire was in disarray, and its vulnerabilities could be taken advantage of. Thus, the scarcity that the failure of the urban provisioning apparatus and the food system generated, exposed the vulnerabilities of all (the subjects, the sovereign, and the mechanisms through which the sovereign governed) and as such, corroded the *body politic.*

Yet, even with all the attention the Ottoman central authority paid to the provisioning of its capital, Istanbul still suffered from high prices, food scarcities, and occasionally, hunger (Karademir 2017; İstanbul 1993e). In addition, prioritizing Istanbul's provisioning often put the peripheries at a disadvantage (Tabakoğlu 2014). The institution of *narh*, bulk purchases in locations of production and the redirection of shipments, caused or exacerbated scarcities in these regions. They, therefore, had to take their own anti-scarcity measures. Dynamics similar to those in Istanbul were at play, especially in the regional capitals where the seats of the local governments were located. Governors appointed from Istanbul had to be diligent about the provisioning of the regional capitals; at the same time, their provisioning apparatus ought not hinder the supply of foodstuffs headed to Istanbul. Still, in the event that the conditions worsened in the peripheries and scarcity turned into hunger, things could suddenly escalate: hunger could become famine and individual acts of violence, theft, and looting could turn into a riot or a rebellion that could, in turn, threaten the entire Empire's stability. The priority was thus to keep regional problems as contained – in other words, as regional – as possible. Nonetheless, the food system failed frequently, and the food regime was not devoid of riots and/or rebellions that followed such instances of failure (Karademir 2017).

For the residents of the capital, however, a well-provisioned city was as representative of Ottoman sovereignty and the reigning sultan's *kudret,* as were hunger and scarcity. A functioning provisioning apparatus made the fruits of the peripheral subjects' labor present for the consumption of Istanbulites; and as such, it made present – literally and figuratively – the Ottoman sovereignty over lands and peoples far and wide: an apple picked in Corfu, for example, or wheat harvested in Ukraine, butter churned in Bulgaria, rice grown in Damietta, to be consumed by the residents of Istanbul, represented Ottoman rule over these lands and their peoples to all parties concerned. In other words, the literal act of making food from far corners of the Empire present in the capital, made the sultan's sovereignty over his territories figuratively present for his subjects.[15] The urban provisioning apparatus thus established a direct relation between the sultan and the producing-consuming bodies of his subjects, through the stomachs of everyone involved. It indicated to the subjects – in the peripheries and in the capital, gastronomically and corporeally – the priorities of the Ottoman central authority, the lands and peoples the Ottomans reigned over, and how well (or ill) they could govern.

4 Timelines and Macro Processes

In the period between 1453 to 1838, the Empire's capital was provisioned from the peripheries that had direct access to the sea trade: Ukraine, Croatia, Bulgaria, Greece, Syrian, Lebanon, and Egypt, all fed the city. Through the 18th and the 19th centuries, however, the Empire lost its control over these regions, and had to increasingly rely on the remaining territories and the global sea trade for Istanbul's provisioning. This constituted a multifaceted problem: the Anatolian mainland and the Levant were landlocked and inaccessible, due to the absence of transportation infrastructures; their aggregate surplus production was not enough to regularly feed the capital; and the towns and cities that had access to the sea trade had begun to switch to export-oriented commercial

---

15   This conceptualization (making something figuratively present by making something else literally present) follows Hannah Pitkin's influential analysis of the concept of representation in her now-canonical work *The Concept of Representation* (1967, 144).

agriculture – and thus, as far as local provisioning agents were concerned, Istanbul's demand for food had to compete with the global demand.

These three problems were interrelated, and they arose from the structural instabilities the Empire faced in the 16th and the 17th centuries. Most importantly, from the mid-16th century to the mid-17th century, the Jelali Revolts (*Celali İsyanları*) wrecked the Anatolian heartland. Though a discussion of the complex socio-economic and political dynamics that led to the Revolts is beyond the scope of this book, their consequences were among the factors that shaped Istanbul's provisioning apparatus, and thus merit mention here. As İlhan Tekeli points out, the Jelali Revolts resulted in what is called "Büyük Kaçgun" – the *en masse* desertion of plain and lowland villages for the highlands. Aside from the huge demographic shift, "Büyük Kaçgun" revealed the insecurity and instability engulfing the Anatolian heartland, while the Empire was at its zenith. It upset the *timar*[16] system and altered the production patterns (Tekeli 1985, 881). As the numbers of peasants who were uprooted and became landless rose (Pamuk 2015, 150–151), so did the prices of agricultural commodities. The merchants who traded in those goods in the hinterland and the military classes who relied on the *timar* system were slowly squeezed out of their profits, and both gradually lost their prominence in the Ottoman social and economic structures (Tekeli 1985).

In the long run, the disarray caused by the Revolts had two fundamental consequences: First, the population-to-land ratio remained rather small, even though the Empire was shrinking in terms of territory and expanding in terms of population. Following the "Büyük Kaçgun", certain parts of mainland Anatolia became quite hollowed-out (Tekeli 1985, 881). Diseases, rural insecurity, and corruption among local authorities and military classes throughout the 18th century worsened the instability (ibid). The situation did not get better until the 19th century, when the Sublime Porte settled the Muslim emigrants from the Balkans into these sparsely populated regions of the Empire, aiming to counter the spiral of death, insecurity, disease, and corruption that had wreaked havoc in the Anatolian mainland (ibid, 878–881). As a result of these efforts, the population gradually increased, though the land-to-labor ratio did not improve.[17] Chronic labor shortages thus significantly hindered the switch

---

16   A complex land structure that densely intertwined certain branches of the Ottoman military with the Ottoman taxation system and the peasantry. Note that the Jelali Revolts were not the reason why the *timar* system was becoming dysfunctional; though they were among its symptoms. A discussion of why and how the *timar* system became dysfunctional and was eventually replaced is, unfortunately, beyond the scope of this book. (For this, see Pamuk 2014, 12–15, 132–139).

17   Labor continued to be short in comparison to land, until the 1950s (Silier 1981).

to export-oriented commercial agriculture (Keyder 1985, 643), as Anatolian peasants could resist the production and price imperatives of the market, and continue with subsistence farming or small-scale commercial farming on the plots allocated to them.

Second, there was a shift in trade routes. Artisans and merchants in the port cities, who could reorient their production and increase agricultural output in the port cities' immediate hinterlands, began to command more economic power (Tekeli 1985, 881). The port cities were quickly integrated with the Europe-dominated global economy, especially after the 1838 trade agreement (Keyder 1985, 642–645; Tekeli 1985). Landlocked mainland Anatolia, in contrast, had to wait until the railroads connected it with the port cities (Tekeli 1985). As a result, the Anatolian cities and the towns on the land trade routes lost their allure as commercial centers, and Anatolian populations remained much less influenced by global consumption trends, political currents, and economic tides.

Trade agreements following the one in 1838,[18] further confounded the diverging trajectories of the Anatolian mainland and the port cities. Plus, with the introduction of steam ships, Ottoman trade volume had begun to expand, from the 1820s onward (Keyder 1985, 644). Thus, to prioritize the provisioning of the domestic market and to ensure the continuation of domestic artisanal production, the Ottoman authorities issued an export restriction on certain goods (Toprak 1985, 668). Titled *Yed-i Vahid*, this restriction was applied initially only to hashish, but was gradually expanded to cover silk, fleece wool, angora wool, cotton, olive oil, and grains (ibid). Following the trade agreements and Mahmud II's reluctant recognition of the legitimacy of his subjects' private property in conjunction to the Tanzimat, *Yed-i Vahid* was considered a violation of free trade principles, and subsequently, removed. Moreover, with the trade agreements, customs duties and taxes on imported commodities were lowered to 1% by 1861, which helped the traders in the port cities immensely (Toprak 1985, 668; Pamuk 2012, 30–31). In comparison, transportation taxes and internal customs duties for exported commodities continued until 1874

---

18   These agreements were: with France on November 25, 1838; with Spain on March 4, 1839; with Sardinia at the end of March 1839; with Hamburg on May 20, 1839; with Federal Dutch Provinces on March 20, 1840; with Belgium on August 11, 1840; with Prussia on October 22, 1840; with Sweden on January 21, 1841; with Denmark on May 1, 1841; with Toscana on June 7, 1841; with Hamburg (again) on September 15, 1841; with Portugal on March 6, 1843; with Russia on April 30, 1846; with Sicily on September 19, 1850; with Sicily (again) on March 5, 1851; with Sardinia (again) on March 31, 1984; with Brazil on February 5, 1858 (Kurdakul 1985).

(Toprak 1985, 668). These changes made foreign trade much more profitable than domestic trade. Consequently, traders in the port cities of the remaining Ottoman lands and the peasants in their immediate hinterlands began to turn towards export-oriented production (Pamuk 2012, 14–17). This increasingly destabilized the networks that provisioned Istanbul.

The first half of the 19th century, then, signaled a disjuncture in Istanbul's provisioning. The areas initially provisioning the city had seceded from the Empire, thus pushing the Ottoman central authority to turn towards the Levant and the Anatolian mainland to feed the city. Yet, Anatolia still suffered the structural effects of the peasant revolts from the 16th and the 17th centuries: even with the settlement of Muslim subjects in the 19th century, the land-to-labor ratio was still high, productivity was comparatively low, and peasants tended to stick to subsistence farming. Plus, a lack of investment in transportation infrastructures (until the late 19th century) locked in any surplus produced in these regions.[19] In contrast, in the port cities and their immediate hinterlands, the removal of domestic customs' duties and transportation taxes had created incentives for some traders and peasants, but even for them, producing for export was more profitable than supplying the domestic market. After all, the sharp decline in the customs duties and taxes for imports, had made imported commodities much more competitive in the domestic market.[20]

With the trade agreements in the 19th century, provisioning apparatuses thus began to change. Once the railway network began to connect the Anatolian mainland to the port cities, trade picked up significantly (Pamuk 2012, 12–13).[21]

---

19   The lack of transportation infrastructures should not necessarily imply that peasants
      and the commodities produced by them were stuck in the villages. Pamuk, for example,
      does a very good job of showing that peasants in the countryside were indeed part of the
      Anatolian urban economies (see Pamuk 2014, 19–30, 77–102, 103–122). It should be noted,
      however that, the type of trade these peasants engaged in was very different from the kind
      of trade – or rather, the kind of operation – necessary to keep Istanbul provisioned. The
      scales and stakes of provisioning Istanbul were much higher than the caravan trade the
      Anatolian hinterlands could offer and provide.
20   The Anatolian hinterland was closed off to Istanbul until railroads were built in the
      19th century. Even then, according to some sources, transporting wheat from mainland
      Anatolia was 75% more expensive than shipping it from New York. (Boratav 2007, 28).
21   I should add that, in the 19th century, the characteristics of commodities traded also
      changed. As Aktüre notes, before the 19th century, most of the goods traded out of major
      Anatolian trading cities were value-added commodities, such as Angora (Ankara) wool,
      silk carpets and textiles, copper kitchen utensils, for example (1985). After the trade agree-
      ments, however, raw materials (unprocessed wool and goats; unprocessed silk; copper)
      became the primary commodities of trade (ibid). I should also note that because there
      was very little to no export previously, early numbers of growth in the volume of trade

Nevertheless, transportation difficulties and the relative surplus of land in comparison to the shortage of labor, kept the costs of provisioning the capital from mainland Anatolia high (even though the Empire continuously took in Muslim emigrants throughout the 19th and early 20th century). Consequently, Ottoman authorities began to turn to the global market to provision Istanbul.

5   Transitions: Global Wheat, Local Plum

During the long 19th century, Istanbul's provisioning continued to occupy the agendas of the Ottoman authorities. The reasons, however, had changed: Initially, the well provisioned capital was a sign of the Empire's – more specifically, the reigning sultan's – *kudret*. It symbolized the extent of his reach over distant lands and peoples; it reflected his health, both mental and physical; and it represented his power over his subjects who – willingly or unwillingly – laid down the fruits of their labor to feed his city. If the city went hungry, it meant the Empire – but more so, the sultan – had become weak and unhealthy; and by implication, had to be removed. Thus, violence, accompanying hunger and scarcity, took over the city; and unless appeased, it did not stop until it claimed some heads, whether of the sultan or the members of the Imperial Court.

By the 19th century, urban provisioning was no longer a representation of the sultan's *kudret*. It had become a logistical and an economic issue – with significant political consequences. On the one hand, trade agreements with Europe inhibited Ottoman authorities from intervening into the provisioning networks, and/or enacting various laws, rules, and quotas to ensure the smooth flow of food into the city. As the proponents of these agreements argued, such interventions would clash with the principles of free market economy that the trade agreements espoused. On the other hand, Istanbul was growing in population. Migrants from the seceding Balkan regions, people running away from the instabilities in the Caucasus, North Africa and the Middle East, were coming to Istanbul either to settle or were passing through the city to settle elsewhere. Plus, the Janissary Army was dissolved, and a permanent standing army was instituted in its place. Barracks, hospitals, schools, and training areas were established in Istanbul, thus increasing the capital's population, urban density, and concomitantly, exacerbating the provisioning needs.[22] In other

---

tended to be high, and as such, are not necessarily representative of long-term tendencies (Pamuk 2012, 79).

22   For example, to respond to these needs, a flour mill specifically for military use – *Askeri Tahiniye Fabrikası* –was established (see Dölen 1993).

words, due to increasing population, it was becoming more difficult to keep the city fed (Tekeli 1985).

The shared provisioning apparatus of perishables had also begun to change. First, through global trade and better transportation technologies (most notably railways and steam ships), produce from longer distances began to be available for public consumption. Also, new fruits and vegetables, alongside new dishes, cooking techniques, serving styles, and utensils began to circulate in the capital and in the major port cities. Even though regional specialties, like Bursa peaches, Malatya apricots, Aydin figs, kept their fame, New World fruits and vegetables, such as tomatoes and potatoes, started to find a place in the local cuisines. At the same time, due to changing production and trade dynamics, local production gained more prominence. Stark fluctuations in prices, wages, and the value of the Ottoman currency throughout the 19th and the early 20th century (Pamuk 2014, 123–132, 144–146, 155–180), made imported foods increasingly unreliable as a source of provisioning for Istanbulites. Instead, gardens, fields, and orchards in and around Istanbul provided the residents with easy and fast access to FFVs. Especially during wars, when the global trade routes were interrupted, local production kept the capital fed. Thus, production sites in and around the city were vital; and they needed to be protected.

Yet, population pressures and new urban planning efforts set different priorities for in-city production locations. With the 1857 Land Statute (*Arazi*

Candie (le marché)

Edit. R. Behaeddin, Photogr., Candie-Crète. No. 23

FIGURE 5   A *manav* (fruit and vegetable seller) at the market, 19th century
PHOTO COURTESY OF THE SEYIT ALI AK ARCHIVE

Kanunnamesi), arable lands around Istanbul (and in the countryside) had become inheritable private property (Tekeli 1985); and with the increasing demand for housing and space from the emigrating populations, the Statute had contributed to a spiraling increase in land prices in and around the city. Consequently, Istanbul began to expand. In addition, foreign firms began to operate ferries and trams in the city (ibid, 882), turning inaccessible outskirts into natural extensions and establishing new expansion routes. Plus, the royal family, high officials of the Imperial Court, and the nouveau riche adopted horse carts for their daily travels and gradually moved out of the city's old quarters (İstanbul 1993e).[23] They thus contributed not only to the expansion of the city, but also to its reconstruction: Their horse carts required streets to be expanded and more orderly city grids (without dead ends, for example) to be planned (Tekeli 1985). For the in-city locations of production, these trends led to a counter-trajectory. Rather than sites of food production, they came to be perceived as potential construction areas, offering ripe opportunities for landowners, urban administrators, and planners to make quick money.

The first zoning plans of the city, which were drawn in this period, often reflected the latter of these two counteracting tendencies. In Tekeli's words:

> With the changing urban fabric, the purpose of green spaces also began to change. Green spaces within the city began to move away from being agricultural production sites that had contributed directly to the residents' provisioning. Some of these became new residential areas. [Plus,] "municipality parks" which were open to everyone's enjoyment began to appear in the city. These were usually repurposed from cemeteries, which ended up in the middle of the city, as a result of the city's expansion (1985, 882; author's translation).

In the earlier codes, Ottoman urban planners primarily emphasized fire prevention and focused on changes in the construction materials of buildings[24], but later codes[25] more systematically took up mapping, expropriation and allotment issues, street widths, and building heights (Tekeli 1985). The 1882 *Ebniye Nizamnamesi* also allowed construction over the *bostan*s and empty lots, with certain stipulations (ibid, 886–887): to undertake construction in

---

23 As Tekeli notes, the sultan himself can be thought of as the last of the wave out of the old center of the city – from Topkapı Palace to Dolmabahçe Palace (Tekeli 1985).

24 For example, 1839 *İlmühaberi*/Code of 1839 and 1848 *Ebniye Nizamnamesi*/1848 Code of Building Regulations.

25 Such as the codes of 1864 and 1882.

these spaces, permission was required exclusively from the sultan; and construction firms were asked to donate a portion of the lot to the municipality, which would use the space to build either a school or a police station (ibid). Moreover, newly constructed buildings needed to have modern sewers; and the construction firms were asked to pay for the street and the pavements their newly erected buildings would have access to (ibid, 887).

Through the war years (1912–1914, 1914–1918, 1918–1923), the structural problems of the Empire begun to intensify. Agricultural surplus remained limited, even with the emigrants settling in Anatolia[26] and the increasing connectivity between the Anatolian mainland and the port cities due to improving transportation infrastructures. In this respect, the relative abundance of land in comparison to labor, and the lack of incentives to move out of small- or mid-scale subsistence agriculture into an export-oriented commercial agriculture, were effective. Moreover, trade agreements with various European states (1838 onward) prevented the Ottoman authorities from instituting protective tariffs, quotas, and/or taxes. As such, Istanbul and other larger port cities became good markets for imported commodities. Due to the dissolution of the guild structure and the difficulties of competing with cheaper imported commodities, artisans too gradually disappeared. In the long run, the Empire's exports remained limited to raw materials – cotton instead of muslin, raw hide rather than leather, corn instead of corn starch, etc. More importantly, the value-adding capacity of the Empire did not grow; and in conjunction, both the production of surplus value (and from that, the generation and accumulation of capital), and the generation of tax revenues – which financed the construction of infrastructure and the modernization of the Empire's administrative, military, and educational structures – were severely restricted. For an Empire fighting tooth and nail to reform, none of these prospects were promising. At first, the Ottoman authorities tried various modifications to their tax systems (such as *iltizam*, *malikane* and *esham* practices) to increase tax revenues; then, by altering the value of the Ottoman currency – by adulteration and by printing and selling title deeds (until 1844); and finally, they borrowed heavily from domestic (1840s onward) and foreign (1854 onward) brokers (Pamuk 2014, 123–146; Pamuk 2012, 21–24,97–115, 117–124).[27] These actions, however, fell short of

---

26   To help encourage agricultural production, the migrants settling down in the Anatolian hinterland were given a 12-year tax immunity (Pamuk 2012, 12). For the migrants settled in the Thrace, the immunity was for 6 years (ibid.).

27   *Düyun-u Umumiye* (Institute of Public Debts) was established when the Empire became unable to pay these debts.

mending the structural problems of the Empire; in fact, in many cases, they worsened the conditions.

With the financial crisis in the early 20th century (which was exacerbated during the war years and spilled over to the early Republican era), the Ottoman authorities once again became more interventionist. However, until World War I, which finally provided them the conditions to abolish the stipulations of the trade agreements and enact protective measures, their hands were effectively tied. Meanwhile, Istanbul's reliance on imported foods grew. This wasn't much of a problem in times of peace, as trade networks and routes functioned well enough. However, in times of war, food scarcity in the city bordered on famine (Toprak 1994b). Yet interestingly, even in these times of crisis, the former tendency – that of protecting the *bağs*, *bahçes*, and *bostan*s in the city to ensure some degree of provisioning – did not gain much prominence. Some staples like wheat, for example, continued to be imported. All else was provisioned by redirecting some of the production from within the Ottoman territories, most notably from the Marmara and the Thrace regions. Yalova, Çatalca, Tekirdağ, and their hinterlands began to provision the city more consistently.[28]

6   The *Urban Food Provisioning* Food Regime

Within the politico-economic world order of the 19th century, the Ottoman Empire's territorial, economic, and political vulnerabilities had clearly surfaced. Structural weaknesses arising from the low labor-to-land ratio, and the lack of sufficient transportation infrastructures, had prevented capitalist market imperatives from seeping into peasant communities engaged primarily in small commodity production and subsistence agriculture. As a result, the Empire remained in a pre-capitalist mode of production while the world increasingly moved towards a capitalist one. Plus, the Ottoman central authority could not maintain the Empire's territorial unity against European imperial forces. In addition, various nationalist-secessionist movements rising from within the Empire managed to break away

---

28   This is not to say that all production in the city disappeared. Reşat Ekrem Koçu, writing 300 years after Kömürciyan and Evliya Çelebi, still mentions, in his gargantuan *İstanbul Ansiklopedisi* (1944–1973), various FFVs specific to Istanbul's villages and neighborhoods. Today, as in Koçu's time, it is possible to trace some of the production sites from the names of the city's many neighborhoods: Bağlarbaşı (Üsküdar), Bağcılar, Bostancı (Kadıköy), Cevizlik (Bakırköy), Çiftlik (Beykoz), İncirli (Bakırköy), Tarlabaşı (Beyoğlu), Acıbadem (Kadıköy), Zerzevatçı (Beykoz), Küçük Armutlu (Etiler), Bostan (Beyoğlu), Çukurbostan (Fatih), Yeldeğirmeni (Kadıköy), Cevizlibağ (Zeytinburnu), Gülbağ (Şişli).

from the Ottoman rule. Structural weaknesses, combined with long wars against imperial interventions and secessionist movements, had led to a chronic fiscal crisis, which was then intensified by heavy adulterations in the Ottoman currency. Looking for a breather, the Ottoman central authority had borrowed heavily from domestic and international donors; however, it had quickly become unable to pay back even the interest, thus exacerbating the economic crisis. In short, the Empire's vulnerabilities had been rendered visible, and the parties – domestic and foreign – had taken advantage of them, hastening the dissolution of the Ottoman *body politic*.

In such circumstances, the dismantling of the urban provisioning apparatus seemed almost inevitable. The trade treaties of 1838 (and after) had removed import and export barriers, thus making the (re-)institution of *narh* impossible. Plus, they incentivized export-oriented production and facilitated a tight-knit production and trade network between the port cities and their hinterlands. While these developments contributed to capital accumulation, they also effectively took these regions out of the apparatus that provisioned Istanbul. In addition, the *Düyun-u Umumiye* (Institute of Public Debts) limited the Ottoman central authority's jurisdiction over economic policy and public spending. Coupled with the inability to institute *narh*, the acceleration of imports, and the redirection of resources for export-oriented production and trade, Istanbul began to be fed by a network of actors that operated according to global demand and supply dynamics. And yet, because the city continued to contain the seat of power and the residents were still politically active constituents of the Empire, Istanbul's provisioning remained on the Ottoman central authority's agenda. However, unlike before, the central authority did not – and more importantly, could not – make sure that food was affordable for the residents, for example, or that the city did not face scarcity and hunger, or that the merchants sufficiently followed the codes and the edicts regulating profits, transportation, storage, distribution, and sale of foodstuffs. Rather, in this emerging provisioning apparatus, as the central authority's interventionism lessened, Istanbulites' access to FFVs became increasingly dependent on their individual purchasing power.

There are two important points of emphasis, with respect to these changes: first, the experience of accession to global free trade, the lessening interventionism on the part of the central authority, and the increasing significance of the citizens' purchasing power as the determinant of their access to food – none of these are unique to the Ottoman Empire. In his analysis of the urban provisioning practices of 19th century Latin America, for example, Thomas C. Wright draws a similar picture:

The politics of urban provisioning in Latin America can be divided into two distinct stages. The first extended from the establishment of Spanish and Portuguese cities to the 1870s and, while complex, took place in a relatively narrow spatial and political context. Most cities were supplied from local or regional sources, and the weather, crop or animal diseases, official policy, and manipulation by producers and middlemen determined the conditions of the urban food supply. (...) From the 1870s onward, the determinants of the politics of urban provisioning became more complex. Latin America became enmeshed in a new world economy in which food, along with other commodities, was an object of global exchange (Wright 1985, 24–25).

The difference between the Latin American case and the Ottoman case lies in the ways in which the urban residents reacted to the failures of the urban provisioning apparatus, and the central authorities' responses to the transition to a global supply chain. As I argued above, in the Ottoman case, before 1838, Istanbulites held the Ottoman central authority directly responsible for hunger and scarcity in the city. This was also the case in Latin America. Wright argues; "during [the pre-1870] period, the urban poor were disenfranchised and limited to playing a role in the politics of food only through the implicit threat of disorderly behavior, or tumult, which erupted occasionally" (Wright 1985, 24). After 1870, however, the urban poor in Latin America "took an increasingly active political role, achieving direct influence over food policy in the twentieth century" (ibid, 25). In contrast, in the Ottoman case, Istanbulites continued to hold the sultan and the Sublime Porte responsible for the city's provisioning. Although tumults undoubtedly continued in both cases, in Latin America, the urban residents could effectively intervene in to the provisioning apparatus; whereas in the Ottoman Empire, the decisions regarding the provisioning agents, prices, profits, transportation routes, transportation and storage infrastructures, distribution and sales practices remained under the shared purview of the Ottoman central authority and the provisioning agents.

The Latin American case also shows us that an urban provisioning apparatus that institutes price controls, regulates transportation routes, storage facilities, distribution and sales practices was not unique to the Ottoman Empire, nor was it necessarily rooted in Islamic political economy. Practical concerns (the proximity of politically active constituents to the seat of power, perishability of foodstuffs, logistical difficulties due to transportation infrastructures, and seasonal weather conditions, etc.) were much more significant in determining the

dynamics and the perimeters of urban provisioning practices, rules, and regulations. Islam offered, perhaps, an added benefit of further public legitimacy
– not only because it was the religion of the ruling cadres and a portion of the
population, but also because it recommends an anti-monopoly, anti-hoarding,
and anti-speculative approach to the economy, endorses practices that prevent scarcity (including by way of imports), and encourages just prices and free
competition (Tabakoğlu 1987, 113–115). From this point of view, the provisioning apparatus of the pre-1838 Ottoman food regime seems in line with Islamic
principles. Nevertheless, looking at the urban provisioning apparatus in Latin
America under Iberian dominance (what Wright describes as the first stage),
we can see similar sensibilities and organizing principles at play: "The politics
of food was closely directed in the public interest. Regulation was based on
the concept of a moral economy in which food, as a necessity of life, was not
considered an object for lucre or speculation" (Wright 1985, 25). Thus, we can
conclude that the organizing principles of the pre-1838 Ottoman food regime
were not specific to Islam or to the Ottoman Empire. Indeed, we find urban
provisioning apparatuses organized around similar *mentalité* in various *ancien
regimes*, including France, Italian and German principalities, colonial North
and South America, and Japan.

Considering these parallels, then, we can say that the urban provisioning
apparatuses in which price controls were instituted and transportation routes,
storage facilities, distribution and sales practices were regularly (and sometimes forcibly) intervened upon, were markers of the political economy of
the pre-capitalist *ancien regimes*. Their dismantling (in the Ottoman Empire)
came at the heels of the legal recognition of the owner's absolute dominion
over his private property with the Tanzimat reforms, and signaled the severing
of the economic power from the sovereign power that Meiksins Wood underlines in the transition to the capitalist mode of production (Meiksins Wood
2016; 2017). Yet, in this case, and in contrast to her analysis – where the market
opportunities turning into market imperatives, enabling the appropriation of
surplus labor through economic means (Meiksins Wood 2016; 2017) – the transition to purely economic appropriation unfolded as a result of the transition
to a *laissez faire* approach, following the trade agreements.

For the Ottomans in particular, the dismantling of the provisioning apparatus and the food system, implied the dissolution of the Ottoman *body politic*. The *body politic* had depended on the Ottoman central authority to bring
foodstuffs from different corners of the Empire to feed itself. Indeed, this act
of making food present in the capital represented the Ottoman sovereignty
and *kudret* of the reigning sultan. However, once the *laissez faire* policies set
market imperatives in motion, it became impossible for the Ottoman central

authority to intervene into the provisioning actor's decisions and set prices (institute *narh*), for example, or redirect their shipments to Istanbul. The provisioning of the city became dependent on what the merchants were willing to bring in to sell, and the residents' purchasing power – not the sultan's and the Sublime Porte's capability to govern peoples and territories. As the sovereign power and the economic power began to be separated (Meiksins Wood 2016, 28–36), the vital connection between the bodies of the subjects and the body of the sovereign was completely broken – yet again, literally and figuratively.

It is possible to read the changes the Ottoman *body politic* experienced, as an instance of the market – particularly the *laissez faire* market– replacing the sultan and the Sublime Porte, and/or the market becoming the new force that governs peoples and territories. In my opinion, such a reading would be a misinterpretation of what happened. The market did not eradicate the Ottoman central authority, nor did it undertake the responsibilities and obligations that were the central authority's purview. What it did was to change the Ottoman central authority's parameters of operation, reorient its priorities (so that urban provisioning was not one of them), and limit its interventions to the subjects' economic activities (the legal recognition of owner's dominion over his private property, and the transition to *laissez faire* approach in trade previously mentioned). These new parameters of operation required not only that the Ottoman central authority not disappear, but in fact be strengthened to serve new purposes (protection of private property, for example, instead of provisioning of the city).

Interestingly, the populations who did not necessarily benefit from these changes, also did not respond to them by taking advantage of the newly acquired protections and liberties gained through the limiting of the Ottoman central authority's interventionism. Rather, the subjects tried to reverse the central authority's parameters of operation yet again and re-establish their bodily connection with the sultan. And to some extent, they succeeded: during the war years of the early decades of the 20th century, interventionist practices came back, and the Ottoman Leviathan was again in a position of directing, managing, and controlling Istanbul's provisioning. Nevertheless, as the policies and approaches adopted after the war years show(roughly known as *Milli İktisat*; national economy), this 'comeback' was quite limited, both in scope and success. It was more a product of the volatile years and the wars, than a foundational re-establishment of a corporeal connection between the subjects and the sovereign. The next chapter delves more deeply into these years, and the provisioning apparatus that was established during that time – which was neither fully Ottoman nor fully *laissez faire* – and the new food regime that emerged as a result.

CHAPTER 3

Unruly Transitions

> The most opulent nations, indeed, generally excel all their neigh-
> bors in agriculture as well as in manufactures; but they are com-
> monly more distinguished by their superiority in the latter than in
> the former.
>
> ADAM SMITH[1]

∴

Perhaps the Empire's 'unruly transitions' began right after the Treaty of 1838. After all, the trade agreements had upset an already fragile political-economic order and triggered major changes in a wide range of fields, from urban planning to architecture to cuisine. Yet here, with 'unruly transitions', I refer predominantly to the 10 years of political (and economic) instability, inter-ethnic/religious conflict, and secessionist wars, and finally World War I, that broke the Empire open. Indeed, between the years 1908 and 1918, the Empire saw so many violent and fundamental changes, that it is difficult to describe them as anything but 'unruly'. The 5 years following World War I were not easy either, with the Independence War raging on all fronts in Anatolia. Though some level of international stability was achieved following the Treaty of Lausanne (which concluded the Independence War and provided legal and international recognition to the sovereignty of the central authority operating out of Ankara, over whatever lands and peoples that remained of the Ottoman Empire in Anatolia), the domestic political-economic scene was much less settled. Ethnic, religious, and ideological violence of various kinds continued to devastate the war-weary populations. Together with the population exchange of 1923 (*Mübadele*), which altered the demographic makeup of the country, and the Great Depression of 1929 (which razed down whatever capital had been generated and accumulated, but also limited the 1838-esque trade statutes of the Treaty of Lausanne, and provided an opportunity to get out of paying the debts of the Empire), the 'unruly transitions' extended to the beginning of the 1930s.

---

1 Smith, Adam. 1982. *The Wealth of Nations: Books 1–3.* New York, NY: Penguin Classics, 111.

© KONINKLIJKE BRILL NV, LEIDEN, 2021 | DOI:10.1163/9789004424500_004

For the provisioning apparatus of Istanbul, these political and economic events constitute major breaks – not only because they are regime-changing events, but because they have had foundational effects on the food system, and as such, on the food regime. They have, for example, greatly altered the labor-to-land ratio – the *Mübadele* for the positive and the war years for the negative – which have resulted in increases and decreases, respectively, of agricultural yields. More important still were the changes in the *mentalité* of government. The *İttihat ve Terakki Fırkası* (Committee of Union and Progress; CUP from now on) cadres, that came to power alongside the sultan in the aftermath of the Young Turk Revolution in 1908, came with the vision of generating a national (read as: Sunni Muslim and Turkish) bourgeoisie. To do so, they had to institute protective measures and limit the *laissez faire* policies the trade agreements had let loose on the economy. The same trade agreements, however, tied their hands, and they had to wait until World War I gave them the 'opportunity' to rescind the policies. Even then, the annulment was not permanent. *Laissez faire* statutes came back with the Treaty of Lausanne; and this time, the Republican central authority had to wait until the Great Depression for an 'opportunity' to institute protective measures. Yet, amidst this back-and-forth, the crucial lesson for the central authority was that a crisis (like a global war or economic breakdown) could generate local opportunities – so long as one was focused on economy and/or agriculture in general, and not on provisioning and/or urban provisioning in particular. Plus, if the 'economy' was a base that could easily disrupt the political superstructure, and lead to the limiting and/or restructuring of the relationship between the sovereign and the subjects(-citizens), then it could also be used to do the exact opposite. That is, under the right conditions, the 'economy' could be a base on which a strong, mutually beneficial relationship of protection and obedience could be cultivated, between the central authority (the sovereign) and the (subjects-)citizens. Yet, as the experiences of the 19th century show, these cannot be just any subject-citizens; they have to be the right ones or '*friends*' deemed appropriate by the central authority.

The period I am going to cover in this chapter delves more deeply into these unruly transitions and disentangle the emergence of the new provisioning apparatus, in conjunction with the new food system, from the remnants of the previous one. The first section, 'The War Years and Republican Istanbul's Codependent Provisioning', is split into two sub-sections: the first, '15 Years of War', covers the volatile 1908–1923 period; and the second, 'Republican Istanbul', focuses on the back-and-forth that characterized the early years of the Republic. Since the Republican central authority brought back so many of the directly interventionist practices and measures of the urban provisioning food regime during World War II (Metinsoy 2012), I have extended this section until 1950. While the first section thus focuses on more macro-level political-economic events, forces, and trajectories, the second and third sections, 'Urban Provisioning during Unruly Transitions' and 'Scarcity in War vs. Scarcity in Peace' respectively, are intended to provide a snapshot of Istanbul's chang-ing provisioning apparatus during those times. Finally, the fourth section, 'The Emerging Food Regime', draws the rough contours of the emerging food system and the food regime (which I have called *codependent provisioning*) that really settles in the post-1950s period.

I should note that the unruly transitions engulfing the country during these hard years continue to constitute both the foundations and the axes of ongo-ing debate for the social, political, cultural, and economic imaginaries in cir-culation today. Plus, while the generation that went through the Balkan Wars and the migrations that followed may not be around anymore, the generation that participated in the population exchange and experienced the scarcity and the long ration lines of World War II are still alive; and like my Grandma, their tales of hunger have shaped the imaginaries of many. While consumerist ten-dencies reigned more freely after the economy opened up in the 1980s, and changed the ways in which the generations of 1980s and after relate to and interact with commodities, the previous generations' spending, consumption, and saving habits are inextricably linked with the food scarcity that character-ized the years I discuss this chapter.

1   The War Years and Republican Istanbul's Codependent Provisioning

To recap some of the discussion from the last chapter: The Treaty of 1838 was a turning point for the Empire. With the shift to *laissez faire*, not only did cus-toms taxes for all sorts of imported goods – from wheat to textiles – have to be eliminated, but also, with new foods coming into the city, tastes and prefer-ences began to change. Though domestic producers did continue to provision the city to some degree, Istanbul was fed a global diet, until naval blockades during World War I plugged off the trade routes. However, these changes in the trade and consumption patterns, along with the disbanding of the Janissary Army and the guild system that was interlinked with it, led to the gradual dis-appearance of the Anatolian artisans, small-scale workshops, and the long-distance caravan traders whom they supplied (Tekeli 1985). In addition, a two-tier system of agricultural production emerged. On the one hand, because of increasing import and export trade along the coastal regions, the hinterlands of port cities like Izmir, Adana, and Samsun (Köymen 1999, 2) began to special-ize, in their production (ibid). That is, specific regions began to focus on specific goods. Plus, property sizes increased. Both debts and the numerous forced migrations and displacements that wreaked havoc on the region throughout the long 19th and early 20th century, fed the expropriation of small-scale family farmers and appropriation of their lands into large estates. The landlords of these large estates preferred, in turn, to produce for export. Moreover, they kicked off villagers and families living on the land, opting instead for seasonal laborers. In the Anatolian hinterland, in contrast, production for the market remained limited, until the construction of railway infrastructure in the latter part of the 19th century made it easier, faster, and cheaper to transport the goods produced in the region to the ports in the coastal cities (Tekeli 1985). Moreover, the availability of agricultural land, relatively low population, and sparse population density, prevented agricultural yields from increasing. Even the large landowners in the Anatolian hinterlands were disinclined to increase their production (Silier 1981, Tokdemir 1988). In some cases, they would even leave some of their land idle since agricultural labor was either scarce and/or simply too expensive (Tokdemir 1988). Finally, the lack of agricultural machinery, irrigation techniques, better practices and know-how, and a dependence on human and animal labor, and low yielding seeds, slowed down the growth in the agricultural output (Tokdemir 1988; Pamuk 2012, 10–11).

1.1   *15 Years of War*

The protectionist measures the Committee of Union and Progress (CUP) cadres instituted at the beginning of World War I, were significantly different from the market-friendly policies of the 1830s. For example, prices were set by the central authority; in other words, *narh* was back (Toprak 1994a). Capitulations (*imtiyazat*) granted to foreign nationals and their trading partners in the Empire were rescinded (Pamuk 2015, 164), and foreign companies were asked to pay taxes on par with domestic companies (ibid). In conjunction, in 1915, customs taxes were re-adjusted to remove certain taxation practices that applied blanket taxes on every imported good (Pamuk 2015, 164–165; Boratav 2007, 31). This meant that the Ottoman administrators could regulate taxation however they wanted and enforce more protectionist measures (Pamuk 2015, 164; Boratav 2007, 31).[2]

The effects of these protectionist measures were pronounced. Prices began to go up almost immediately in the coastal towns. The French and the British

---

2   The CUP administration also stopped the payment of debts to foreign debtors and effectively suspended the activities of the Institute of Public Debts (Pamuk, 2015, 165).

were the Empire's primary trading partners before the war (Pamuk 2015, 165); whereas during the war, they fought against the Empire. Their naval blockades in the Mediterranean brought the imports into the Empire practically to a halt (ibid.). Plus, in the aftermath of the Russian invasion of the Caucasus and Northeastern Anatolia, and the forced migration and massacre of the Armenians in 1915, the deployment of what was essentially the agricultural labor force, to the various fronts, had significantly reduced the domestic agricultural production (ibid, 166–167). Thus, the Empire was suffering from major food shortages.[3] Wheat, flour, and sugar had become particularly scarce. Indeed, the crisis continued until the German invasion of Serbia towards the end of 1915 (ibid, 166). The invasion enabled railway transportation through Bulgaria and Serbia, and food was again supplied to the Empire.

The war conditions also stifled the supply of provisions coming into Istanbul. The most fundamental problem was transportation. The existing railroad infrastructure, already quite limited, primarily carried soldiers and supplies for the army. The transportation of foodstuffs was deprioritized, unless there were serious, recurring reports of hunger and scarcity. As such, and unsurprisingly, people in rural areas and the Anatolian hinterland suffered less than Istanbulites (Pamuk 2015, 167). Although the peasants in these regions had lost a significant portion of their manpower to World War I (1914–1918), and their cattle to the Independence War (1918–1923)[4], those that had access to land continued to cultivate it. Yields and the efficiency of production were both undeniably low, especially compared to the outputs of their contemporaries in Western Europe and America (Tokdemir 1988). Nonetheless, subsistence farming continued and often there was some level of surplus production, especially in the regions where small family farms were still prevalent (Pamuk 2012, 140–144). Similarly, until after World War I, the coastal regions could rely on their immediate hinterlands to supply the more densely settled towns and cities. Since they had previously been integrated with European markets as exporters of various agricultural goods, they had already established trading networks and a relatively functioning transportation infrastructure, that could carry foods from their locations of production to those of consumption (ibid.).

---

3   According to Pamuk, by 1916, the foreign trade volume of the Empire had gone down by 20%, relative to the pre-war period (2015, 166). By 1918, the domestic income of the Empire had fallen 40% below pre-war levels (ibid, 167). The production of most exported commodities, such as wheat, tobacco, raisins, hazelnuts, olive oil, raw silk, and cotton, had fallen by more than 50% (ibid).

4   The army confiscated cattle (among other things) from the Anatolian farmers during the Independence War.

Food scarcity regularly turned into famine only for the urban and the rural populations of Istanbul and the Eastern regions of Anatolia, where the Russian invasion and the Armenian massacres had wreaked havoc on the regional supply lines and networks (Pamuk 2012, 155, Pamuk 2015, 168).

Population movements were the other crucial factor exacerbating scarcity in Istanbul. Throughout the 19th century, the Empire had lost control over various parts of Eastern Europe, the Balkans, and the Caucasus. The Muslims living in these regions had migrated to the territories still under Ottoman control (Pamuk 2012, 128–129). For these migrants, Istanbul was a significant geographic and symbolic gateway. Passing through (and as often, remaining in) the city symbolized making their way back to the imagined Ottoman homeland. In the 20th century, especially during the Balkan Wars (1912–13), these inflows increased (Akad 1994), adding to the burden on the city's provisioning apparatus. Plus, the newly established and modernized Ottoman army was housed and trained in various military schools and barracks around Istanbul. This meant another substantial population in the city and more pressures on the city's already stretched provisioning apparatus.

In an interesting pattern, most locations that housed the army, experienced multiple waves of food scarcity throughout World War I – and in that, Istanbul was no exception. On the one hand, the presence of the troops guaranteed that the resources of the Ottoman central authority (whether money, administrative attention, or simply a few additional train wagons) would be directed to that location to provision the army (Toprak 1994b). On the other hand, such redirection of resources did not necessarily guarantee that the civilian population would be fed. In fact, the population increase caused by the troops, often worked against the civilians in multiple ways. When the foods were transported to the locations where the troops were, the troops were prioritized over the local civilian population. Plus the Ottoman administrators gave the army the right to confiscate surplus production in its immediate vicinity for its own consumption. As such, the hinterland's resources were already depleted. Local populations were thus left to choose between purchasing food through the black market at skyrocketing prices (see Table 1), or simply having to live with seemingly unending scarcity (ibid).

Moreover, the Ottoman central authority's own policies and practices were contributing to price increases and the expansion of black markets in Istanbul. For example, both the agricultural surplus and the transportation infrastructure (that connected Istanbul to the rest of the Empire) were allocated to the army (the latter, to carry supplies and personnel) (Boratav 2007, 28–29, Toprak 1994b). As a result, the volume of FFVs and other foodstuffs coming into the city had decreased, though the demand had effectively increased, or at the very least, stayed the same. Large landowners, riding on this demand increase, hiked up their prices. Plus, when possible, they would keep some of their surplus from being confiscated[5] and sell it to traders for high prices (Temel 1998). Traders, in turn, would hoard these, pushing the prices further up and causing more scarcity in the city (Pamuk 2012, 151–157, Toprak 1994b).[6] Between 1914 and 1920, food prices thus increased by 1350% in Istanbul (Temel 1998, 40).

The Ottoman central authority's response to these price increases was contradictory. To slow down the price increases and prevent black market activities, excess profiteering, and stockpiling, the CUP cadres tried to institute fixed prices in retail, thus reviving the *narh* practice (Toprak 1978). *Narh* was applied first to wheat; later, it was extended to cover other staples like olives, sugar, and bulgur (Toprak 1978, 213). Following in the footsteps of their 17th and 18th century counterparts, the Ottoman central authority also pushed for strict policing of the set prices and enforced heavy fines and corporal punishment for those who did comply (Toprak 1978, 1994a). However, unlike their predecessors, the CUP cadres gave certain rights to municipal administrators within Istanbul. According to a statute passed in early May 1916, for example, municipal administrators could confiscate grain mills and bakeries, and/or determine base prices for bread and other staples (ibid). Furthermore, the CUP government established various administrative units to further plan and coordinate Istanbul's provisioning (Toprak 1978, Temel 1998, Toprak 1994b).[7] Most of these administrative units were tasked with organizing the logistics of bringing wheat and flour into the capital, fixing prices, and enforcing the prices and weights (Toprak 1994b). After the first year of the war, the jurisdiction of the administrative units was expanded to include olive oil, sugar, cheese, rice, bulgur, and kerosene (ibid). By the third year of the war, they were entitled to regulate the transportation and the sale of grains and legumes in the city as

---

5   Note that when the agricultural surplus was confiscated, farmers were paid a fixed price – which was considerably lower than the market price (Pamuk 2012, 154–155). As such, farmers preferred to sell their produce in the market, and often declared their production as less than what it actually was.

6   Yet, even for traders, transportation was the most difficult challenge to surmount. Only those who had government connections could secure a few train wagons to carry the produce; and once they managed to actually bring the shipment into the capital, they sold the cargo for exorbitant sums (Boratav 2007, 28–29; Pamuk 2012, 151–157; Temel 1998).

7   Other than potatoes and onions, I have found of no mention of any fresh fruits and vegetables that came under the control of these administrative units (Toprak 1994a). Even in the case of these two FFVs, the organization of their logistics was mostly for military and bureaucratic personnel (ibid).

well (ibid). However, these management strategies were not enough to deal with the scarcity Istanbul was experiencing.

One of the most important factors that contributed to the scarcity, was the decline of the shared provisioning apparatuses that supplied the city with FFVs and other perishables. As I mentioned in the previous chapter, the modernization movement of the early 19th century had led to lifestyle changes. While the urban-administrative elites moved out of the old quarters to locations where they could commute with a carriage, they had also become much less inclined to protect the traditional in-city locations of food production in the new urban planning schemes and statutes (Kuban 1994, İstanbul 1993b). Plus, the trade agreements had helped imported goods (including food) to come to the city more freely, feeding both the fashion frenzy of the modernizing elites and offering alternatives cheaper than goods (including food) produced locally and in Anatolia. Just before the war, for example, the import trade had become the

FIGURE 6   Patisserie Baylan, Istanbul – One of the few pastry shops in Istanbul that survived both world wars, the occupation of the city, the Independence War, and the structural adjustments of the 1980s. This photo is of the now-closed branch in Karaköy. Baylan continues to serve delicious cakes, chocolates, cookies, and desserts to its customers across its other locations in Istanbul.
PHOTO COURTESY OF THE SALT RESEARCH ARCHIVE

primary source supplying the city with grains (Pamuk 2012, 37), even though shared provisioning continued, particularly for FFVs and other perishables. Yet once the naval blockades closed off the trade routes during the war and protective measures made it more expensive to import, this global supply route came to a stop (Pamuk 2012, 139–168). Rather, the city began to rely, primarily, on its remaining in-city locations of production and its immediate hinterland (the remaining Thrace region, Yalova, İznik, and the region around the Marmara Sea), and secondarily, on the central Anatolian hinterland (since the western, northern, and southern coastal regions and sea transportation were threatened by the Allies) for its provisions. Yet the allocation of rail lines to the army for the transportation of personnel and supplies significantly stagnated the supply of provisions coming from these locations of production.

Still, Istanbul did receive provisions from the relatively sheltered central Anatolia during the war years. Indeed, economic historians consider this a positive development for the region (Boratav 2007, 28). According to Korkut Boratav, for example, such a provisioning effort incentivized the central Anatolian farmers to leave subsistence farming and to start to produce for the market (ibid). However, there were significant problems. First, due to the central authority's waning control over the peripheries, the rural administrators often disregarded the central authority's orders to immediately send provisions to the capital (Temel 1998), or they acted slowly, delaying transfers, keeping the food for local consumption, or even sending it somewhere else altogether (ibid). Second, the prices of almost all food items rose during the war years (Pamuk 2012, 151–157). Third, because of inflation, the purchasing power of those who had fixed incomes dwindled (such as bureaucrats, diplomats, soldiers, teachers, etc.) (ibid). Fourth and finally, because the army

TABLE 1   Official (O) and black market (BM) prices of some of the staple products in Istanbul (Annual average in Kuruş) (Toprak 1982, 327)

Year	Bread		Sugar		Beans		Mutton	
	O	BM	O	BM	O	BM	O	BM
1915	1.65	7.5	7	8.5				
1916	1.6	9.5	30	15	16			
1917	2.5	18	20	112	10	40	30	35
1918	2.5	34	30	195	15	65	50	125

was prioritized over the civilian population, food scarcity continued for many (Toprak 1994b). As such, even if the Anatolian farmers began to produce for the market, Istanbulites did not immediately feel the effects of such a shift. The scarcity in Istanbul frequently bordered on famine.

For the CUP cadres, however, the food scarcity in Istanbul was an opportunity to put in place policies that could be broadly categorized as *iktisadi milliyetçilik* (economic nationalism). The protectionist measures enacted at the beginning of the war (termination of trade agreements, reform, and reinstitution of customs taxes) had the effect of redirecting some of the production in the central Anatolian hinterlands to the market. This could be considered the first step of the CUP's attempt to constitute a national economy; and it did work to the benefit of predominantly the Sunni Muslim-Turkish[8] peasants, especially the large landowners, of the Anatolian hinterland. The preferential treatment the Committee bestowed upon some of the traders was even more significant. For example, during the war, the rail line between Anatolia and the capital was particularly busy, transporting soldiers and ammunition (Toprak 1994b, 1978). Plus, because of various technical problems in the coal mines and continuing naval battles with Russia, coal production in the Black Sea region (where the most active coal mines were) had stagnated; and as a result, train travel had become both costlier and less frequent (Boratav 2007, 28–29; Pamuk 2012, 151–157). Securing a few wagons without appropriate connections in the government – and in the military – was almost impossible. In these conditions, the CUP granted access to a few, handpicked merchants. For other goods that had to be imported, the Committee gave permissions to a select few it had close relations with, effectively establishing monopolies in the import and distribution of imported staples. In both cases, the CUP was careful to work with Sunni Muslim-Turkish merchants (Boratav 2007, 28–29; Pamuk 2012, 151–157). This was, thus, the second and the more fundamental step the CUP took to help create what it considered to be a 'national bourgeoisie': Through preferential treatment of some, the CUP enabled them to amass a significant amount of capital. Boratav, for example, rightfully classifies this as a form of primitive accumulation (2007, 27) and argues that such mechanisms of rent and accumulation caused the CUP-oriented 'national bourgeoisie' in Istanbul to take their time in recognizing the significance of the Ankara-led national struggle, and to lend their support to the independence struggle (ibid.).

---

8   Note the change in the meaning of 'national' here: By the time the CUP was in government, the nation came to be considered less the peoples of the Ottoman Empire (composed of different ethnicities and religions), and more the political community of Turkish Muslims (For more on this, see Mardin 2017; 2015a; 2015b; Keyder 2017).

In the war period, then, a fundamental change occurred in the way Istanbul's food provisioning was thought of. For the reigning CUP cadres, feeding the city was surely important. As the capital, Istanbul continued to house the sultan and the royal family, as well as the CUP cadres themselves, their families, and the military elites. Plus, all the major financial institutions and diplomatic envoys were in Istanbul. For the Muslims migrating to the Empire, it retained its symbolic power and acted as a gateway to the Ottoman homeland. Yet, when food scarcity began to hit the city, because of protectionist measures and naval blockades, the Ottoman authorities chose to institute policies and practices that aimed to cultivate a 'national bourgeoisie', rather than instituting policies and practices that aimed to ensure that the city was fed. This resulted in an increase in prices, and an exacerbation of scarcity. In other words, not only was the provisioning of the residents deprioritized, but also, sacrificing many to hunger just so a handful of entrepreneurs could accumulate enough capital was considered acceptable – if it were not planned for.

Equally significantly, the provisioning of the city no longer represented the sultan's – and through him, the Empire's – 'kudret'. Earlier, the wellbeing of the Empire was represented by the sultan's capability to reach into his territories far and wide, and to bring the fruits of his subjects' labor to feed his capital. After the trade agreements, however, private – and foreign – actors began to provision the city without much supervision; and until the war broke out, Istanbul was fed on a global diet. Ottoman authorities, in contrast, had to deal with territorial losses, domestic political squabbles (which eventually led to regime change), and regular diplomatic crises (which often turned into conflict). More importantly, trade agreements made the relation between economic power and sovereign power clear. The provisioning of the city continued to be on the agenda – albeit as a low priority item. No longer able to exert sufficient influence over either market mechanisms or economic actors, the Ottoman authorities instead had to deal with the Institute of Public Debts (Pamuk 2012, 121–122). In other words, the link between the sultan's persona, the Empire's *kudret,* and the provisioning of the capital had now completely been broken.

1.2   *Republican Istanbul*

Istanbul underwent some very significant political, demographic, and social changes during the early Republican period (1923–1946). To begin with, it lost its status as the capital city. The new Republican central authority had chosen Ankara as its home base, and after almost a millennium of serving as a capital city for two large empires, Istanbul suddenly became a provincial – yet still important – city. Fueled by a desire to seal off the Ottoman past, the early

Republican elites had initially boycotted the old capital, diverting economic, cultural, and political investments to Ankara and to other Anatolian cities. Even though this boycott began to be slowly lifted by the late 1930s, a deep, unsettling fissure was already present, between Ankara and Istanbul. While Ankara symbolized the serene and determined progress of Republican Turkey to the *level of contemporary civilizations*, Istanbul stood for the lost, glorious, yet disgraced past. Concomitantly, every division of Republican society came to be entangled in this axis between the old and the new capital: Secular, progressive, well-planned Ankara vs. religious, backward, disorderly Istanbul; devoted, hardworking bureaucrats and public employees of the Republic vs. lazy, greedy, extravagant private entrepreneurs of Istanbul ... Although these stereotypes changed in the decades to follow, the fissure between the two cities and the visions they symbolized remains to this day.

Second, as a result of 15 years of war, Istanbul's population had dwindled. Before the war, the population of the capital was approximately 900,000; however, after the war, it was estimated to be under 700,000 (Pamuk 2015, 176). Although diplomatic envoys continued to stay in the city, most of the merchants, creditors, and artisans who had fueled the urban economy in the long 19th century had left (ibid.). Plus, the few industrial production facilities[9] in the city had suffered during the war years: Labor had become scarce; machinery was damaged or had become defunct (ibid.). Consequently, economic output was reduced. Finally, with the abolition of the sultanate and the exile of the Ottoman family, the Ottoman palace, which had been an economic and a cultural powerhouse for the city, disappeared. As the unwavering attention of the elites continued to focus on Ankara, Istanbul quickly lost its former glory.

---

9 Boratav cites that according to the 1915 inventory, the total number of industrial production facilities in the Ottoman Empire was 225 (Boratav 2007, 33). 28% of these (72 of them) were established after 1908 (ibid.). Most of these facilities were producing basic textiles (processing cotton, silk, wool, and leather) or food (such as processing wheat, sugar, or tobacco) (ibid.). Their overall contribution to the Ottoman economy was also relatively small. In 1915, they could produce only 9.5% of the overall textiles consumed and 20.5% of the overall silk thread consumed (ibid.). The Empire had to import the rest to keep up with demand (ibid.). The industrial production facilities that were established before 1908 included: "20 flour mills, 2 pasta-making facilities, 6 canning facilities, 1 beer brewery, 2 tobacco shops, 1 ice-making facility, 3 brick-making facilities, 3 lime-making facilities, 7 tin-production facilities, 2 oil presses, 2 soap-making facilities, 2 porcelain ateliers, 11 tanning facilities, 7 carpentries, 7 wool, 2 cotton, 36 raw silk weaving facilities, 6 other weaving facilities, 35 presses, 8 smoking paper production facilities, 5 metal factories and 1 chemical production facility" (Boratav 2007, 20). Boratav rightfully points out that the list does not include the facilities that were opened and closed before 1908 as well as the few facilities in Adana, Samsun, and Tarsus (ibid, 21).

FIGURE 7   Sugar refinery in Etimesgut, Ankara
              PHOTO COURTESY OF THE SALT RESEARCH ARCHIVE

Two junctures mark this period: The Great Depression and World War II,
although the period between these cataclysmic events contained equally significant yet more gradual developments: demographic adjustments to peace,
ideological shifts vis-à-vis the course of the economy,and the new alliances
between the political and the economic elites – all of which helped restructure
how Istanbul was fed.

The period between the establishment of the Republic (1923) and the Great
Depression (1929) could be considered a period of recuperation. After 15 years
of almost continuous war, men finally began to go back to the countryside,
and within a few years, Turkey saw a population increase (Boratav 2007, 51).
The population exchange with Greece (*Mübadele*) also contributed to this
increase – though the change in this case was not purely numerical: During the
Mübadele, approximately 1,200,000 Greek Orthodox Christians from Anatolia
were 'exchanged' for 500,000 (Sunni) Muslims from Greece (Arı 1999, 97). Most
of the Christians who were exchanged were either urbanite traders and artisans, or farmers who produced for the market – groups who were more in tune
with global market pressures, produced relatively higher value commodities,
and had higher productivity (Pamuk 2015, 174). The newcomers were equally

specialized in the production of specific agricultural commodities, depending on the place or province in Greece they came from (Arı 1999). Although the government at the time made efforts to settle newcomers as quickly as possible, paying attention to their specializations and skill sets (for example, they tried to settle tobacco growers in the tobacco-growing Black Sea region), production levels among the newcomers remained relatively low[10] (ibid). As such, while the population grew and became allegedly more homogenous in terms particularly of religious identity, the population exchange stagnated agricultural and manufacturing outputs.

The demographic adjustment to peace, in turn, had a positive effect. During the war years, agricultural output had fallen by about 50% in most major commodities (Boratav 2007, 51); and as a result of certain measures that the CUP government had initiated, low output had generated a planned scarcity in many Anatolian cities. Once the wars were over, however, agricultural production picked back up. Now supported by governmental measures and practices (such as changes in taxation and pricing), output quickly grew back up to its pre-war levels (ibid). For example, according to Boratav, by 1929, wheat production had moved up to 2 million tons, from 1 million tons in the early years of the Republic (2007, 51). More importantly, growth in the agriculture sector in this pre-Great Depression period was larger than the growth of the overall economy (ibid) – which implies a resource transfer from agriculture to other sectors of the economy.

The Great Depression upset this fragile growth in multiple ways. With the crisis, grain prices began to plummet globally. At that time, due to the trade agreement signed in conjunction to the Treaty of Lausanne, the newly sovereign Republican government had limited control over its economic policies (Boratav 2007, 44). It could not, for example, change its customs taxes or apply tariffs (ibid). Thus, when the Depression hit and grain prices began to fall, cheap grain flooded the Turkish markets, causing a price crush that shook the already quite fragile economy. At the same time, the term limits for the trade agreement were expiring in 1929; and business circles were well aware of the government's intentions and efforts to institute more protectionist measures (Boratav 2007, 49). To undercut the policy change, they began to increase stockpiling and speculative activities – subsequently intensifying the already tight fiscal situation (ibid.). Thus, by the time the Depression fully hit the young Republic of Turkey, a major fiscal crisis had broken out, and the

---

10   To encourage production, newcomers who were settled in Rumeli and who undertook farming were exempted from paying taxes for 6 years; and those who were settled in Anatolia were given tax exemptions for 12 years (Arı 1999; Pamuk 2012, 12).

government had intervened and reregulated the exchange rate (ibid.). To top all of this off, the first installment of the readjusted Ottoman debts was due 1 June 1929 (Özdemir 2009, 118). At approximately around 15 million Turkish Lira (Boratav 2007, 49) or 1,435,000 British Sterling (Özdemir 2009, 118), the installment signified a substantial sum for the struggling economy.[11]

Yet, certain other mechanisms and processes slowed down the crush: For example, in 1925, *aşar* (or, *öşür*; tithe tax) was removed (ibid, 47). This had been a major tax on agricultural goods since the early Ottoman times and was a consistent income for the treasury (including during the 15 years of war). Because *aşar* was calculated based on weight (10% of the overall commodities produced), it adversely effected smaller farmers (Pamuk 2015, 177). With its removal, more peasants could sell more of their agricultural commodities in the market (Boratav 2007, 54). In other words, the abolition of *aşar* tax incentivized – albeit indirectly – more farmers to produce for the market; farmers – small and big – managed to accumulate some capital (though who, amongst them, could reinvest that capital and increase capacity, is a slightly different and a much more complicated question); and the early Republican state faced a significant reduction in tax revenues. To make up for it, the central authority increased the taxes on sugar and kerosene (Boratav 2007, 54). This meant, essentially, shifting the tax burden from the agrarian countryside to the urban economy (ibid). By the same token, it indicated that the Republican elites saw the urban economy and industrial production – rather than the rural economy and agriculture – as the motor of development for the country.

However, there is a contradiction here: Targeting the urban economy might imply an increase on the taxes on profit or on capital – and as the proponents of liberalism would have it, both would inhibit (if not prevent) foreign and/or domestic entrepreneurs from investing in the country. Given the already limited number of industrial production facilities and even fewer entrepreneurs who had enough capital to invest, implementing such a policy would counteract the developmentalist goals of the Republican elites. Then, by taxing sugar and kerosene, what the Republican elites were doing was to shift the tax burden not only to the urban economy, but more specifically, to the consumers within the urban economy – the workers, bureaucrats, and small shopkeepers (ibid). Because of this resource transfer from (the consumers within) the urban economy to (the producers of) the rural economy, the agricultural sector managed to achieve growth rates higher than the overall economy (ibid, 55).

---

11   According to Boratav, it was equal to 10% of the total export revenues for that year (2007, 49).

Interestingly, in the long run, this had the effect of directing resources back into the urban economy, by way of initiating capital accumulation within industry and manufacturing.

The primary effects of the Great Depression on the food provisioning of Istanbul were two-fold. First, because of falling prices and the fiscal crisis, both urban and rural economies suffered. In the city, real wages dropped, thus pulling down Istanbulites' purchasing power. In the countryside, especially in the regions which were more integrated with the global market, Boratav estimates a 68% price decline in wheat (2007, 67), and a 22% shrinkage within agriculture (ibid, 73) between 1929 and 1932. To balance these effects, the central authority instituted the protective measures it had been planning for: New tariffs and customs taxes were imposed; and following the establishment of the Republic's Central Bank in 1930, a new law[12] gave the government the right to set the exchange rate (Boratav 2007, 68). In addition, the central authority instituted base prices for certain agricultural goods and made bulk purchases from farmers to slow down price declines (Köymen 1999, 10–11). Finally, the central authority began to look for initiatives to encourage investment, particularly in the processing of agricultural products, such as wheat (milling), sugar beet (processing), and cotton (textiles) (Boratav 2007, 64). In conjunction with the Republican elites' dream of conceiving a 'Muslim-Turkish bourgeoisie', investments (like these) that brought together agriculture and industry, and thus, tied the urban and the rural, were considered to be ideal (Karaömerlioğlu 2000, 125–126) and were prioritized.[13]

Following the Great Depression, the government changed its economic policies. In conjunction to instituting protectionist measures, it began to undertake industrial investments. Generally known as *étatisme* (*devletçilik*), this implied

---

12 *Türk Parasının Kıymetini Koruma Hakkında Kanun*; the Law Regarding the Protection of the Value of Turkish Currency.

13 The Great Depression, however, made finding the necessary capital for large-scale investments difficult. In fact, even during the first 6 years of the Republic, when the economy was relatively liberal (1923–1929), such direct investments were extremely slow to materialize. Although conditions created by the Treaty of Lausanne and the subsequent trade agreement countered their visions of *milli iktisat*, the Republican elites still made it clear that they were willing to work with foreign investors for the sake of setting off an industrial revolution that would help develop the country (Pamuk 2015, 180–182). In the 1st *İzmir Iktisat Kongresi* (Izmir Economic Congress), for example, officials signaled that so long as foreign and domestic entrepreneurs worked in equal conditions and were subject to domestic laws, foreigners could freely invest in the country (Boratav 2007, 61). By 1929, however, it had become clear that such calls were not resonating within entrepreneurial circles, and that most of the investments made fell short of initiating the kind of industrial revolution Republican elites dreamed of (ibid, 61–62).

a state-led, macro-level policy initiative to set off capital accumulation and to transfer resources from the rural-agrarian economy to the urban-industrial economy (Boratav 2007, 59–67). Since it prioritized industrial production over agricultural production as the motor of development, in the long run, it also triggered certain other processes (such as rural-to-urban migration, increasing concentration of capital and labor in the city) that have fundamentally altered the topography and the demography of Istanbul – which, in turn, shaped how the city was fed. As such, the move to *étatisme* could be considered the second major effect of the Great Depression on Istanbul's provisioning. Indeed, laws enacted in this period aimed to slow down price declines in agricultural goods, provide cheap credit to farmers, and establish a more direct line between new, state-funded industrial initiatives and farmers (Boratav 2007, 69–70; Pamuk 2015, 195; Tekeli and İlkin 1999, 45). Moreover, through investments into the railway system (nationalized during the 1920s), rural producers were better integrated with urban consumers and the domestic market (Pamuk 2015, 179–180). As such, throughout the 1930s, there was a steady growth of agricultural output, and by the end of that period, Turkey had succeeded in reversing its position from a grain importer to a grain exporter (ibid, 196).

Still, two major and interconnected problems remained: First, capital accumulation within agriculture was very slow. Although the demographic recuperation and abolition of *aşar* had increased agricultural output (even amidst the Great Depression (Pamuk 2012, 173–175)), this growth was reaching its limit by the end of the 1930s. Most producers remained as small to mid-size farming families, who owned enough land to cultivate on their own, but did not have enough to justify hiring extra labor (Tekeli and İlkin 1999, 44–45). As such, they could not accumulate capital, and in conjunction, shift to the commercial, intensive agricultural production model. Second, the low labor-to-land ratio continued throughout the early Republican period[14] (Tekeli and İlkin 1999, 44). Even if farmers wanted to hire extra labor, there simply was not enough to meet the demand. World War II had exacerbated the labor shortage and halted the demographic recuperation since World War I (1923–1941). With more than one million men drafted and farm animals, especially the cattle, seized for the war effort, growth in agricultural output was bound to be limited.[15] Consequently, prices of agricultural commodities began to rise, which,

---

14   According to Tekeli and İlkin, in the 1930s, 10.9% of the lands in the Republic of Turkey were *tarla*s (agricultural fields), 2.6% was *bağ*s and *bahçe*s (vineyards, orchards, gardens), 15% uncultivated but arable land, 31.1% pasture, 31.1% woods and bushes, and 27.3% non-arable land (1999, 44).

15   Agricultural production at the time was still not machine intensive.

FIGURE 8   Celebrating the 10th Anniversary of the Republic with sugar: From the 10th
             Year Anniversary Fair organized by İş Bankası. Here, the Bank is advertising
             its investments in two sugar refineries – one in Istanbul, the other in Alpullu,
             Kırklareli
             PHOTO COURTESY OF THE İŞ BANKASI ARCHIVE

coupled with inflation, made it difficult for the urban wage-earning classes to
be adequately fed. In addition, the expansion of the military required more
substantive planning of food provisioning. As a result of all of these factors,
the early Republican central authority enacted a series of laws, taxes, and measures to restructure agriculture and industry, and through these, to reorder
urban food provisioning (Metinsoy 2012).

In Pamuk's analysis of economic policies during World War II, urban food[16]
provisioning policies are divided into four groups, based on how interventionist they were (Pamuk 1986; 1999; 2012, 183–198). According to this schema, the
period from September 1939 to February 1941 is somewhat non-interventionist.
The Republican central authority aimed to rely on its stocks to provision the
city (Pamuk 1999, 61–62). However, due to price increases in agricultural commodities, it could not make enough bulk purchases. Once the stocks began to

---

16   These policies primarily targeted grains, especially wheat. After 1943, they were expanded
       to include legumes as well.

FIGURE 9   From the same exhibit as the previous one. The model of a publicly owned sugar
            refinery
            PHOTO COURTESY OF THE İŞ BANKASI ARCHIVE

dwindle, scarcity worsened and triggered further price hikes (ibid.). To slow
these down and to replenish its stocks, the central authority passed a law
called *Milli Korunma Kanunu* (National Protection Law) in 1940, which gave
the government the right to set prices, to set quotas for government purchase,
and/or to seize the cattle if a farmer had less than 4 hectares of land (ibid).

The relative failure of these measures to alleviate scarcity in Istanbul pushed
the central authority to become more interventionist in the period between
February 1941 and July 1942 (Pamuk 1999, 62–63). For example, new measures
required farmers to sell all their output to the central authority at predeter-
mined fixed prices, after the farmers had set aside the amount necessary for
seeding, animal feed, and yearly self-subsistence (ibid). Meanwhile, the prices
of the agricultural commodities continued to rise under war conditions, leaving the prices set by the central authority significantly below the market price
(ibid). Consequently, underreporting the output, bribing the provisioning officials, stockpiling, and black market transactions became common practices.
Urban scarcity, thus, intensified (ibid).

In August 1942, the central authority changed the provisioning policies yet
again (Pamuk 1999, 63–65). Rather than buying all the output, it instituted
quotas: 25% of the output of those who produced up to 50 tons, 35% of 50 to

100 tons, and 50% of more than 100 tons (ibid). Farmers were free to do whatever they wanted with their remaining output (which included selling to the traders) (ibid). However, because the purchasing prices for the quotas were fixed earlier, this new policy failed as well (ibid). Stockpiling, underreporting, and black market transactions continued (ibid).

By the beginning of 1943, urban food scarcity had turned into a major crisis (Pamuk 1999, 63–65). Subsequently, the central authority increased the quotas and began to purchase legumes in addition to grains (ibid), and in June 1943, it issued a series of new taxes (ibid, 65–66). According to these new taxes, 8% of the output of those who produced up to 50 tons and 12% of those who produced more than 50 tons were expropriated and for the remaining, the central authority would make a bulk purchase at a fixed price (ibid). After April 1944, the rates were changed to 10% and applied to everyone, regardless of quotas (ibid). Thus, practically, *aşar* – which was abolished in the early years of the Republic – was brought back, until the end of wwii. However, this too did not alleviate the scarcity. As both small and large farmers protested, prices continued to rise and urban consumers suffered, because food was either simply not making its way into the cities, or, given skyrocketing prices and inflation, whatever was available was also inaccessible to significant portions of the urban populations.

Boratav argues, perhaps controversially, that these provisioning policies were neither total failures nor total successes (Boratav 2007, 86–87). On the one hand, major cities and the military were provisioned under war conditions – which were successes; on the other hand, corruption, underreporting, and stockpiling could not be prevented – which were failures (ibid). While inflation skyrocketed, and wages and purchasing power declined, the measures undertaken brought back practices long thought to be over. Most importantly, however, the food provisioning policies had long-lasting consequences for different populations (Metinsoy 2012). In the cities, traders who had strong connections with the ruling *Cumhuriyet Halk Partisi* (chp; Republican People's Party) ended up accumulating significant sums, even when tight war conditions had stagnated growth and exacerbated labor shortages. Through *Varlık Vergisi* (wealth tax), by 1944, 315 million Turkish Lira was raised, which roughly amounted to 38% of public spending in 1943 (Boratav 2007, 88).[17] The working classes and bureaucrats, in contrast, suffered under inflation (which axed their

---

17   Just as a point of reference, the 10% tax on agricultural produce could only generate 167 million Turkish Lira (Boratav 2007, 88). Given that about 80% of the population at the time was living in the countryside and engaged in agriculture, whereas only 114,000 people were wealthy enough to be taxed under the Wealth Tax, this should provide us with some idea about how wealth was distributed in the early Republican era, and how

purchasing power) and increasingly tight food rations (Dokuyan 2013). In the countryside, the effects of the policies were more pronounced, since they had almost exactly opposing consequences for large landowners and small to mid-size farmers (Metinsoy 2012). For small farmers, the 25% quota had the effect of pushing them out of commercial agriculture back into subsistence farming or to sharecropping. For large landowners, in contrast, it enabled a rising proportion of black market activity, stockpiling, and hence, increasing accumulation of capital – even after substantial bribes had been paid out to tax officials and regional bureaucrats.[18] Similarly, the seizing of cattle, from which large landowners were exempt, essentially expropriated small to mid-size farmers, and enabled the means of production to be concentrated in the hands of large landowners (Silier 1981). By the time *aşar* was effectively reinstituted in 1944, the socio-economic differentiation in the countryside had already become substantial. Coupled with a chronic labor shortage (and land abundance), the concentration of the means of production in the hands of large landowners hindered small and mid-size farming families from producing more and producing more efficiently – and thus, from accumulating capital (Silier 1981; Pamuk 2012, 210–211).

Following the war, the Land Reform Act aimed to engage with some of these problems and to alleviate the economic hardships suffered by small and mid-size peasantry during the war. Scholars agree, however, that it fell short of

---

profoundly unequal (in terms of wealth, among other parameters) early Republican society was at the time.

18   Pamuk describes the opposing tendencies patiently in his study of the period:
       In the conditions of the day, wheat was yielding 1 to 5; as such, 20% of the produce needed to be set aside for seeding. In that case, peasants who cultivated less than 600 decares [au: 60 hectares] and who made up the majority of the population, had to set aside about half of their produce (20% + 25%) for seeding and for taxes. For example, a farming family who had 50 decares [au: 5 hectares] and who produced about 4 tons of wheat would retain about 2000 kg [au: 2 tons] of grains after taxes and seeding were set aside. This was barely enough to sustain the annual consumption of a family of 5–6. In this way, the "25% decision" was seizing the entire surplus of small farmers; and even coercing those farming families who cultivated less than 50 decares of land and were sharecropping, to cut down on their own consumption. (...) In contrast, the situation of the large landowners was getting better. As the amount of land cultivated increased, the amount of produce that was left to the farmers to be sold in the market for higher prices also increased. After large landowners sold 50% of their produce to the state, they could use the high grain prices in the market to their advantage. While others were selling their wheat to the state at 20 kuruş/kg, these [large landowners] could sell theirs [the remaining 50%] in the market at 100 kuruş/kg (1999, 65; author's translation).

achieving any of these aims: Republican elites misdiagnosed the problems; the solutions they proposed were not supported by the peasantry; and the large landowning faction within the elites themselves managed to sabotage certain aspects of the reform, which, they thought, might upset the status quo in the countryside (for more, see Karaömerlioğlu 2000; Pamuk 2012, 199–213; Boratav 2007, 93–94; Sencer 1999).

In many respects, the provisioning difficulties that Istanbul experienced during the early Republican years were indicative of other, larger problems the Republic had to deal with. On the one hand, a more fundamental transformation was necessary vis-à-vis agriculture: The country was barely able to feed itself; and as the provisioning difficulties during the war made it quite clear, it quickly became unable to, during times of emergency (Dokuyan 2013). Chronic labor shortages, relatively low technological input, and the concentration of the means of production in the hands of the few, stifled the agricultural advancement. Moreover, the profit-motive pushed different actors along the food system to act in disharmony, causing the supply chain to malfunction and scarcity to arise. On the other hand, exactly how that fundamental transformation vis-à-vis agriculture was going to happen was ambiguous: Not just in this period, but throughout the Republic's history up to the present, different governments made different – if not oppositional – decisions, and some even changed their decisions during their time in government. However, the provisioning needs of the country and the large size of the rural population (hence the voting power) kept the idea of advancing agriculture (with high capital inputs) and spearheading development via agriculture (as opposed to urban economy and industrialization) steadily on the table.

As Boratav points out, it is possible to see the early Republican period as a continuation of the economic policies (and effects) of the late Ottoman period (2007, 39). The problems identified above vis-à-vis urban food provisioning also give weight to Boratav's observation. At the same time, compared to their Ottoman predecessors, early Republican elites were more vigilant about the imperatives of the 'free market' infringing upon their sovereign authority. As their careful attention to the post-Treaty of Lausanne trade agreement demonstrates, they understood that low quotas, tariffs, and customs taxes could lead to strengthening certain domestic actors, who, in turn, could challenge the central authority's capacity to exert control over producing-consuming bodies of the Republic, and alter the relationship between the ruler and the ruled. This precautionary streak also distinguished them from their predecessors in the late Ottoman era and signaled a discontinuity between successive central authorities.

2   Urban Provisioning during Unruly Transitions

In a span of 40 years (1908–1948), Istanbul's provisioning apparatus went
through a series of changes, due primarily to the wars. As I mentioned before,
from 1838 to roughly 1914, Istanbul was fed by a shared provisioning apparatus: Global suppliers brought in wheat, legumes, and other grains, and the
locals supplied the perishables (FFVs, dairy and dairy products, ice, herbs, etc.).
While the unloading and storage facilities in the Eminönü area continued to
serve the wholesalers and retailers of the city (in some cases, until the 1970s),
the abolition of the Janissary Army and the weakening of the guild system led
to the disappearance of practices and mechanisms that sought to balance the
interests of public and private actors. Instead, the interests of those who had
access to capital – that is, the merchants who bought the goods from producers
and transported them to the city – began to govern the provisioning apparatus.
    Once World War I broke out and it became clear that the global actors sup-
plying the capital were now the Empire's enemies, the merchants switched
to domestic producers to provision the city. Thus, between 1914 and 1918, the
provisioning apparatus became – or rather, had to become – predominantly
domestic. Local supply lines and locations of production thus began to attract
higher demand. While the population increase in the old quarters stretched
thin the output of the neighboring Bosporus villages, scarcity and high prices
led institutions like hospitals, schools, military barracks, and orphanages to
plant gardens and keep animals. Even then, many residents of the city lived in
a condition of constant food scarcity (from both Type 1 and Type 2 failures of
the food system[19]). At times, wheat could not be brought in and as such, bread
became unavailable; and at other times, wheat flour was heavily adulterated
with ground barley and acorn to supply the bread demand (Temel 1998).
    Following the end of the war, Istanbul once again began to be provisioned
by a combination of global, domestic, and local actors (1918 to 1929) (see
Table 2). Wheat coming from the US was particularly significant in overcoming the grain and bread scarcity that had left the city so hungry during the
war. Yet, unlike the pre-war years, Istanbulites did not fully rely on imports.

---

19   Type 1 failure refers to the lack of food due to interruptions in the production or trans-
      portation of food. We see this type of scarcity usually during wars, epidemics, disasters,
      etc. Malnourishment or hunger that follows from it are usually experienced *en masse*.
      Type 2 failure, in contrast, refers to cases where food is available yet is inaccessible due to
      high prices. While it may not be experienced *en masse* like Type 1, it can be the chronic
      condition of living for certain populations – usually lower-income households, and mar-
      ginalized groups.

They continued to cultivate FFVs and other perishables in local gardens. Other locations of production, those along the Marmara coast for example, were also prominent suppliers of FFVs during this time. However, because the experiences of *en masse* scarcity (Type 1), due to food simply not making its way to the city, remained as a keen *aide mémoire*, domestic producers and locations of production were retained as primary suppliers in the provisioning apparatus. Nonetheless, for the domestic supply lines to become fully functional, Istanbul first had to be liberated from the Allied occupation – which would not happen until 1923. Meanwhile, the residents made use of the opportunities the city offered to grow food. While those wealthy enough to hire and/or spare labor could take advantage of the relatively rural hinterlands of the city, middle and lower class residents relied on the production in the neighborhood gardens and orchards (particularly if they were in the small and relatively more quiet Bosporus villages) and in-house gardens (which primarily depended on women's labor).

The gap between the rich and poor residents of the city also widened during the war years– not just in terms of how much they consumed, but in terms of what they could consume. For example, during the war and the occupation, poor residents could barely get even adulterated bread (Dokuyan 2013); whereas the wealthier residents could get – through the ever-expanding black market, of course – even luxuries like sugar, spices, rice, and coffee (Doğan 2018, 51-22). Another telling sign was the city's many European-style pastry and sweet shops, which had opened in the late 19th and early 20th centuries and remained open during these difficult years. While bakeries had to make do with adulterated flour and deal with ration regulations (Dokuyan 2013), these boutique shops drew in well-connected Istanbulites, diplomats, and higher military officials of the Allied Powers, who were able to afford the expensive delicacies.

In an interesting twist of history, for many of these shops, supplying the necessary ingredients became more difficult after the Great Depression. As I mentioned above, the early Republican government used the shock to stop enforcing the free trade policies of the Treaty of Lausanne and to institute protectionist measures. This meant higher taxes and quotas for import goods, which included certain food items like coffee, cocoa, and spices. Because these could not be grown in the country, the sweet and pastry shops that used them had to rely on imports – which were admittedly more erratic and expensive during this protectionist period. Alternatively, these shops could change their menus around or look for substitutes. To a certain extent, all of these options were explored: For example, while the country amped up its sugar beet and rice production and established publicly-owned processing facilities for them,

TABLE 2   Some of the staple foods imported to Istanbul between 1919–1922 (Doğan 2018, 48)

Product	Type	Origin
Grains & flours	Corn	Bulgaria
	Barley	Romania
	Rye	Russia
	Wheat flour	The United States
	Corn flour	Canada
		Australia
		Marseilles (France)
		Alexandria (Egypt)
Fats & oils	Butter	The United States
	Margarine	Bulgaria
	Vegetable oil	Macedonia
	Cottonseed oil	Marseilles (France)
	Sesame oil	
	Coconut oil	
Sugars	Granulated sugar	Java (Indonesia)
	Cube sugar	The United States
		The Netherlands
		Belgium
		Czechoslovakia
Rice		The United States
		Baku (Azerbaijan)
		Yangon (Rangoon/Myanmar)
		Saigon (Vietnam)
		Siam (Thailand)
		The UK
		Italy
		Egypt
Legumes	Beans	Romania
		France
Coffee		Java (Indonesia)
		Rio de Janeiro (Brazil)
		Santos (Brazil)
		Guatemala
Tea		Ceylon (Sri Lanka)
		Java (Indonesia)
		China

TABLE 2   Some of the staple foods imported to Istanbul between 1919–1922 (Doğan
           2018, 48) (*cont.*)

Product	Type	Origin
Potato		Marseilles (France)
		Italy
		Malta
		Bulgaria
		Cyprus
Fruits	Banana	Jaffa
	Orange	Egypt
	Watermelon	Canary Islands

public campaigns were also launched to trigger a switch in the preferences from coffee to tea, which could be (and after subsidies and know-how transfer to the farmers in the region indeed were/are) grown in the northeastern Black Sea coast of the country (Öğüt 2009; Hann 1990; Biryol 2016).[20]

Perhaps one of the most enduring impacts of these years was the memories of scarcity and hunger. While times of peace did offer some respite, already heavy bouts of scarcity and hunger were exacerbated by population increases. Though most of the new arrivals were only temporary residents (migrants passing through, disbanded soldiers, wounded transported back from the fronts, etc.), they still put a strain on an already stretched provisioning apparatus. Yet, it was the long lines for rations, a characteristic of the provisioning practices during the "Great War" (World War II) (Dokuyan 2013), that shaped people's imaginaries for years to come – particularly when the import substitution system begun to crack, due to its own inherent contradictions (one of the major points of discussion in the next chapter), and long lines for basic commodities like cooking oil and gas, became visible again, not unlike the ration lines of the "Great War". And for many, this was the most obvious sign that the economy was not well, and that the days of (hunger and) scarcity had returned.

---

20   A similar effort to incentivize the production and consumption of domestic produce
      was the *İzmir İktisat Kongresi* (Izmir Economic Congress). The Congress was essential
      for not only drawing up the framework of the *milli iktisat* (national economy) approach
      of the early Republican years, but for also demonstrating to foreigners and nationals alike
      what the newly established Republican regime aimed to do economically (Zürcher 1997;
      Finefrock 1981).

3   Scarcity in War vs. Scarcity in Peace

The difficult years I discussed in this chapter correspond approximately to 4 stages: the open economy period of 1908–1914 (when Istanbul was provisioned by global and domestic actors), the closed economy period between 1914 and 1918 (when, due to the war, the provisioning apparatus had to be primarily local and secondarily domestic), the open economy period from 1918 to 1929 (when global provisioning actors once again begun to supply the city), and finally, the closed, import substitution economy period from 1929 to 1980. This last period can further be divided into three sub-periods: the national economy period between 1929–1940 (when domestic and local suppliers fed the city), the war period from 1940 to 1945 (when amidst major scarcity, people had to rely on whatever local suppliers could offer), and the developmentalist period from 1945 to 1980 (when Istanbul came to rely increasingly on the domestic suppliers for its provisions, which will be covered in the next chapter).

These 'back-and-forths' between open and closed economy, local, domestic and/or global suppliers, and scarcity and sufficiency, occurred primarily because the country oscillated between war and peace, which generate different dynamics for urban provisioning and agricultural production in general. Hence, when the men were drafted, for example, agricultural yields were measurably reduced (on this, see Köymen 1999; Metinsoy 2012), whereas peace contributed to increases in both the agricultural production and the (rural) population. Second, however, these 'back-and-forths' had to do with the central authority (first the CUP, then the early Republican) negotiating its position vis-à-vis the subject-citizens' economic activity and what that activity may entail for the central authority itself and for the *body politic* as a whole (scarcity, abundance, profits, poverty, legitimacy crisis, etc.). Thus, the central authority had to settle both its approach to interventionism (whether it should be more or less interventionist, for example, whether it should set prices, grant import and export rights, etc.) and its practices, mechanisms, and tools of intervention (different apparatuses of practices, procedures, and mechanisms for directing, regulating, managing – in short, 'governing' – economic activity). In other words, what was at stake was how and how much the central authority should (the emphasis being on the normative as well as the practical) intervene into 'the economy'. Moreover, both the central authority's decisions and the apparatuses of government they generated, were met with a significant amount of different types of resistance from the subject-citizens: Widespread black market activity, farmers hiding some of their produce from tax collectors, complaints about tax hikes from peasants as well as large landowners, at the local and the parliamentary level, are a few such examples.

In contrast to the *urban food provisioning* food regime, however, the resistance of the subject-citizens could not generate as much traction over the central authority; and in this sense, the emerging food regime differed from the previous one: In the *urban food provisioning* food regime, provisioning practices and mechanisms linked the body of the sultan to the bodies of his subjects. Whenever there were scarcities, and the provisioning apparatuses malfunctioned, the sultan's own vulnerability became visible. Therefore, the sultan and the Sublime Porte did whatever they could to make sure that the provisioning apparatuses functioned, and the city was fed. However, this created a complicated dynamic between the central authority and the actors of the provisioning apparatuses: While the actors wanted to maintain their business networks and to profit, the priority of the central authority was to feed the city. If a merchant was caught tampering, stocking, or trying to cheat the authorities, the Sublime Porte considered him a deceiver of the *body politic*. He was punished severely, and his cargo was confiscated, and delivered to the Istanbulites as provisioning. To put it differently, the Istanbulites' right to be protected against their corporeal vulnerabilities, which surfaced particularly at times of scarcity and famine, was prioritized over the "merchants' absolute proprietorship of [their merchandise]" (Hill and Montag 2015, 286). In the emerging *codependent provisioning* food regime, in contrast, the "absolute proprietorship" (ibid) of the merchants began to be prioritized over the residents' right to be protected against their corporeal vulnerabilities. This, combined with lengthy wars, labor-intensive agricultural practices, and macro-level financial difficulties, led to the more frequent occurrence of Type 1 and Type 2 failures: That is, not only did subject-citizens become unable to afford what was available, but also, what was available itself became scarce. The response of the central authority to the string of crises, however, was not to provision through various punitive and coercive mechanisms (as was the case in the previous food regime) but to try to find solutions without violating the merchants' right to 'absolute proprietorship' (via rationing, for example). Yet, for the residents of the city, this meant that their corporeal vulnerabilities were no longer prioritized. The bodily link between them and the central authority was broken, and the central authority no longer considered protecting them from their corporeal vulnerabilities[21] as its obligation. Food had become just a commodity – essential for survival undoubtedly, but still, just a commodity.

---

21   To reiterate, with vulnerability, I mean, the imminence of death, the shifting of the limits of one's mortality and endurance due to external or internal infringements, the breaking down of one's bodily order, harmony, constitution, and/or balance.

Equally importantly, by no longer considering the protection of the subjects against their vulnerabilities its obligation, the central authority also relinquished the idea of keeping mutual vulnerabilities in check. To recap, in the *urban food provisioning* food regime, the central authority and the members of the *body politic* (the people) looked after each other. The members believed in and exalted the sultan's *kudret*, which represented Ottoman territorial unity in the sultan's body and in his rule; and the central authority made sure that its capital was provisioned. The proper functioning of the provisioning apparatuses signaled the health of the Empire; scarcities and profiteering, however, indicated that the sultan's vulnerabilities were surfacing and that his rule over the producing-consumer bodies of his subjects was weak. In the emerging *codependent provisioning* food regime, in turn, the ceding of urban provisioning to market mechanisms meant that the people and the central authority were not keeping each other's vulnerabilities in-check. The failures of the provisioning apparatuses (scarcity, profiteering, corruption, etc.) were thus no longer representative of the central authority's weaknesses or the limits to its rule.

An unfortunate implication was that the central authority was left with a sense of limitless capability and control: Places and localities not reached could still be reached; development, industrialization, and capital accumulation could be achieved even at times of intense crisis. For the residents of the city, this sense of limitless capability and control – or rather, the central authority's disregard for any limits of its capabilities and control – meant that they could no longer contest, or threaten to contest, the central authority, or remove them from their position of governance. For example, even when scarcity due to high food prices, transportation malfunctions, production failures, exposed the residents' corporeal vulnerabilities, Istanbulites could not make their discontent heard or felt.

Its link with the members of the *body politic* thus severed and unable to recognize their discontent, the central authority began to perceive itself as an entity distinct from the political community and to cultivate relationships, networks, practices that ensured its own survival aside from – and sometimes, regardless of – the survival of the political community as a whole. In the long run, the central authority's awakening to itself as a separate *body* led it to redefine what it is, what it does, what kind of a relation it has with the political community, and how it engages with the various members of the political community. At the same time, the survival of the central authority could not be completely divorced from the survival of the political community. It needed to maintain *"some* of its traditional functions" (Hill and Montag 2015, 263; emphasis added) for *some* members of the political community, so that it could continue in its position of governance. And this is exactly where the intersection of two fundamental fissures that have shaped the political-economic dynamics of Istanbul's provisioning in the new food regime become clear: the people–population fissure and the insider-outsider fissure.

Without necessarily indicating a chronology, the first fissure refers to the emergence of a separation between protections against vulnerabilities offered at the individual and the collective levels. That is, the central authority continues to provide protection against certain corporeal vulnerabilities at the collective level, but it does not necessarily offer protection against the same vulnerabilities at the individual level. For example, at the collective level, the central authority works to ensure the 'national security'; that is, the *body politic* as a whole is protected against, displacement, death, loss of land or property of its members due to foreign invasion, and so forth. At the individual level, however, members of the *body politic* could – and in the present case, did – experience all of these: they could be (and were) displaced, their lands and produce could be confiscated, etc. Critically and relatedly, not every member of the *body politic* experiences this fissure in the same way: Some members could be more protected than others, and some members could be more exposed than others (Armenians in 1915, Shia Kurds in 1938, Jews in 1942, Greeks in 1955, etc.). Moreover, this difference is not generated randomly. The central authority fragments the political community (the people) into 'populations' according to particular identity markers (religion, sex, class, ethnicity, mother tongue, literacy, etc.) and directs resources to those it considers 'insiders' and away from those it considers 'outsiders'. Finally, how 'insiders' and 'outsiders' are constituted remains contextual and impermanent (Kurds as 'insiders' during 1915, Shia Kurds as 'outsiders' during 1938, etc.), their members can overlap (Sunni Kurds as 'insiders', Shia Kurds as 'outsiders'); and depending on the zeitgeist, subject-citizens can travel seamlessly between the two categories.

The central authority thus used this 'people-population' fissure to make some live ('insiders'), and let others die ('outsiders'). Yet, this was not a matter of mere (!) resource allocation. It also entailed the cultivation of a new kind of link between the central authority and some populations ('insiders') within the political community, *and the exclusion of others* ('outsiders'). This meant that various populations became/were instituted in an existential opposition to others. Furthermore, some were willing to let the central authority leave others to fare for themselves – if not (in)advertently to goad them to do so – to perish even, so long as they themselves were protected against their own corporeal vulnerabilities. In the long run, this new link thus established between the central authority and the 'insiders' helped normalize an economy of death and decay within the political community itself. Hill and Montag call this *necro-economics*: "a deliberate refraining or withdrawal from action – not simply the inertia of non-action, but a strategically conceived retreat, a leaving alone or an abandonment, often in the face of powerful counterforces, whose effects could be far more devastating than any advance of government controls" (Hill and Montag 2015, 263–264). During these unruly years, *necroeconomics* became the new constituting and the binding dynamic of the *body politic*.

4   The Emerging Food Regime

What shaped the food system of the war years and later, the early Republican era, is the response the central authority developed to deal with the geographic and the political-economic division between the coasts and the hinterlands. On the one hand, this response was the institution of mechanisms of control, that signaled an almost complete reversal of the liberalization of the economy (that defined the post-1838 era of globalization): Prices were set; import quotas and customs taxes were reinstituted; shipments were closely monitored, and when necessary, state forces were deployed to provision Istanbul. On the other hand, the very same mechanisms and the crises of wartime provisioning were used to generate opportunities for capital accumulation for certain populations (*friends*), in collusion with and under the careful guidance of the central authority.

   This partnership – sometimes out in the open and other times more closeted – between the central authority and the *friends*, is the primary characteristic of the food system and the food regime that emerged after the *urban food provisioning* food regime. While 'friendship' with the central authority was the primary way to accumulate capital for the members of the political community, soliciting recognition and support from *friends* was how the central authority was able to secure any kind of legitimacy. Thus, the central authority chose venues of intervention (indirect and direct supports, specific projects for investment, policies for development, etc.), established who the *friends* were (in terms of ethnicity, religion, sexual orientation, gender, etc.), decided in what capacity they should be able to participate in the market (as bourgeois, or industrial workers, land-owning peasants, sharecroppers, landless laborers, etc.) and granted permissions of operation. *Friends*, in turn, respected and obeyed the central authority, ran operations (produced, processed, transported foods), delivered commodities and services, and provisioned the city. Hence, the name, "*codependent provisioning*" . Though this partnership and its effects became more prominent in the era following World War II (which is the focus of the next chapter), the signs had already appeared during the unruly years.

FIGURE 10   Uşak sugar factory
             PHOTO COURTESY OF THE SALT RESEARCH ARCHIVE

Yet, this closed-circuit of codependency was also prone to crisis. City-level scarcities due to lack of food (Type 1) were particularly prevalent during the war years, and the high prices made whatever was available, inaccessible to many (Type 2) when the country was at peace. Critically, however, while the central authority intervened and, to the extent possible, alleviated the scarcity in Istanbul during war years – through price controls and rationing (Dokuyan 2013) – the scarcity experienced during peace went unnoticed. So long as the city was provisioned on the aggregate, and the country as a whole produced enough to sustain itself, some populations' experiences of hunger and scarcity was not perceived as a problem that needed to be tackled by the central authority.

To top this off, these oscillations between Type 1 and Type 2 failures of the food system, the recognition of the experiences of some and disregard for others, intervention into some problems and non-intervention into yet others, unfolded within the *milli iktisat* (national economy) framework. That is, the central authority used the already existing conditions (and more often than not, created the very conditions) to create a national bourgeoisie, encourage domestic investment, and the accumulation, and/or concentration of capital in the country. As such, the shift I mentioned in the introduction – from frequent yet political community-wide scarcities (Type 1) to scarcities that are continuous yet contained to specific populations within the political community

(Type 2) – went hand-in-hand with the dissemination of the capitalist mode of production and relations of exchange. The central authority thus spearheaded the intensification of [free] market pressures on the economic activities of the political community, which had already shaped the political community by leading to a rift between the port and the hinterland cities during the later Ottoman era. In addition, the central authority managed the hazardous and beneficial effects of these market pressures by distributing them among the populations it carefully picked. Those who were made to live (*friends*) were protected and supported in various ways, their experiences of suffering due to scarcity and hunger were recognized as problems and addressed, and they were able to benefit from this food system and food regime, in return for their support of the central authority. In contrast, other populations (*enemies*) were either left to deal with the market pressures themselves or in certain cases, actively exposed – by way of forced displacement and/or relocation, heavy taxes, appropriation of land, animals and/or other resources, etc. – and let (and/or made) to die. Not only were their experiences of scarcity and hunger not recognized as problems, but the central authority even elicited these experiences so as to be able to offer *friends* a wider breadth of resources and/or opportunities to accumulate and/or concentrate capital. Normation (*a la* Foucault) of *friends* and *enemies* and the increasing tolerance of Type 2 failures were, in other words, expected and desired outcomes of this food system and food regime. I will explore this aspect further in the next chapter.

Before concluding, I want to address two additional questions: First, the populations who were categorized as '*enemies*' – did they not resist? Did they not come up with various ways to contain, deflect, alter, and/or reduce the hazardous effects of the market, and the central authority's ingenious methods of governing [through] its pressures? Second, how exceptional is the case at hand? Can we find corollaries elsewhere, in terms of shifts in the *mentalité* and/or practices, for example, or is this juxtaposition of [free] marketization, *necroeconomy,* and government particular to a central authority that has been associated with one of the first genocides of the modern era?

With respect to the first question: Populations and members of the political community categorized as '*enemies*' did in fact use wide-ranging practices to deal with hunger and scarcity. For example, to deal with exorbitant prices, inflation, and falling purchasing power, poor Istanbulites grew FFVs in times of peace and war. Less well-to-do migrants to the city squatted on public land. They set up gardens and fields, from which squatter communities were provisioned. Similarly, so long as transportation lines remained open, migrants from the countryside were regularly supplied by their kin who remained back in the villages. For their experiences of hunger and scarcity to be recognized and addressed by the central authority, however, these less well-to-do residents had to wait until the end of World War II, when the national political scene became ripe for multiparty politics (Boratav 1981; 1995). Particularly from the 1950s onward, the numbers among populations transiting between the *friend-enemy* categories increased, in parallel to growing rural-to-urban migrations, partisan violence, and ethno-religious tensions. Political parties then began to voice the experiences of these populations at the national level and articulate them as urgent problems that needed to be addressed by the central authority. Though not always successful, these iterations and practices of resistance helped some populations to move out of the *'enemy'* category. With that, the iterations and practices of resistance also gradually shifted from being illegal (for example, squatting on public land) and informal (hawking) to legal (privatization of squatted land through amnesty ordinances) and formal (converting hawkers into regulated and taxed street vendors). Most importantly, neither the gradual legalization-formalization of these iterations and practices nor the eventual acceptance of some of these populations into the *'friend'* category, contested and/or tackled the *friend-enemy* binary. In other words, even if certain populations moved between the *friend-enemy* categories, neither the categories and nor the food regime that enabled the central authority to govern through the categories, were altered.

The answer to the second question is relatively more complicated. On the one hand, in terms of shifts in the *mentalité* and practices, it is indeed possible to find corollaries elsewhere. During both world wars, for example, blockades on sea and land pushed many to rely primarily on their domestic producers, while also triggering price increases and local scarcities. At such times, rationing was a common recourse to alleviate urban provisioning crises (Hionidou 2013; Blum 2013; Davis 2000a; Goldman and Filtzer 2015; Mouré 2010; Seidman 2008). Yet even when there was not a targeted blockade going on, inflation, falling wages and purchasing power, were widespread as were scarcity, adulteration, black market trading, and hoarding (Blum 2013; Davis 2000a; Mouré 2010). The central authorities of the Allied and the Axis Powers alike tried to deal with these problems through methods and mechanisms similar to what I have explored in this chapter. In some cases, scarcities did become famines (Goldman and Filtzer 2015; Tanielian 2018), and the crises were exploited by either side to secure victory. Plus, the movement of large numbers of men (armies and auxiliaries) as well as the concentration of wounded, sick, and displaced in cities, put extra pressures on the food system, leading to frequent Type 1 and Type 2 failures.

Yet these parallels in mechanisms and methods to deal with scarcity and hunger do not necessarily correlate to similar shifts in the *mentalité* of government. In other words, just because a central authority utilized price controls and/or rationing to contain city-wide scarcity and hunger during war, doesn't mean that it also began to think about agricultural production and food consumption in the aggregate, rather than primarily provisioning its capital, or even other cities for that matter. Though such a shift did happen pretty much everywhere eventually, how and when it happened differed widely. In what we call the Global North, for example, the shift in the *mentalité* of government unfolded over a few centuries, whereas in most parts of the developing Global South, it has happened over a few generations.

Perhaps the more salient question is the pervasiveness of *necroeconomics* as a tool of government. That is, how common is it for central authorities in different contexts to deliberately take (or not to take) actions that would lead to scarcity and famine [and/or famine-like] conditions for the sake of accumulation and/or concentration of capital, or [further] marketization (Çalışkan and Callon 2009; 2010) of economic relations? This question informs one of the fundamental arguments of Polanyi's *The Great Transformation*:

> Our thesis is that the idea of a self-adjusting market implied a stark utopia. Such an institution could not exist for any length of time without annihilating the human and natural substance of society; it would have physically destroyed man and transformed his surrounding into a wilderness (2001, 3).

While Polanyi makes a more generalizing claim about the destructive tendencies of the market, Mike Davis points out that these destructive [and productive] tendencies have unfolded differently in different contexts precisely because they were utilized as tools of governments:

> How do we explain the fact that in the very half-century when peacetime famine permanently disappeared from Western Europe, it increased so devastatingly throughout much of the colonial world? Equally, how do we weigh smug claims about the life-saving benefits of steam transportation and modern grain markets when so many millions, especially in British India, died alongside railroad tracks or on the steps of grain depots? And how do we account in the case of China for the drastic decline in state capacity and popular welfare, especially famine relief, that seemed to follow in lockstep with the empire's forced 'opening' to modernity by Britain and the other Powers?
>
> We are not dealing, in other words, with 'lands of famine' becalmed in stagnant backwaters of world history, but with the fate of tropical

humanity at the precise moment (1870–1914) when its labor and products were being dynamically conscripted into a London-centered world economy. Millions died, not outside the 'modern world system', but in the very process of being forcibly incorporated into its economic and political structures (2000b, 8–9).

In other words, metropoles could be provisioned sufficiently only because the produce was drained out of the colonies through the markets. Central authorities that governed the metropoles eradicated peacetime famines, not by guaranteeing a fairer and/or a more efficient distribution of food, but by displacing scarcity and containing it in the colonies. Thus, the metropoles were fed – let live – only because colonies were starved – made to die.

For Foucault, this preferential treatment (protection of some and the exposition of others) is founded upon racism. He suggests, in the final lecture in *Society Must be Defended*, that racism is "a way of introducing a break into the domain of life that is under power's control: the break between what must live and what must die" (2003, 255) and as such, it "justifies the death-function in the economy of biopower by appealing to the principle that the death of others makes one biologically stronger insofar as one is a member of a race or a population" (ibid, 258). Achille Mbembe, building on this reading, argues that the racism-inflected "perception of the existence of the Other as an attempt on my life, as a mortal threat or absolute danger whose biophysical elimination would strengthen my potential to life and security (...) [is] one of the many imaginaries of sovereignty characteristic of both early and late modernity" (Mbembe 2003, 18). Indeed, Mike Davis's comprehensive and stark analysis of the death of millions in the colonies due to market-enforced famines in the late 19th and early 20th century (Davis 2000b) confirms both Foucault's and Mbembe's analyses.

Not only was the use of *necroeconomy* as a tool of government pervasive (and, as I will argue, it still is), but following Foucault and Mbembe, *necroeconomy* is inherent to the relationship between the sovereign and the subject-citizens, in political communities where marketization and accumulation of capital have come to determine the dynamics of [urban] provisioning. Once the central authority transfers its duty to provision and guarantee the right to subsistence of the members of the political community to the market, people will fragment into populations that will be and can be killed, and populations that will be made to live. Yet, while racism undoubtedly shapes who will fall into these categories, it is not – as I will show in the next chapter – the only factor.

CHAPTER 4

Planned Scarcities

Even the capitalist business itself had to be sheltered from the unrestricted working of the market mechanism.

KARL POLANYI[1]

∴

"When the 'Great War' ended," my Grandma used to say, "poverty and scarcity did not". In fact, following the war, the conditions got worse for a while. Lacking either animals, manpower, or machinery to work the land, her family had to leave the small town that had been their home for generations and move, first to Izmir and then to Istanbul, looking for wage work. Compared to many others also migrating, Grandma and her family were actually quite lucky. Grandma's father and her grandfather had worked in Izmir and Istanbul before, and they had lived in both cities for short durations. So, the family was not going into completely unknown territory. Still, Grandma says, they felt "rootless" for a while. Even after the men got wage work, and she got married to my Grandpa (who, as a police officer, also had wage work, social security, and job security), food scarcity did not abate – even if poverty did.

Unfortunately, neither the persistence of scarcity conditions, nor the migration, is unique to my Grandma's story. Indeed, following World War II, the country's infrastructure and its agricultural yields were in shambles: Because men had been drafted, labor power had been drained off of the land. Heavy taxes had pushed peasants to their limits, leading to a dramatic rise in rural poverty. Rations, high inflation, and dwindling purchasing power had fed urban scarcity and the black market. By the end of the war, only the rich in the city and the large landowners in the country could eat adequately. Moreover, like most episodes of post-disaster recovery, it took a while for conditions to improve. It wasn't until the end of the Korean War, that both the population and the agricultural yields picked back up, and scarcity in the cities began to abate. Yet

---

1 Polanyi, Karl. 2001. *The Great Transformation: The Political and Economic Origins of Our Time.* Boston, MA: Beacon Press, 201.

© KONINKLIJKE BRILL NV, LEIDEN, 2021 | DOI:10.1163/9789004424500_005

[urban and rural] poverty, now articulated in juxtaposition to 'national economy' and 'development', persisted, fueling waves of [im]migration.

This chapter continues the discussion on the *codependent provisioning* food regime. Though the previous chapter explored the dynamics and relations that were foundational to it, the food system underwent some significant changes in the aftermath of World War II, which shaped the ways in which the food system and the food regime responded to the frequent global and domestic political-economic crises of the Cold War era. These changes need further elaboration. Plus, the *codependent provisioning* food regime is a transitory food regime. It contains characteristics of the food systems and the food regimes that both preceded and succeeded it. While the previous chapter dealt with the similarities with the *urban food provisioning* food regime, this chapter focuses on the convergences with the one that followed it, that is the *urban food supply chain* food regime.

The first section of the chapter, 'Growing Istanbul: The Pangs of Development or the Crisis of Capitalism?' unravels the changes in the food system in conjunction with political-economic policy shifts throughout 1950s, '60s, and '70s. The next section, 'A Rationed Sovereignty', takes another look at *friend-enemy* (Schmitt 1976) dynamics and the role of *necroeconomics* for government, particularly in light of import substitution industrialization. The following section, 'Urban Provisioning in Import Substitution', offers a comparative analysis of food systems and urban provisioning practices, in contexts where an import substitution approach to development was adopted. Rather than juxtaposing peace vs. war time provisioning, as in the previous chapter, the emphasis here is on the oscillations between industry (manufacturing) and agriculture as the motor of development. While capital can be accumulated through either, whether the resource transfer will be from industry to agriculture or vice versa, has divergent implications for urban provisioning. The chapter concludes with a discussion of how the dynamics inherent to the food system led to frequent crises, the emergence of a new food system, and to the contemporary food regime, in the final section titled, 'The *Codependent Provisioning* Food Regime'.

1   Growing Istanbul: The Pangs of Development or the Crisis of Capitalism?

1.1   *The 1950s: Menderes' Istanbul*
By the end of World War II, the *Cumhuriyet Halk Partisi* (CHP; Republican People's Party) which had been in power since the establishment of the Republic, had alienated most people: The taxes instituted during the war had

effectively brought the Ottoman *aşar* (tithe tax) back and pushed the economic burden of the war on to small and mid-size farmers. Disincentivized to
produce for the market, these peasants either turned to subsistence farming or
lost their lands due to debt and crippling interest rates. Following the war, the
CHP tried to address these issues with a Land Reform Act, that aimed to settle
landless peasants and give them land (Pamuk 2015, 225). The discussions at
the time included redistributing public land as well as appropriating unused
land from large landowners. Yet given the already prevalent labor shortages,
the proposed law worked only to alienate more people – particularly large
landowners. On the urban front, the Party had managed to upset both the big
bourgeois and the small merchants, the lower level bureaucrats, and the still
relatively small urban working class. The big bourgeois was alienated from
the Party due to the Wealth Tax of 1942, whereas the latter groups had seen
their purchasing power fall drastically, as a result of war-time inflation, which
they attributed to bad leadership and economic mismanagement. Plus, the
Party had provided special permits and incentives to the big bourgeois, which
enabled them to accumulate sizable fortunes during the war (Boratav 2007, 97;
Pamuk 2015, 215). When this preferential treatment became public, it further
fed the prevalent negative sentiments against the Party.

The alienation of these groups had two interrelated effects at the macro-
level: First, the cracks within the CHP had widened to the point that a group
from within left the Party and established the *Demokrat Parti* (DP; Democrat
Party). Spearheaded by Adnan Menderes, a large landowner from Western
Anatolia, the DP contested the first multiparty elections in 1946 and took
over the government with an electoral victory in 1950. Second, between 1946
and 1953, Turkey shifted its economic policies to take a slightly more liberal
approach to 'development'. Agriculture, especially export-oriented commercial agriculture, was prioritized, in conjunction with an emphasis on private
entrepreneurship over public investments (Boratav 2007, 99–102). Similarly,
import and export quotas were lowered, to enable an easier flow of commodities; and with a devaluation of the Turkish Lira in 1946, Turkish export goods
were made more competitive within the global market (ibid, 100–104). Such
a policy shift was in line with a discursive shift to 'free trade' unfolding in the
post-World War II Western bloc at large, and had significant backing: US-
sourced investments, foreign aids, and credits flowed in conjunction with the
Truman Doctrine and later, through the Marshall Fund (ibid, 98–104).[2]

---

2   It should be noted that at the time when Turkey was receiving 'aid', the budget of the Republic
    showed a surplus and there was enough foreign currency in the reserves to fund a gradual,

Most of this aid was directed towards 'modernizing' Turkey's agricultural sector (Köymen 1999, 13). For example, tractors and agricultural machinery, endowed by the US, were distributed among select farmers. While these endowments further fed intra- and inter-regional income disparities (resulting from property distribution), they also structurally altered Istanbul's provisioning. To begin with, due to the replacement of animal-powered ploughs by tractors, overall reliance on farm animals decreased. Farmers began to switch to cash crops (wheat and cotton) and in some cases, increased the land under cultivation. Given that most small to mid-size farmers had fallen back into subsistence farming by the end of the war, this implied an expansion in the agricultural sector (Boratav 2007, 103) and concomitantly, abundance of produce, and lower prices. Overall, larger urban populations could access more produce.

Second, these 'modernization' efforts exacerbated the structural inequalities in agriculture, due particularly to landownership. For those who were already landless, mechanization meant the loss of (or at best, significant reduction in) even seasonal manual agricultural work and necessitated an almost immediate migration out of the countryside. Small farmers, in comparison, had to become sharecroppers to survive. They would rent machinery from local large landowners, in return for the right to work the land. In regions where land distribution was already highly unequal, this meant that large landowners could find enough small farmers to work their land, and thus accumulate capital more quickly (Akçay 1999; Keyder 1999d; Köymen 1999).[3]

Once it became clear that capital accumulation was possible through agriculture, agriculture-oriented economic development began to be seen as a strong possibility and a feasible alternative to industrialization-oriented economic development. Within this framework, the village and the lands attached to it came to be thought of as 'resources' rather than 'living spaces'. Thus, lands owned but not used to their utmost capacity, for example, were seen as resources wasted; and especially for those looking to expand (like mid-size farmers), they came to stand for potential, future gain. Similarly, each

---

controlled process of industrialization and capital accumulation within the domestic economy (Boratav 2007, 101–104).

3   That is, in regions with high inequality in landownership, the concentration of agricultural capital increased with the increasing 'modernization' of agriculture. In contrast, in regions where mid-size landownership (50 to 500 decares) was common, farmers would take longer to accumulate capital; the concentration of capital would be less stark; and for many, who tried to accumulate enough to buy their own machinery, diverse strategies would have to be put in place to maintain their profit margins. Often, small commodity production was the most commonly used strategy; and it slowed down the dissolution of rural structures, to the extent possible (Keyder 1999d).

household was considered to be a unit of production, and their social status came to be attached to their economic status, which in turn, was attached to their output and the market value thereof. Given that the availability of small farmers who were willing to engage in sharecropping, and/or seasonal agricultural labor force who could be hired for temporary work, varied greatly between regions and overall remained limited, self-exploitation of the household unit became a significant method through which farmers could produce surplus value and accumulate capital.

At the micro-level, both tendencies – to expand the area under cultivation, and to think of rural spaces (land in particular, but also populations) as resources – had major implications for Istanbul's provisioning. To begin with, increasing mechanization in agriculture had triggered a series of rural-to-urban migrations. This had caused Istanbul's population to increase, from approximately 850,000 in 1945 to 1,500,000 in 1955 (Keyder and Öncü 1993).[4] However, at the time, Istanbul had neither the housing supply nor the infrastructural capacity to deal with such a population increase. Consequently, throughout the 1950s, the city underwent a series of urban transformations, that altered the demographic, architectural, and socio-economic composition of the older neighborhoods. In addition, the city expanded in all directions, engulfing what used to be its immediate hinterlands. For the urban provisioning mechanisms, these changes implied both a decrease in in-city production and an increase in the demand thereof, to which the food system and the provisioning mechanisms needed to respond.

Three factors merit mention, vis-à-vis the urbanization and urban transformations Istanbul underwent in the 1950s: Changes in the architectural styles of the houses; increasing urbanization in the older parts of the city; and the expansion of the city. First, the migrations to the city triggered an architectural alteration in the older parts of the city, from large, Ottoman-style wooden or stone houses, to apartment buildings (Keyder 1999a, 173–174). Initially, the apartment buildings were two to four stories tall, with each floor containing two apartments (Tanyeli 2010, 137). Eventually, however, the buildings grew taller; and the gardens and the lots between them disappeared, to make space for larger and even taller buildings (Yaltırık 1993). Moreover, as "in the 1950s, the apartment building became the standard building type in Istanbul" (Tanyeli 2010, 137), construction codes and property laws were changed to adjust to the new construction trends in the city. Thus in 1954–1955, a new property law (*Kat*

---

4   Note that not all of the increase in population could be attributed to rural-to-urban migrations. As Tekeli notes, Turkey was undergoing a 6% annual population increase at the time; therefore, some of this increase is from the residents of the city (Tekeli 2009, 117).

Mülkiyet Kanunu) was legislated (Sey 1993). Before, each parcel of land had a single owner (Tekeli 2009, 119). This usually meant that a single-family unit[5] was housed on the family-owned land. The new law, in comparison, enabled multiple ownership over the same parcel of land, which essentially made it possible for people to own apartments in an apartment building.

While the new property law gave a legal push to architectural transformations, the demographics of residents in the older neighborhoods were also changing. Those who could take advantage of rising wages and purchasing power throughout the 1950s were moving to the new suburbs[6]; and those who could not, had to stay in the older neighborhoods with the migrants (Keyder 1999a). Yet, for some of the migrants, renting an apartment even in the older, working class neighborhoods, was not economically feasible. Shantytowns, instead, proved to be a cheaper alternative, albeit a legally uncertain one (Ekinci 2010a). Established at the city's outskirts, shantytowns thus contributed to Istanbul's expansion outward throughout the 1950s.

This early urban expansion, however, came at the cost of the *bağ*s, *bahçe*s, and *bostan*s adorning the city. While the changes in architectural styles led to the disappearance of home gardens, increasing housing demand put the neighborhood fields, gardens, vineyards and orchards in the sights of the developers (İstanbul 1993b; Yurt Ansiklopedisi 1981). Production in the immediate hinterlands of the city was also gradually pushed out. Consequently, in-city food production significantly decreased, and by the late 1950s, Istanbul's population outstripped the provisioning capacity of local production (Yurt Ansiklopedisi 1981).

For Istanbul's provisioning, another micro-level reverberation of the two tendencies – to expand the area under cultivation, and to think of rural spaces (land in particular, but also populations) as resources – was the rise of the intermediaries. Experiences during World War II had made clear – to both consumers and the central authority alike – the difficult relationship between interventionism and scarcity: If the central authority did not intervene, prices could go up; food could become inaccessible; scarcity, perhaps even famine, could haunt the city. With intervention, however, favoritism, nepotism, and

---

5   The family unit could be nuclear or extended, depending on circumstances.
6   Such as the Levent neighborhood, for example, which is considered a central location today. In the mid-1950s, when my Grandpa was stationed there, his patrol unit of 4 police officers (all with horses) got stuck in Levent during a particularly bad snowstorm. The roads were completely blocked, and they couldn't make their way back to the 'city' for 3 nights and 4 days. On a day with calm traffic today, Levent is about 20 minutes (by car) from Ortaköy, the small seaside neighborhood they lived in at the time.

corruption would become rampant, and the residents of the city would still be left to deal with high prices and possible scarcity. What was essential, as earlier experiences showed, was the establishment of a framework, within which provisioning actors would compete with each other. The central authority – whether the state or the municipality of the city – would play the role of an arbitrator between competitors and enforce rules that would keep the public interest in mind.

There were a few ways in which such competition could be generated: the central authority could favor *friends*, as it did during the war, and by providing subsidies, special permits, and/or tax cuts, generate competitive entrepreneurs within the food retail and wholesale sectors. However, given the extremely fragmented state of the sector, such a strategy would likely have failed. Alternatively, the central authority could have devised base and ceiling prices and ask the municipality to enforce them. Similar methods had been tried various times, with unsatisfactory results. The retailers and wholesalers both found ways around the enforcement. Finally, the central authority could have let the market determine prices; and instead, enforce and control taxes, and delegate to the municipality the job of enforcing sanitation and hygiene codes. In the end, the central authority decided to make use of all these methods: In 1954, the Istanbul Metropolitan Municipality (*İstanbul Büyükşehir Belediyesi*; IBB)established a joint venture with Swiss Migros Cooperatives Union (Migros 2011), with the aim of instituting price uniformity, and standardization in sales, labeling, and packaging. Although Migros operated as a mobile vendor in its early days, using trucks to visit various neighborhoods and selling mostly dry produce (legumes, grains, etc.), by 1957, the joint venture had enough capital and political support to open its first shop in the famous *Balık Pazarı* (Fish Market) district in Beyoğlu (ibid.).

The establishment of Migros Türk should also be seen in the context of macro-level developments. Good weather, increasing mechanization in agriculture, and the use of synthetic fertilizers and higher efficiency seeds had increased yields and created an abundance of produce. Market-friendly policies, high prices sustained by the US policy on stocking raw materials during the Korean War (Pamuk 2015, 229), and competitive prices achieved through the devaluation of the Turkish Lira in 1946, had spurred profits from exports. *Demokrat Parti* governments (1950–1960) further fueled this boom, by increasing the transportation capabilities of the country. Backed by the newly up-and-running automobile industry and the Marshall Fund, the DP shifted public resources to the construction of highways and incentivized private transportation (Pamuk 2015, 230). As the roads between villages, town, and cities improved, it became possible to ship FFVs easier, quicker, and cheaper. Finally, in the late 1940s and early 1950s, a few cold storage units and canning facilities were set up across the country, through public and private investments (Milli Prodüktivite Merkezi Tarım Şubesi 1968). As a result, FFVs could be transported over longer distances and offered to urban consumers at competitive prices. In other words, in the 1950s, agriculture and provisioning became profitable sectors and as such, it made sense for private investors and entrepreneurs to turn their money and attention to the food supply chain. The launch of Migros Türk was thus no accident.

1.2 The 1960s and 1970s: Volatile Growth

The transformations of the 1950s were not absolute. While the first half of the 1950s had been a relatively good time for the Turkish economy (increasing wages, capital accumulation, foreign investments, and infrastructural investments, and growth in both agriculture and manufacturing), the second half was strained by economic and political crises: increase in the domestic money supply had triggered high inflation, which depreciated purchasing power; and the falling demand for agricultural commodities on the global market, coupled with the effects of a relatively liberal trade policy in the absence of strong currency reserves, had initiated a currency crisis (Pamuk 2015, 231–234). The DP government tried to take control of the situation by devaluing the Turkish Lira on the one hand, and instituting interventionist measures on the other (ibid). In Istanbul, for example, *narh* came back for many food items, as well as other basic consumer goods; similarly, long lines and scarcity, reminiscent of the war era, once again became part of Istanbulites' everyday experience (ibid). Political unrest initiated by the economic downturn also pushed the DP government to take strict measures that restricted fundamental rights and freedoms (ibid).

The economic and political crises that started in the second half of the 1950s culminated in the 1960 coup. Consecutively, significant alterations were made in both economic policies and governmental structures. While the new constitution rearranged the relationship between the executive, legislative, and judiciary; economically, an industrialization-oriented outlook was adopted. There was also a move away from export-led growth towards import substitution. The liberal trade policies of the DP era were dropped, and quotas and tariffs were raised to balance out the foreign trade deficit. Given that most imports were oriented towards basic consumer goods, this change in policy could have worsened the long lines and scarcity. However, devaluation, trade deficit, and high quotas and tariffs, had created an impetus for domestic investors. With abundant support and protection from the central authority, private investments expanded in manufacturing, starting with finished consumer goods to consumer durables, and then to intermediary goods and machinery (Pamuk 2015, 237–239; Boratav 2007, 121). Indeed, between 1962 and 1977, the Turkish economy grew 6% annually, on average, with manufacturing growing by 10% on average and per capita income rising by 3% (Pamuk 2015, 238–239).

These political-economic changes had multiple and contradictory effects for Istanbul's provisioning. On the one hand, they rolled back some of the achievements of the 1950s, especially in agriculture. When the focus of economic policies shifted away from agriculture to industry, resources were also directed away from supporting farmers, farmers' cooperatives, and agricultural commodities. More importantly, import substitution had an adverse effect on the importing of agricultural inputs (synthetic fertilizers, pesticides, machinery, and spare parts). Given that oil was one of the most prominent imports, changes in oil prices also directly affected agriculture. Thus, overall, compared to the early 1950s, it became more difficult to generate profit within agriculture. Nonetheless, the political-economic changes continued to favor mid-size farmers and strengthened the connections between rural peripheries and urban centers (Pamuk 2015, 245). The number of tractors in the country continued to rise, from 42,000 in 1960 to 100,000 in 1970 and 430,000 in 1980 (ibid). Moreover, increases in efficiency and land brought under cultivation continued. As a result, in terms of food production, Turkey remained a self-sustaining country until the end of 1970s (ibid).

For FFV retailers and wholesalers, on the other hand, the post-1960 coup changes proved to be quite profitable. The expansion in the domestic manufacturing of consumer durables pushed the prices of these commodities down; and with sustained increases in wages and incomes, refrigerators entered the household (Boratav 2007, 122). Although often unreliable, electricity had also become available throughout most of the city – including in the shantytowns. Thus, Istanbulites' food shopping habits began to change. Now able to keep perishables for slightly longer periods of time, trips to the greengrocer decreased from once a day to several times a week. In addition, many preferred to shop weekly from the bazaars, where FFVs were somewhat cheaper. Plus, the city was expanding. Sustained industrialization and economic growth had pulled more people into Istanbul. As the number of people that needed to be fed increased, it became clear that the wholesale ports in Eminönü, which had been the point of entrance and distribution of foods into the city since the Ottoman era, had neither sufficient space nor organizational capacity, to handle the expanding food supply chain (Tekeli 2011, 64). By 1965, there was already talk of rearranging the ports and moving them out of Eminönü. Meanwhile, Migros Türk, largely privatized in 1975, started to create its own "infrastructure for a healthy distribution of fruits and vegetables", which included "fruit and vegetable offices", and a "gigantic center depot" (Migros 2011) that rivaled the disorganized and unsanitary wholesale ports at Eminönü.

By the mid-1970s, the structural contradictions of the import substitution approach began to seriously stifle the economy. As Pamuk diligently shows in *İthal İkamesi, Döviz Darboğazları ve Türkiye, 1947–1979*[7], industrialization is easier in the earlier stages of import substitution than it is in later stages. In the earlier stages, most of the products are finished consumer goods and basic intermediary products. They do not require advanced technology or capital-intensive investments. If there is a need to import machinery, for example, or other types of input, exports from agriculture or other sectors can be enough to sustain the necessary foreign currency. Problems occur, however, if industrialization stays at these early stages. Pamuk parses the dynamics out (ibid.): Manufacturing constantly needs to appropriate the surplus from agriculture; as a result, income inequality rises, which in turn has an adverse effect on the consumption of the very goods that are produced through import substitution. If industrialization advances to the production of more complex goods, other problems arise: For example, the production of intermediary goods may require more advanced technology, which the country may not be able to import (due to trade treaties, copyright laws, etc.). Alternatively, even if there were no barriers to the importation of technology, a global downturn in agricultural commodity prices (as in 1973 and 1979, for example, in conjunction with the OPEC price hikes) or in environmental conditions (drought, extreme heat or cold, etc.) may prevent the country from generating the necessary currency revenue. In other words, structurally, import substitution is bound to create major currency bottlenecks that are not easy to overcome. As Boratav and Pamuk point out, Turkey suffered regularly from such bottlenecks, the most severe starting out in 1976–1977, and leading to a series of economic and political crises for the following 3–4 years, only to culminate in a more radical liberalization of the economy (24 January Decisions) and a brutal military coup in 1980 (Boratav 2007, 141–146; Pamuk 2012, 249–272) (all to be discussed in the next chapter).

In terms of Istanbul's provisioning, the effects of these structural tendencies of import substitution industrialization were three-fold. To begin with, Turkish agriculture had to maintain (if not increase) its expansion. Given that the surplus generated from the export of agricultural commodities sustained (some of the) necessary foreign currency, Turkish agriculture needed to keep generating a surplus, even as resources were regularly being allocated away from it.

---

7   Import Substitution, Forex Bottlenecks and Turkey, 1947–1979.

The key dynamic here was the low labor-to-land ratio. While increasing invest-ments into agro-tech (which included farm machinery and higher yielding seeds) was spurring productivity and expanding the overall land under cultiva-tion, rural-to-urban migrations were further draining labor out of agriculture. This meant that growth in agriculture could be prolonged (it was!), so long as investments continued (they did) and demand was sustained (it most certainly was). Migrations, in fact, helped labor productivity increase faster within agri-culture than in manufacturing. Consequently, more and more peasants began to produce for the market, specialize in the production of specific agricultural commodities, and steer away from subsistence farming, while prices remained low and FFVs continued to be accessible for the swelling urban populations.

'The urban pull' was another effect, with direct implications for urban pro-visioning. As I have discussed in previous chapters, Istanbul had always drawn [im]migrants; and – to brave a gross generalization – it was mostly able to han-dle newcomers and maintain its cosmopolitan urban identity. From the 1950s onward, however, the incoming numbers proved to be too high for the city to manage. Insufficient infrastructure and the absence of affordable housing were the most immediate problems for newcomers. In this context, shanty-towns – established and maintained through kinship networks – became the solution. Neighborhoods of makeshift houses provided the new residents of the city with accommodations as well as the connections necessary to find work and settle in Istanbul. Plus, shantytowns acted as urban enclaves and enabled migrants to integrate with urban life at their own pace. Most new-comers could maintain contact with their villages, going back regularly to help with the harvest, for example, or to fulfill customary familial and/or religious obligations (Erder 2010; 1999; Ekinci 2010a). In fact, life in the shantytowns often looked like village life: Residents continued to dress like peasants; they cultivated FFVs in their household gardens, raised chickens, sheep, and cows, and self-produced the majority of the processed food items they consumed (such as tomato and pepper pastes, orzo and pasta, yoghurt, cheeses, pick-les, jams, marmalades, and molasses, etc.). In this respect, shantytowns acted as enclaves of the rural in the urban, and enabled migrants to embrace their rural roots explicitly, as opposed to being (perhaps forcefully) assimilated into Istanbul's cosmopolitan urban culture.

The shantytowns also became vehicles of urban expansion. Until gated communities, keen on drawing middle classes, triggered suburbanization, shantytowns pushed into the city's peripheries in an uneven sprawl. In some places, they merged into and expanded the existing villages around Istanbul; in other places, new settlements were constructed; and in yet other places, shantytowns were established between two older settlements, thus generating low-density connections between neighborhoods that were distinct. In any case, shantytowns and the rural-to-urban migration determined the dynamics of urban expansion throughout the '60s and '70s and shaped the conversation on it.

Meanwhile, production in the shantytowns was barely enough to sustain *some* of the needs of *some* of the city's new residents. Unlike before, when production in local *bağs*, *bahçe*s, and *bostan*s aimed to supply at least the neighborhood-level consumption, production in the shantytowns could not go beyond sustaining household needs. It was neither aimed to provision the city, nor could it, even if the migrants were to attempt it. This was primarily because production in the shantytowns had arisen as a response to the perceived inadequacy of the urban provisioning mechanisms of *codependent provisioning*. 'Mainstream' mechanisms either did not cater to the needs of the migrant population (as in, region-specific food items, for example, that were not available) and/or the population did not have the income and/or the purchasing power to access what the 'mainstream' provisioning mechanisms had to offer.

In any case, the emergence of this new 'alternative provisioning mechanisms' in the shantytowns is the manifestation of a few critical characteristics of the *codependent provisioning* food system and the food regime. To begin with, the central authority no longer found it necessary to intervene to feed the city as a whole. Instead, it was now up to the individual members to make sure that they were fed; and in the absence of the central authority's interventions, they were going to do what they could to provision themselves. Household production in the shantytowns was one such mechanism. By providing food (FFVs, milk, eggs, regional specialties, etc.), it helped stretch the already strained low-income family budgets. Second, this absence of intervention affected only certain *populations* in the city. Others, who had the income and the purchasing power, could either use the city's many weekly markets (*pazar*s; bazaars), neighborhood greengrocers (*manav*s), and delis (*bakkal*s), or go to now (mostly) privatized Migros. In other words, the city was no longer being treated as a whole; and while there were mechanisms to feed *some populations* (*friends*), others were left to fare on their own (*enemies*). Or, alternatively, the central authority was intervening to establish provisioning mechanisms that would feed only *part(s)* and not the whole.

Without spoiling the end, we can say that in the long run, not only did these 'alternative provisioning mechanisms' survive, they have flourished. Today, in lower-density neighborhoods, suburbs, and shantytowns alike, self-provisioning practices continue. People raise chickens, tend their front and back gardens (where available) and (try to) turn unused lots into urban gardens. Walking around even higher-density neighborhoods located at the heart of the city, it is not uncommon to come across all sorts of fruit trees and small vegetable gardens. Though these efforts are undoubtedly inspiring, in that they demonstrate the resilience of people against market-generated and central authority-enforced scarcities, Istanbul today is far from being the 'city of gardens' and Istanbulites no longer have the political power to force the central authority to provision them.

2   A Rationed Sovereignty

Codependent provisioning is a transitory food system; and as such, it contains practices, mechanisms, and discourses of both the preceding (*urban food provisioning*) and the succeeding (*urban food supply chain*) food systems. For example, as in the preceding food system, the central authority intervened to bring food to the city and even undertook its distribution. At the same time, unlike the preceding food system, such intervention was done only at times of national emergency, and not on a regular basis. Similarly, as will become clear in the next chapter, the central authority delegated the task of feeding the city predominantly to the market and encouraged private entrepreneurs to engage in provisioning as a profitable economic activity. However, unlike the succeeding food system, in *codependent provisioning*, the central authority established partnerships with private entrepreneurs and entered into the provisioning sector as an economic agent, while also providing all sorts of indirect subsidies and supports to them.

The 1950s was a significant juncture for the *codependent provisioning* food system, as it underwent some major changes. During the reign of the *Demokrat Parti*, the dominant *mentalité* of the food system shifted, from being characterized by the features of the preceding food system to the succeeding food system. For example, as I explored in the previous chapter, the idea that it is the duty of the central authority to protect the *people* against their vulnerabilities[8] (in return for their obedience) was still prevalent during the war years. Whether through taxes or rations, the central authority actively and directly intervened into the food system and provisioned the city. After the 1950s, however, the central authority refrained more and more from such active and direct interventions. Instead, it began to let the market determine the dynamics of provisioning. However, differing from the succeeding food system, it did

---

8 To reiterate: with vulnerability, I mean the imminence of death, the shifting of the limits of one's mortality and endurance due to external or internal infringements, the breaking down of one's bodily order, harmony, constitution and/or balance.

FIGURE 11   Alcoholic beverages production facility for the Public Tobacco and Alcoholic
Beverages Company or TEKEL, 1953
PHOTO COURTESY OF THE SALT RESEARCH ARCHIVE

not fully cast off this duty either. By way of indirect interventions, infrastructure projects, welfare provisions, and planning that led to the establishment of
a complex network of producers and provisioning agents, the central authority
continued to offer limited protections to the selected few among the *people*
(the *friends*).

Second, the 1950s marked the period when rural-to-urban migrations intensified; and in the absence of sufficient infrastructure, housing, and public services, these triggered urban expansion by way of ghettoization. For the food
system, these movements implied the increasing reliance of an increasing
urban population on a decreasing rural population for its food stuffs. In other
words, while de-peasantization was wreaking havoc on the countryside, the
withering away of urban food production was pushing the urban populations
to become more dependent on the countryside for its foodstuffs. In such conditions, if efficiency in agricultural production had not increased, it wouldn't
have been surprising to see incidents of Type 1 failure – unless, of course, markets were opened up for imported foodstuffs. And although these tendencies
and their implications were becoming quite clear by the end of the 1950s, the
central authority still refrained from implementing economic, social, and/or

political measures. The movement out of the countryside and out of agricultural production was not slowed down; help was not offered to ease the integration into urban life and/or to transition to manufacturing and/or service
jobs; and the necessary infrastructure and services were simply not provided.
As a result, not only did proletarianization speed up, but also, the industrial
reserve army in the city continued to grow. Given the focus on industry as the
motor of development in the decades that followed, it wouldn't be wrong to
say that this nonintervention on the part of the central authority, was more of
a deliberate choice and less of an unintentional disregard.

Third, the 1950s was the decade in which the tendencies, practices, mechanisms that would go on to characterize the succeeding food system, began
to become much more pronounced. These included; on the production side,
the use of high-efficiency seeds, artificial fertilizers, and machinery; on the
consumption side, the increasing diversification of consumer preferences
and consumption patterns; and on the retailing side, the emergence of specialized provisioning agents, networks, and mechanisms, that targeted specific consumer segments. Though these tendencies, practices, and mechanisms began to dominate the food system only after the 24 January Decisions
(1980), their effects were already visible, starting in the 1950s, and they were
feeding off of the city's changing demographic makeup throughout the '50s,
'60s, and '70s.

Nonetheless, the predominant *mentalité* in the *codependent provisioning*
food system remained 'codependency'. The central authority regularly established public-private partnerships, and through investments, infrastructure
projects, export and import permissions, and currency controls, generated
public and private co-dependencies. These partnerships not only provided
significant capital accumulation and concentration opportunities for the
most favored among the *friends*, they also showed the benefits of being in the
friends category to others. In other words, co-dependencies enabled capitalist
accumulation on the one hand, and on the other, they acted as carrots for less-
privileged *friends* and *enemies* alike. More pointedly perhaps, as the destructive effects of burgeoning capitalism (coated in the discourse of development)
began to atomize, alter, and commodify even the most personal relations,
every member of the *body politic* had to co-depend on others to manage these
effects and to ensure his/her survival as politically recognized living member
of the *people*: The central authority co-depended on *friends* for obedience;
friends co-depended on the central authority for provisions and other features
of protection (housing, health, various direct and indirect subsidies depending on their occupation etc.); producers and provisioning agents co-depended
on the central authority for capital accumulation; and the central authority

co-depended on the producers and the provisioning agents for the provisioning of the *friends*, and so forth.

In *codependent provisioning*, then, the relationship between the central
authority and the subject-citizens was constructed such that only some were
protected, though the obedience of all was expected and enforced. In conjunction, those who refused obedience and those who were classified as *enemies*,
were either killed and/or let die. The central authority used the destructive
effects of the market to weed out individual subject-citizens who actively
opposed its *mentalité* of government, as also the populations it considered
detrimental to its existence, even if such populations were among the foundational constituents of the *body politic*. Plus, relying on the support and the
obedience of those provisioned, the central authority stifled the power of the
people which, in the previous food regime, could rattle the sovereign whenever the city was not provisioned adequately. To do so, the central authority
generated and/or made use of fundamental oppositions and exclusions within
the *people*, based on the different types and degrees of protections it provided
to different populations: employed vs. unemployed, wage worker employed
in a formal sector with job security and pensions vs. wage worker employed
informally with no job security and no pensions, middle class urban dwellers
who could afford what the urban provisioning apparatus had to offer vs. lower
class shantytown dwellers who had to rely on their own gardens and relatives
elsewhere for provisioning, rural poor still in the village vs. rural poor who had
migrated to the city, etc.

These oppositions were also fed by other societal tensions, ideological divergences, ethnic and religious conflicts. The central authority never refrained
from exploring and exploiting these, to declare some populations as *enemies*
and concurrently, withholding and/or refusing 'public' services and infrastructures, knowing full well that such denials were forms of letting die, and in certain cases, could even escalate to killing[9]. *Necroeconomics* (Montag 2005) thus
served *necropolitics* (Mbembe 2003): Without having to generate exceptions, the
central authority eliminated *enemy* populations by making it difficult and/or
impossible for them to engage in the productive and reproductive labor necessary for subsistence. In other words, to let die and/or kill through the market,
within the law, while the political community is maintained – at least discursively – as a single, unified entity.

Yet these inactions, non-interventions, and refusals were not just destructive. The protections that were offered (and not offered) to specific populations,

---

9   See, for example, the pogroms of 6–7 September 1955.

also determined how reproductive labor was going to be distributed in those populations and who was going to engage in that labor. In other words, the co-dependencies cultivated by the central authority also (in)advertently produced notions of gender: The household gardens that were quite widespread in the shantytowns, for example, were – unsurprisingly – planted, tended, and harvested mostly by the migrant women. Upper class women, in contrast, able to afford what the provisioning apparatus had to offer, kept flower gardens and employed others (primarily men) as gardeners.

Nevertheless, cooking and provisioning within the confines of the home remained women's duty – irrespective of class (Bora 2018; Kandiyoti 2015; Özbay 2019). Even if women engaged in productive labor, they were still expected to do groceries, cook, and if need be, garden. Upper class women could employ others to do these tasks, and yet they were still responsible for 'feeding the family'. The ability to cook and to serve was strongly associated with femininity, though the execution thereof, depended on class. Moreover, girls of a certain age were expected not just to know how to cook, but again, depending on their class, to cook regularly for their families. Similarly, the ability to prep certain dishes signaled that a girl was ready for marriage, acting as a referent for the performance of femininity. In turn, the failure to cook, serve, and provision, according to class-based senses of appropriateness, was perceived as a manifestation of insufficient 'femininity', making clear that the person was either incapable of performing their assigned gender role (usually considered their fault) or that they were not disciplined sufficiently in what their gender role entailed and how to perform it (usually considered the fault of their upbringing). In either case, the economy of reproductive labor and constructions of (class-dependent) gender were shaped by the central authority's provision, withholding, or denial of protections. Roughly, then, any reduction in provisioning by the central authority, had to be compensated for by more reproductive labor by women; at the same time, regardless of how much the central authority provisioned, the onus remained on women, discursively ingrained into a class-specific sense of 'womanhood', to provision. Through the *friend-enemy* dynamics, then, the central authority constructed not only senses of femininity (and masculinity), but also gendered subject-citizens in opposition to one another.

In this context, how is the right to subsistence articulated? The difficulty of this question lies not in its theoretical acumen, but the contradiction inherent in the context: On the one hand, the right to subsistence is a right that can only be recognized at the level of the political community, between the sovereign and the subject-citizens. Indeed, in the previous food regime, for example, the right to subsistence materialized through the Ottoman sovereign and the comprehensive web of regulatory agents he had appointed, though the people's threat of disobedience was a significant factor in the public recognition and enforcement of this right. Yet, as I have shown in this chapter and the previous one, beginning with the *codependent provisioning* food regime, not only did the sovereign (central authority) distance itself from such political community-wide recognition and enforcement (except during certain emergencies, like wars), it also used the very social and economic conditions that necessitated the right to subsistence in the first place, to eliminate *enemy* populations.

Yet, following Polanyi, markets cannot be allowed to become the sole directors of the "fate of human beings and their natural environment" (Polanyi 2001, 76), as that would obliterate the political community. As such, so long as capitalist relations of production and exchange are around, the right to subsistence needs to be articulated, publicly recognized, and enforced – in some fashion or another. Indeed, in *codependent provisioning*, in tandem with public reticence, we see new spaces opened up, new opportunities emerging, for discursive rearticulations of the right to subsistence. The most important among these were made by the *enemy* populations, who have reclaimed and rearticulated what the right to subsistence entails, in reaction to the central authority. Broadly speaking, demands for better working conditions, the right to organize, and to bargain for higher wages, voiced by the revolutionary leftist movements of the '6os and the '70s; and more controversially, Kurdish demands for ethnic recognition, enhanced civil rights, and better political representation, can be mentioned as examples of these rearticulations. A more common rearticulation was of the right to subsistence in reference to the right to the city. As I have discussed previously, the lack of affordable housing in the city pushed the rural-to-urban migrants to the shantytowns mushrooming on Istanbul's peripheries. The city's housing crisis was – to some extent – thus alleviated. However, most of these shantytowns lacked essential infrastructures (water, sanitation, electricity, roads) and public services (transportation, education, and health). Living standards were low, poverty was high, and more often than not, both aspects adversely effected the new residents' health, mortality rates, and class mobility. Politically active residents from these neighborhoods, in alliance with politically invested actors from both the left and the right, reclaimed the right to subsistence and rearticulated it as the right to the city in this context. The state's provision of basic necessities, usually associated with the struggle for the right to subsistence, hence became one of the main items of the political agenda throughout the '6os and the '70s – in effect, well into the 1990s. These demands and the political impetus of the populations behind them were so strong that – in a marked contrast to today – political

parties asking for votes from all ends of the political spectrum had to make
a pitch for how they would provide these public services and infrastructures.

Accordingly, the central authority could not remain completely oblivious
to these public demands – particularly when the demand came from those
populations who were potential *friends* (or, who were certainly not *enemies*).
In other words, the demands for access to public infrastructures and services
were being voiced by those populations who the central authority were letting
live – or, at least, were not actively or passively killing (making die or letting
die, respectively). Plus, as *friends* – or potential *friends* – who were getting the
short end of the stick, these populations could as easily change their attitude
towards the central authority. Some indeed had already done so, by allowing
those associations the central authority considered a 'threat', an '*enemy*', or a
'traitor', to recruit and organize in their neighborhoods. In response, the central authority followed a 2-tier strategy: on the one hand, it provided the infrastructures and services to select few shantytown neighborhoods, or through a
series of intermittent amnesties, legalized whatever make-do infrastructures
and services the residents of these neighborhoods had already pirated or
cobbled together. The neighborhoods were thus drawn into the formal urban
economy (of housing, taxes, energy, etc.), and the residents were able to accumulate capital more quickly (both rent and social capital), and to move up the
socio-economic ladder. On the other hand, for another select few, the central
authority not only did not provide any services and infrastructures, it in fact
destroyed whatever housing, infrastructures, and services the residents had
developed for themselves.

The intention here was not solely to make an example of those 'perfidi-
ous' neighborhoods that had opted for a more radical stance against the sovereign. It was to generate a strong, highly polarized division between loyal,
*friend*ly winners, who could benefit from what the city could offer, and the
enemy-esque losers, who had to keep on struggling. The message, as such, was
clear: How the right to subsistence was rearticulated was not as important as
who rearticulated it. The central authority maintained the division between
friends and *enemies* and continued to utilize access to the public infrastructures and services necessary for subsistence, as a tool for making some live
and letting others die. To reiterate, then, *necroeconomics* (Montag 2005) served
necropolitics (Mbembe 2003): Letting die and/or killing through the market
became the strategy of operation for the central authority.[10]

---

10   The effects of this 2-tier strategy are still visible in Istanbul. Banu Bargu, for example,
      begins her book *Starve and Immolate: The Politics of Human Weapons* (2014), with the
      touching story of Mehmet, a hunger striker who holds fast to resistance, despite being

3   Urban Provisioning in Import Substitution

It is quite difficult to assess whether *codependent provisioning* failed, and if it did, exactly how so. Because in this food system, some were expected – indeed, targeted – to not be provisioned. That is, from the get-go, the food system focused on feeding some (*friends*) and not others (*enemies*). Therefore, that some populations were not provisioned, was not a failure; it was how the food regime was designed to work. The hunger and scarcity that *enemies* struggled with, as well as the abundance *friends* experienced, were planned for. Failure, then, could occur only if a population who was supposed to be provisioned, was not (that is, when a *friend* was treated like an *enemy*); and when *en masse* scarcity and hunger (Type 2[11]) hit the country. Fortunately, instances of both

---

"reduced to a skeleton wrapped in a thin, almost-transparent layer of skin, with the greenish gray hue of death" (Bargu 2014, 37). As Bargu articulates Mehmet and his agency in his death-imbued resistance, she also situates Mehmet and the neighborhood in which he lays thus. We learn that he is in *Küçükarmutlu*,

> [a] shantytown neighborhood upon a hill overlooking the Bosporus, the many one-story houses – some partially constructed, some left without the final coating – were of the familiar kind in Istanbul built under the radar of municipal officials by the influx of immigrants who came to the city from rural Anatolia in search of a better life. Built with cheap construction materials, reflecting the poverty of their inhabitants and the precariousness of their status, and without official construction permits, these houses were of the kind that sprang up overnight, became part of the ever expanding contours of the city, and yet faced continuous danger of demolition by authorities. Separated from one of the most expensive and chic districts of Istanbul by the highway that led up to the Fatih Sultan Mehmet Bridge, connecting Europe to Asia, the neighborhood had unpaved, dusty roads, intermittent bus service, plumbing and electricity legally provided after long struggles and populist land grants from incumbent governments, and a population that served as the informal and flexible labor force of the growing metropolis. This new working class was essential in the economies and functioning of the largest cities and yet unable to earn their deserved share in them. At the same time, this neighborhood was one of several shantytowns, which had their own traditions of organized resistance that developed through the mobilization of their inhabitants for access to urban services and violent struggles between radical leftist and ultranationalist militants who parceled different neighborhoods in the ideological battles of the 1970s. Like their Islamist counterparts in the late 1980s and 1990s, though less successfully than they, leftist militants had been organizing in these shantytowns since the late 1960s, offering their inhabitants informal networks of relief, economic solidarity, and even physical protection (Bargu 2014, 38).

11   Type 1 failure refers to lack of food due to interruptions in the production or transportation of food. We see this type of scarcity usually during wars, epidemics, disasters, etc. Malnourishment or hunger that follows is usually experienced *en masse*. Type 2 failure, in contrast, refers to cases where food is available yet inaccessible due to high prices. While

were relatively rare – that is, until 1974, when a string of political and fiscal crises led to a breakdown in the food system down, and concomitantly, led the carefully managed *friend-enemy* dynamics to go haywire.

The costs and benefits of the larger structures and principles that made and broke the *codependent provisioning* food system (such as import substitution, *étatisme, milli iktisat*) are still up for debate. However, it is indisputable that the contemporary food system and its associated food regime – what I have called the *urban food supply chain* food regime – would not become dominant, unless the *codependent provisioning* food system was undone. And even though that undoing might have been due to the food system's own internal dynamics, and it may have started to unravel with the 1974 crisis, the vital blows that took the food system apart came with the 'structural adjustments' in the 1980s.

In this sense, Turkey is not unique at all. During the long 1980s – if I were to re-appropriate Eric Hobsbawm's famous analogy – a host of countries underwent comparable dissolutions and reconstitutions of their food systems, and more gradually, their food regimes (for examples, see Hopewell 2016; Baer and Kerstenetzky 1964; Bagchi 1977; Balisacan 1989; Botella-Rodriguez 2018; Debowicz and Segal 2014; Oshima 1986). Similarly, in those cases, it is unclear when exactly the dissolution begun and whether it was due to the dynamics inherent to the *codependent provisioning* food system. For India, for example, Raj Patel identifies dependency on foreign food aid as the factor that destabilized the food system (Patel 2007, 121–122). He traces the beginning of the dissolution of the food system to the 1950s and 1960s, when *codependent provisioning* was, in fact, in full force. More interestingly, as in the Turkish case, this dependency on foreign food aid was result of a crisis that was due to the central authority's oscillating focus between industry and agriculture as the motor of development (ibid.). While the Indian central authority initiated the "shifting [of] local capital away from rural areas and into the development of urban industry and technical skill" (ibid.), farmers decreased production – though the demand was increasing. This widening gap supplemented by foreign food aid, which generated the dependency.

One can make the argument that such dependencies (on external agents and/or inputs) can occur irrespective of the food system in place, and that so long as public-private partnerships are fundamental components of a food system, such dependencies are inevitable. Yet, the distinct characteristic of *codependent provisioning* is *necroeconomy* and the ways in which *necroeconomy*

---

it may not be experienced *en masse* like Type 1, it can be the chronic condition of living for certain populations, usually lower-income households, and marginalized groups.

is entangled in the relationship between the sovereign (central authority) and the (subject-)citizens. In other words, the critical characteristic of this food regime is its differentiation between *friends* and *enemies* and the provisioning of some (*friends*) at the expense of others (*enemies*). The important question, then, is if this dynamic plays out in other contexts as well, and how so.

This is a tough question – not because the answer is the difficult to identify, but because the ways in which *friends* and *enemies* are selected, categorized, and governed, vary significantly from context to context. For example, while discussing the formation of capitalist agriculture in Latin America, Anthony Winson points out that until the crisis in the 1970s, state policy favored the development of industry in Argentina, though the country remained pre-dominantly agricultural (1983, 89–90). Gradually, however, industrialization changed the pre-existing social configurations, "strengthening the industrial interests (...), the swelling urban proletariat, and [creating] new popular sec-tors lacking effective political expression" (ibid, 90). Yet when those popular sectors did find political expression, they were deemed dangerous – requiring violent intervention to be quieted. *Friends* and *enemies,* in this context, came to be defined through class (whether someone owns means of production) and adherence to free market principles. In Turkey, in comparison, religion and ethnicity played a more significant role – both in the ways classes were configured, and in the ways those class-based demands found expression.

Regardless of these contextual differences, so long as redistributive policies are not actively enforced, there is going to be some level of governing through *necroeconomy*. However, this is not to say that all government is *necroeconomic* government, unless poverty-induced hunger and/or malnutrition is completely absent. The critical question here is, whether the central authority is using the provisioning apparatus and its role in it, to govern through hunger: either by taking resources from some populations (*enemies*) and giving them to others (*friends*), or by making certain resources inaccessible to some, or by leaving some to fare for themselves, when it is clear that the market is going to eradi-cate their livelihoods. To put it in terms of the Hobbesian protection-obedience formulation: Government through hunger manifests when, in return for the subject-citizens' obedience, the protection the central authority offers – one that is supposed to include the subject-citizens' right to food as a part of their right to subsistence and/or the right to self-preservation – is granted unequally to those subject-citizens, in such a way that the provisioning apparatus itself becomes a tool through which the central authority can actively or passively administer who lives and who dies.

This utilization of the provisioning apparatus as a tool of government is neither unique, nor is it specific to a particular configuration of urban-rural dynamics. It can come about in various contexts, with differing emphases and constellations of local forces. In Brazil, for example, the central authority was much more in tune with the demands of the "urban-industrial complexes [which] were very sensitive to food shortages" (Alves and Pastore 1978, 868). The working class and the bourgeois were thus able to put "pressure on the government to shape an agriculture policy that would increase the production of agricultural commodities at a lower cost" (ibid) as well as push for price and export controls, to "lower or to restrain the increase of the prices" (ibid). While this does not mean that 'government through hunger' was not prevalent in Brazil, the political-economic configuration of the country at the time did allow demands for the right to subsistence to have an effect on the relevant policies. Whether these alterations were meaningful or successful, in the short or long run, of course, remains open for discussion.

Critically, the effects of *necroeconomic* government, in terms of severity, are directly proportional to the involvement of the central authority in the provisioning apparatus. Yet the developmentalist approach itself, which the Turkish case exemplifies, requires the central authority to be substantively involved in the economy – both as an economic agent, and as a law-maker that sets and enforces the rules that govern the markets. While I don't go into the political-economic implications of this involvement here, I do want to highlight that this is one of the primary internal contradictions of the *codependent provisioning* food regime. It does not, however, have only destructive effects. The central authority, rather, utilizes its involvement in the economy to institute and strengthen its position of political power: If it is required to be involved in the economy, then it will use this involvement to encourage those who obey its authority (*friends*) and to impede those who do not (*enemies*). *Necroeconomy* thus manifests as a natural conclusion of the central authority's involvement in the economy, and *necropolitics* thus becomes the *mentalité* of government in this food regime.

So far, I have principally focused on the internal contradictions of the *codependent provisioning* food system and the food regime. Moreover, I have portrayed *necroeconomy* – and *necropolitics* – as components of the food regime that the central authority generated, instituted, and enforced in and of itself. Yet, the impact of external factors on (the dissolution of) the *codependent provisioning* food system and food regime, in similar contexts, merits mention – particularly the 'food aid' Patel mentions vis-à-vis India (Patel 2007, 121–122). Excepting countries like Germany and Japan, where the food system was utterly decimated by World War II, US food aid has had unabated negative effects on domestic agriculture production capacity everywhere it was extended to: It triggered radical price drops, rural-to-urban migrations, socio-political instability, debt dependence, and related political problems.[12] Thus, it is possible – and accurate – to point out that the existential crisis the *codependent provisioning* food system (and the food regime) experienced in the 1970s is, in fact, a result of factors and/or actors external to the food system. Quite a few scholars have indeed argued so (for well-thought out and researched scholarly works on the subject, see for example, Patel 2007; Köymen 1999; Wise 2019). In fact, in most analyses, 'external factors' are emphasized as the causal reason for the unraveling of the *codependent provisioning* food system. This is quite problematic, as it can make it seem as if the 'external factors' were the only reason for the collapse of the *codependent provisioning* food system, thus implying that the system was otherwise free of internal contradictions. As such, and more importantly, it puts the onus of *necroeconomy* – too conveniently, in my opinion – on the shoulders of PL 480, USAID, the Gold Standard, and the General Agreement on Tariffs and Trade (GATT), and clears the central authorities of their involvement in garnering economies of death through the provisioning apparatuses for the purpose of generating obedient subject-citizens.

Similarly, a wide range of ecological, social, and political tensions, that were ignited during *codependent provisioning* and exacerbated in the food system that followed, are generally attributed to these 'external factors'. While not inaccurate, such analyses situate local resistance movements that developed as a response to these tensions, within an anti-globalization framework, casting them as fighting against the negative local impacts of the 'external factors'. What this leads to, in turn, is a failure in recognizing how the internal contradictions of the *codependent provisioning* food system contributed to those very issues, and worse, how certain populations became complicit in their intensification. As a result, not only may new lines of solidarity between various resistance movements not be sought out, but more importantly, the very populations and/or agents who were complicit in the first place, could be championed as the motors of change (see, for example, discussions of neoliberal sustainabilities and the Slow Food movement in Goodman, DuPuis, and Goodman 2012; Leitch 2013; Pilcher 2008). I will explore this dynamic more in Chapter 6, particularly in the section on alternative food networks; but for now, let me illustrate my point with an example.

My current project involves charting out and exploring the market pressures (small and big) farmers on Istanbul's peripheries feel, and how they deal with

---

12   The US itself very quickly recognized the – *necroeconomic* – power of PL 480. Once the
      aid-receiving countries became dependent on US food aid, the US could hold a knife to
      that government's throat just by "systematically withholding a guarantee of food aid sup-
      ply" (Patel 2007, 123).

them. One very common pressure that almost all farmers (that I have talked to) mention, is the effect of rising land prices: Istanbul is growing and expanding – which means the farmlands immediately around the city are under the threat of urbanization. Indeed, with a new law in 2004[13] that reclassified all the 'villages' in Istanbul (and neighboring Kocaeli) into 'neighborhoods' – thus enabling the legal conversion of farmlands into residential zones – such threats became a lot more viable. Furthermore, farmers in Istanbul (and beyond) regularly complain about how farming doesn't pay enough to subsist, that they have to undertake other jobs to maintain themselves and their farms. As they see it, moving forward, they have 2 options: Either sell the land, quit farming, and move to the city proper, or take on loans, buy land, and expand production.

Most small farmers that I talked to, really love what they are doing, and they are not willing to quit farming just yet. Some of them had already taken out loans and were expanding, and/or switching to more labor-intensive[14] yet higher profit crops. Women farmers in particular were very into value-added products; as such, they were looking to invest in processing facilities and machinery, packaging, PR, and social media. For many of them, 'organic', 'sustainable', 'biodynamic', 'clean' or 'toxin-free' production made sense, so long as they could sell their produce for substantially higher prices. Moreover, when asked, almost all of them said they would rather expand and shift to production for export. They knew that the EU, for example, paid much better prices for organic produce.

Yet, these small farmers were also the population the food movement at large, and ethical consumers[15] in particular, saw as the country's only hope, for a food-sovereign future and a sustainable food system. In interviews with consumer cooperatives and buyers at the organic farmers' markets around the city, the need to protect and to be in solidarity with 'small farmers' (especially the women farmers) regularly came up. Consumer cooperatives, for example, said that they support 'small, women farmers', even if they were not doing organic farming, and that they were not looking for certified-organic products, as they were aware that the costs of certification could be prohibitive for small farmers. Most interestingly perhaps, when I asked about the small farmers' tendency for

---

13   5216 Büyükşehir Belediyesi Kanunu. (2004, 07 23). Ankara: Resmi Gazete.

14   And interestingly, at least in agriculture, the recent influx of immigrants from Syria, Iraq, Central Asian republics, and Afghanistan, has 'helped' tremendously in reducing agricultural labor costs.

15   Broadly defined as those who are interested in and knowledgeable about where their food comes from and the social, economic, and ecological conditions under which it is produced.

expansion due to market pressures – horizontally (by increasing production) or vertically (by adding value through processing) or both (by increasing production and switching to organic produce for export) – my interviewees either denied such a tendency or suggested that it was misguided. For the buyers, it seemed that small farming was (or should be) a lifestyle that was best when it remained 'small' and 'local'. The small farmers themselves, on the other hand, reading the signals from the market and preparing to take the opportunities on offer, were looking to aim high and expand.

At this stage, I don't think this is simply a misreading of the small farmers' position, by ethical consumers, as motors of change, or a theoretical disagreement between agents about the future of the food system – though more time in the field might change my interpretation. Rather, the consumer cooperatives, and the food movement writ large, that are demanding a more sustainable food system with a shorter (a.k.a. local) food supply chain (which they associate with small farmers and small farming), are overlooking the market dynamics the small farmers are subject to. Though the food movement is taking a critical view of the transformation of Turkey's agriculture in the post-1980 period (more on this in the next chapter), the small farmers themselves, who have been participants in and products of that transformation, seem to only want more of the same. And whether the food movement will be able to resolve or reconcile with this contradiction will perhaps determine the course of the movement as well as its success.

4   The *Codependent Provisioning* Food Regime

I want to conclude this chapter with a key observation Polanyi makes in *The Great Transformation*. He points out that neither the rise nor the continuation of what we understand to be *laissez faire* was spontaneous (2001, 145–148). States had to plan and intervene to remove social protections and to protect private enterprise (ibid, 155–156), for *laissez faire* to work as a market principle. Plus, they used 'hunger' or 'nature's penalty' to create a labor market (ibid, 172–173). To put it differently (and to go back to Meiksins Wood's argument), states used their political power to make the extraction of surplus labor possible through purely economic means. Yet, as this chapter also shows, in doing so, states also served a political purpose: They reordered the political community into *friends* and *enemies*, and they reformulated their relationship with the people. Thus, while the political sphere was undoubtedly devalued (Meiksins Wood 2016, 211) for the subject-citizens, it was expanded for the central authority. By making its protections scarce, not only could the sovereign power support and sustain the free market, but it could also compel more obedience to its authority.

Moreover, with the rise of *necropolitics* as the predominant *mentalité* of government, the political community could no longer be maintained or represented as a unified body. In this regard, however, two factors were critical: the central authority's utilization of hunger and the scarcity-generating tendencies of the economy to secure obedience from some populations (*friends*) in return for allocating resources and protections to them; and their acceptance of, and cooperation with, this separation. In other words, if the *friends* had not been such willing participants, perhaps a unified *body politic* might still have been possible. At the same time, planned scarcities do have disciplinary effects (Foucault 1995) – what Polanyi frames as the 'taming' character of "pangs of hunger, on the one hand, (and) the scarcity of food, on the other" (Polanyi 2001, 118–119) in his discussion of Townsend and Hobbes – and it would be reasonable to expect that these disciplinary effects had long ago eroded such a possibility of resistance, or even non-compliance, on the part of the *friends*. In any case, the irreparable fracturing of the political community into *friends* and *enemies* has been one of the fundamental consequences of the *codependent provisioning* food regime.

One can argue that such fragmentations and contestations over who fits into which category are inherent to every political community. Perhaps establishing boundaries between in-groups and out-groups could even be considered 'human nature' (if there is such a thing). While discussions on the subject continue among political theorists, it is important to note that when such divisions intersect with the politics of urban provisioning, the consequences can occur very gradually and can be very stealthy. After all, death and decay are not always Promethean spectacles; the withholding of protections against scarcity, malnutrition, and hunger and/or the creation of circumstances in which one cannot protect him/herself from such aspects, can also be a Kafkaesque trial. Indeed, that is the case in *codependent provisioning*: *Enemies* who are not killed are left either to starve, or to deal with scarcity and malnutrition(through the central authority-managed invisible hand of the market). A politics of death thus becomes the new right to kill, and the market, the new medium of sovereign violence.

In the next chapter, I will turn to the contemporary food system feeding Istanbul and the accompanying food regime, which I call the *urban food supply chain*. I will begin with the move from import substitution to export-oriented economic growth, with each decade from the 1980s onward roughly corresponding to a set of economic transformations: trade liberalization (1980s); the liberalization of capital markets and subsequently, the increasing preeminence of the financial sector over agriculture and industry (1990s); and globalization (2000s). The chapter will show that these processes will lead to a redefinition of economic demands on the one hand (fair wages, job security, unemployment benefits, etc.) which include and enable access to food, among others things; and on the other hand, increasing precarity, both of the market agents who supply the city, and the residents of Istanbul who need to be fed. For the political community, these changes imply not only more fragmentation, but also further institutionalization of *necroeconomics*, by way of free market-induced precarization.

Feeding Global Istanbul

> Force is the only solution open to capital; the accumulation of cap-
> ital, seen as an historical process, employs force as a permanent
> weapon, not only at its genesis, but further on down to the pres-
> ent day.
>
> ROSA LUXEMBURG[1]

∴

There seems to be a deep divide in Turkey (albeit one of many) between those
who experienced the period of import substitution – the era before the 1980
coup – and those who did not: Those who experienced the pre-1980 era roman-
ticize the long-gone solidarity, when commodities were scarce but, they claim,
community was abundant, and they would collectively overcome everything
– from political violence in the streets to impossibly long lines for cooking gas
and margarine, from frequent water and electricity cuts, to torture and death
in prisons. Comparing themselves with the post-1980 generations, they prose-
lytize that the present is the real era of scarcity, even amidst the abundance of
everyday necessities, from cooking gas to cars, luxury porcelain to instant coffee. Community, they suggest, is the missing key ingredient: In this era of globalization, when people are supposed to be more connected, everyone is just
more alone, more individualistic, and more selfish. And there is no possibility
of overcoming one's adverse circumstances collectively. Whatever people are
stuck in – poverty, unemployment, precarity – they have to deal with it alone.
It is a sink-or-swim system, and more people sink simply because they don't
have someone – a community – to look out for them.

While the conservative implications of such commentary might be
unwelcome, the observation about the relative abundance and diversity of
commodities today – food included – in comparison to the pre-1980 import
substitution era, is accurate: For those who can afford them, the liberalization of trade and globalization has enabled access to a wider range and larger

---

1   Luxemburg, Rosa. 2003. *The Accumulation of Capital*. London: Routledge, 351.

supply of goods – and climate change notwithstanding (though of course it is withstanding!), it seems like we always have everything 'in stock'. Indeed, it is in this context – and only in this context! – that my Grandma's habit of saving bread, as if the apocalypse were nigh, seems odd: Stocking up on food for emergencies would only seem weird, if you have grown up with food being available to you, on-demand, all the time.[2]

My aim in this chapter is partly to trace the last piece of the 'how we got here' puzzle. How did our *mentalité* change? How did we go from stocking up on food for emergencies – or rather, always thinking about potential and eventual food scarcity, and acting with prudence – both at the collective and at the individual level; and to arriving at the prevalent assumption of food as an ever-available commodity so long as we are willing and able to pay for it?

And unpacking that sunset clause is my other aim in this chapter: In the years following the liberalization of markets and the 1980 coup, the lines for cooking gas and margarine have largely disappeared. At the same time, poverty, unemployment, and precarity, have all grown exponentially – to such an extent that particularly among the young (ages between 15 and 24), they have become utterly unexceptional (unemployment in this age group was 21.7% in 2010[3] (Turkish Statistical Institute 2019)). Moreover, compared to the pre-1980 era, what poverty looks like has radically changed – thanks partly to the availability of commodities, and partly, to the spread of credit cards, and the technologies and infrastructures that support their expansive use. It is entirely possible, and wildly problematic, that a person might be carrying an expensive-looking smartphone or own a widescreen LCD TV but may not be (and have not been able to) afford to eat well. Plus, the disappearance of lines for cooking gas and margarine have been followed by an increase in the (sizes of) waistlines and diet-related diseases – not just in Turkey, but all around the world, and particularly among lower-income and minority populations (Albritton 2008; Jacobs and Richtel 2017a; Julier 2013; Searcey and Richtel 2017). So, again, how did we get here? Why has a nutrient-rich diet, with fresh and un- or less-processed ingredients, become both more available and yet more unaffordable for most people?

My intention here is not to offer a grand narrative, that provides a single explanation for a complex, content-dependent, yet universal shift. In the Turkish case, however, the transformations underlining these 'how' and

---

2 Especially since today, even the traditional preserved foods – pickles, pastes, jams, smoked and dried meats, cheeses, etc. – are consumed as if they are available on-demand.

3 Just as a reference, the rate had gone up from 13.1% in 2000, and it has increased again yet to 25.3% in 2019 (Turkish Statistical Institute 2019).

'why' questions, came in the wake of the liberalization of trade (particularly in commodities and capital, but not in labor), the country's move towards a more [neo-]classical free market economy, and a shift in the *mentalité* of economic development – from being spearheaded by import substitution industrialization, to focusing on export-oriented growth (the emphasis being on both sets of changes: from 'import substitution' to 'export orientation', and from 'industrialization' to 'growth'). The chapter thus untangles these footsteps, with each decade from the 1980s onward corresponding to a different set of political-economic transformations, and each set of transformations having specific implications for agriculture, urban provisioning, and food consumption. The 1980s, for example, was the era of the 24 January Decisions, which brought in trade liberalization, and the coup, which enforced them. As I discuss in the section 'The 1980s: From Import Substitution to Market Liberalization', the Decisions not only altered the structural dynamics of agriculture in the country, but in conjunction with the coup, overhauled whatever social and political power the country's peasants – big and small – had. The 1990s, in turn, entailed the liberalization of capital markets. Subsequently, the financial sector became preeminent over every other sector, including agriculture, logistics, and food – retail and wholesale. It seeped into and inadvertently connected seemingly unrelated actors and sectors, and gradually accumulated the capacity to unleash the cataclysmic volatility of global finance on the economy writ large – hence the section title, 'The 1990s: A Decade of Crises'.

The 2000s involved further integration with foreign markets, and while such increasing integration obviously has political-economic implications for urban provisioning and agriculture, I want to emphasize here the debates over globalization and Istanbul's identity that unsettled the political community. Aside from the relative abundance of analysis on the political-economic implications of the integration (Aydın 2010; Aysu 2008; Kazgan 1999; 2003; Keyder 2014; Keyder and Yenal 2014a), the identity debates revolved around food and foodways quite a bit. Not only were new meanings attributed to the production and consumption of certain foods (which then came to change the city's foodscape), but also, and I think more importantly, the movement for localism/localization (as opposed to globalization) and alternative food initiatives (as opposed to conventional provisioning chains) began to gain significant momentum at this time. I explore these initiatives and the social movements they are connected with in more detail in the next chapter; for now, in the section 'The 2000s: A World City? Globalization and Istanbul', I focus on how the penetration of the contradictions of global capitalism into local dynamics have been critical in the rise and increasing prominence of the movement toward localism/localization, alternative food initiatives (AFIS, in short), and their unruly alliance with the environmental movement in Turkey.

That is not the end of the story, however. After tracing how the contemporary provisioning apparatus works (in the eponymous section), I delve into the implications of all these economic and socio-cultural transformations, for the relationship between the central authority and the political community, in 'A Precarious Sovereignty or the Sovereignty of Precarity?'. Here, I argue that at the macro-level, these transformations (trade liberalization, financialization, globalization) established the market as the sole mechanism through which the city was provisioned and removed the central authority from its position of governance. The provisioning of the city thus came to depend exclusively on the profit motive of the provisioning agents. Meanwhile, certain economic demands of subject-citizens (fair wages, job security, unemployment benefits, etc.) were reformulated into social and civic freedoms. Concomitantly, the emphasis regarding the *mentalité* of government shifted, from the central authority guaranteeing certain rights and services, to the central authority enabling, sheltering, nurturing the market, so that the subject-citizens could access these services (and related commodities) through the market.

More problematically, and equally importantly, this thorough and hegemonic affirmation of the market unraveled the central authority's sovereign right (Foucault 2003, 241) to target anything and everyone that could potentially hinder the smooth and efficient functioning of the market: Those who cannot compete effectively, those who challenge the profit motive, those who look for alternatives to the market mechanism. Yet the volatilities of the global market, fluctuations of the currency exchange rate, and the crisis-prone political-economic structures at home, could push every member of the political community into one of these categories of new public '*enemies*' – if not today, certainly tomorrow, or the next day. Precarity thus became the defining condition for the members of the political community – as always, more so for some (urban poor, marginalized, lower-income, etc.) than for others (rich, politically well-connected, etc.).

I should note that this chapter is a little different from the preceding ones. To begin with, I have chosen to leave out a section that compares Istanbul with other cases – an aspect I address in the subsequent chapter. Second, the analysis I present in this chapter, particularly in the section 'The Contemporary Provisioning Apparatus', is on the basis of data gathered over almost a year's fieldwork in Istanbul. This involved participant observation at 17 periodic markets, 10 branches of domestic and 20 branches of multinational supermarkets all across Istanbul, and a series of semi-structured interviews (32 in total) that I conducted with almost all actors of the provisioning apparatus: Farmers who produce FFVs in on the peripheries of the city, shop owners at the wholesale ports, intermediaries who go from village to village buying produce from the farmers, bazaar vendors, street vendors, municipal police who inspect the bazaars, representatives of all multinational supermarkets, representatives of 7 domestic supermarkets (including regional and hard discount ones), representatives of bazaar and mobile vendors' associations, representatives of the federations of domestic and multinational grocery retailers' associations, municipal agents who inspect the wholesale ports, truckers who transport the foodstuffs to Istanbul, and residents of the city – or customers – who, one way or another, have to rely on this vast network of people, mechanisms, infrastructures, laws and regulations, in order to be provisioned. I rely on this data to understand how the provisioning apparatus changed in the aftermath of the Decisions and the socio-cultural and economic transformations they initiated. As such, unlike other chapters, my reliance on the literature here is limited to the analysis of the effects of the Decisions on agriculture and rural *lifeworlds*. I conclude the chapter with a reflection on the defining features of the current food regime and food systems, the transformations that have led to it, and the path that lies ahead.

1   The 1980s: From Import Substitution to Market Liberalization

To understand how and why trade was finally liberalized in the 1980s, it is necessary to first identify the series of political and economic crises that rocked Turkey throughout the 1970s. In 1971, the US had unilaterally ended the convertibility of the US Dollar to gold; the oil crisis in 1973 pushed prices up globally; and finally, the embargoes imposed due to Turkey's initiation of Operation Peace in Cyprus in 1974 put further constrictions on an already stumbling economy. With the culmination of the Bretton Woods system, international pressures had increased on Turkey to move away from import substitution and to liberalize its economy. Responding to these pressures, in the aftermath of the 1971 coup, strikes and collective bargaining had been temporarily banned, wages were frozen, and some of the International Monetary Fund's (IMF) recommendations were implemented. However, socio-political polarization was increasing as were the numbers of failed coalition governments. Elections had become frequent, and political elites were doing their best to evade, ignore, and postpone taking measures against the global crisis spilling over to the Turkish economy. And to a certain extent, they were successful: In 1975 and 1976, the Turkish economy grew at around 8% (Boratav 2007, 131) successively. Yet, by

1977, the country had fallen into one of the most serious economic crises in its history. Exports declined, imports grew by 13%, and the country's capacity to balance imports with exports eroded by 30% (ibid, 142). The foreign trade deficit surmounted 4 billion dollars (ibid); and Turkey could not find foreign debtors to finance the country with more loans, such that it was unable to pay even the interest on its debts.

Price increases and devaluations followed. Although these had the potential to erode the purchasing power of wage workers and peasants, populist politics spurred by frequent elections pushed governments to implement policies that prevented an immediate dip in real wages and incomes (Boratav 2007, 144–146). At the same time, the increasing costs of imported intermediate goods and rising costs of labor had begun to cut back on profits particularly in the manufacturing sector. In response to unions' growing gains in wages and benefits, the bourgeois effectively initiated a 'capital strike' and halted investments (Boratav 2016, 79–80). In these crisis conditions, all imports, including oil, had to be paid for in cash, at the time of purchase (Boratav 2007, 143). As a result, manufacturing slowed down; the black market became the only way to find consumer goods as the lines to get even basic household items (gas, cooking oils, etc.) became longer and longer (Pamuk 2015, 244).

As the country's dependence on imports and foreign currency grew, the political climate of frequent elections and populism prevented the implementation of austerity measures that would have eroded the artificially high value of the Turkish Lira, as well as real wages and incomes of the urban working class and peasants. By 1979, the inherent problems of the system had become too exacerbated to be ignored. Thus, backed by the domestic big bourgeois and the IMF, measures that came to be known as the '24 January Decisions' (*24 Ocak Kararları*) were imposed, as a response to the crisis, and they have significantly reshaped the country ever since. The Decisions altered the capital-labor relations in favor of the bourgeois, liberalized trade, privatized major public enterprises and opened the way for the liberalization of capital markets in the 1990s.

Overall, the Decisions initiated 8 major shifts:
1) The Turkish Lira was devalued to bring the value of the currency significantly under its market value; subsequently, the system was adjusted for a floating exchange rate.
2) All price regulations were lifted, with price determination left to the market.
3) Interest rates were raised; and then, were left to the fluctuations of the market.

4) In all areas of the economy, public subsidies were removed, as exports had been incentivized.

5) Measures to incentivize foreign direct investment were taken.

6) Measures to liberalize imports were taken.

7) Areas of economic activity into which the state intervened were limited; and through new tax regulations, attempts were made to reduce public deficits.

8) In determining wages and base prices for agricultural goods, a new index (that fell under the inflation rate) was accepted. (Tekeli 1984, 13; author's translation)

Among these eight, only the last one explicitly deals with the pricing of agricultural goods, though each shift had major effects on the country's agriculture, farming populations, and the provisioning apparatus – which, in turn, shaped the food regime. For example, due to the elimination of price regulations and subsidies for agricultural inputs, not only did the costs of production increase, but more importantly, the prices of value-added agricultural commodities increased more than their costs of production (Boratav 2007, 169; 2016, 53–60; Kazgan 2013, 236–238). In other words, profit margins for farmers declined, even though consumers had to pay more for the same goods (Boratav 2016, 53–60; Kazgan 2013, 236–238). Increasingly, substantial profits were appropriated by third parties – intermediaries who bought from the farmers and sold to the retailers and the wholesalers. In the 1990s, however, these intermediaries themselves were eaten up by the expanding retailers and wholesalers, who eventually went on to dominate the entire urban provisioning apparatus (Boratav 2016, 171).

Similarly, the privatization of public enterprises left both urban residents (consumers) and rural producers (farmers) relatively powerless against price fluctuations and the increasing profit margins of the intermediaries. Prior to the Decisions, 3 different types of actors usually functioned as intermediaries: private companies, public enterprises, and the farmers' cooperatives. Among these, the public enterprises were the strongest as they had the most resources. Typically, they would buy from the farmers at higher-than-global prices and sell relatively cheaper, to support various other agricultural[4] and manufacturing[5] industries as well as urban consumers (Pamuk 2012, 267; Kazgan 2013, 236–238). Once the public enterprises completed their allotted

---

4   FFV juices, canned goods, processed foods, for example.

5   Textiles, for example.

bulk purchases, prices would fall to global levels, enabling private companies to take advantage of lower prices and to increase their profit margins. The Decisions unraveled this regulation mechanism and removed the purchasing guarantees[6]. Farmers were thus left to deal with global price fluctuations on their own, which put them put at a significant disadvantage in comparison to their well-subsidized global competitors.[7] They quickly became unable to manage their costs (Aydın 2010; Gönenç and Rehber 2007; Öztürk 2012) and began abandoning farming and the countryside, triggering a new wave of rural-to-urban migrations.

Yet, moving to the city no longer guaranteed jobs or prosperity either. The urban economy was undergoing its own set of transformations, and the opportunities the city offered to these new migrants were significantly limited in comparison to what their predecessors were able to get in the 1950s, 60s, and 70s. Thus, stuck between the urban and rural economies, the migrants of the 1980s had to use (their access to) both to their advantage, to survive in a very volatile economy: They regularly went back to wherever they were coming from (nostalgically referred to as *memleket* in Turkish) to lend a helping hand during the harvest and plantation seasons (Keyder 2014; Keyder and Yenal 2014c; 2014d; Pamuk 2012, 233); they established businesses that connected the city and the village in new ways (tourism, restaurants, food shops, etc.) and they financially supported the 'home land' whenever necessary. Concomitantly, every time the urban economy went through bottlenecks and/or crises, the countryside acted as a shock-absorber, offering temporary relief to the newly proletarianized populations, until the urban economy picked up again. In the late 1990s, this dynamic became much stronger, and mid-size towns – which enabled households to participate in both urban and rural economies – became the new destination for migrants leaving the countryside.

Finally, the Decisions altered production patterns, by incentivizing foreign direct investment and production for export. Agricultural producers targeting foreign markets (as opposed to domestic ones) began to be differentiable,

---

6 Earlier, farmers' cooperatives and the Ziraat Bankası (Bank of Agriculture) provided its members with cheap credits and insurance (Aydın 2010; Kazgan 1999; İlbaş 1999; Kazgan 2003). After the Decisions, these relatively independent cooperatives were first brought under government control, and then, after various international treaties ushered in the country's integration into the global market in the 1990s, they were effectively disbanded.

7 For more on this, see Aydin (2010); Aysu (2008); Boratav (2016, 53–60); Kazgan (1999; 2003; 2013); Keyder (2014); Keyder and Yenal (2014c; 2014d; 2014a); Pamuk (2012, 267; 2015, 271–272); Öztürk (2012).

based on the size of their operations (small and mid-size farmers produced for the domestic market, whereas large ones turned to export) as well as the quality of their produce. As production increased and domestic consumption decreased (due to the curbing of middle and working class incomes (Boratav 2007, 161–162; Kazgan 2002, 134)), the country also managed to substantially increase its export of basic agricultural goods. Industrialization also began to focus on low-technology, labor-intensive, low value-added goods and basic consumer products (Boratav 2016, 48) – which in the short term, maintained the industrial labor demand and sustained the urban pull.

The effects of the Decisions were not as immediate for the provisioning apparatus as they were for the country's agricultural sector. In fact, as it became clearer in the 1990s, the effects were different for the provisioning apparatus than they were for agriculture. Yet in the 1980s, in the discussions on the Decisions, agriculture and farming served as reference points that signaled, depending on where one stood, either exactly what was wrong with import substitution or what could go wrong with the Decisions. For example, for those propagating the Decisions, low capital accumulation and low productivity in agriculture showed exactly why import substitution could not work: The public was directly and indirectly subsidizing the farmers – which was subverting the market's signals to farmers to produce more and to produce more efficiently. Surely, infrastructural problems, price increases for gas and other imported agricultural inputs, and rising transportation costs, were contributing to low efficiency and low production; however, the primary obstacle to more efficient and better globally-integrated agriculture was public intervention through subsidies, price guarantees, bulk purchases, and public enterprises. Moreover, these interventions were not products of sound economic judgement; rather, they were 'populist' implements. As such, they not only countered market logic, causing inefficiency, scarcity (by way of low output), and low quality, but also, they were inherently wasteful (since they prevented a fuller utilization of the rural potential) and crisis-inducing (since they were contributing to the public debt). Counterarguments emphasized the limited options for rural communities and pointed out that if the Decisions were implemented, agriculture would collapse and destroy farming communities. Peasantry, the critics claimed, would simply disappear. The 'populist' concerns, although problematic, were one of the ways in which farming communities could benefit from the redistribution of wealth collectively generated, influence macro-level politics, and compensate for the significant deficiencies of public services in the countryside (education, health, infrastructure, etc.). Even if public interventions had not yielded efficient results economically, they had, critics argued, at the very least, moderately equalizing effects among the people, thus generating and reinforcing a sense of unified political community for the (subject-) citizens in the country and in the city alike.[8]

The Decisions, though effective on their own, were complemented by decrees (such as the 'interest decree' of 1 July 1980), bylaws (such as the unpegging of the Turkish Lira on 1 May 1981) and most importantly, by the military coup of 12 September 1980 (Tekeli 1984; Kazgan 2002; Ekzen 1984). Undeniably, the implementation of the Decisions would not have been possible if the military had not initiated the coup, banned strikes and union activity comprehensively, tried, imprisoned and killed students and union activists, removed the option of collective bargaining, and appointed the High Board of Arbitration to set wages (Boratav 2007, 152–153; Pamuk 2015, 266). The urban working classes and peasants saw a significant decline in their incomes and purchasing power in the 3 years following the coup, as devaluations and high interest rates rocked the country (Boratav 2007, 153; Kazgan 2002). Indeed, by 1989, when (following a strike) the government was finally coaxed to soften its adherence

---

8 In the backdrop of these conversations, the brutality of the 1980 coup erased most of the resistance and contestation to the Decisions, and although the military junta lasted for about 3 years (1980–1983), the center-right government that initiated the Decisions remained in power until 1991. The significance of Turgut Özal during this era cannot be overemphasized (Boratav 2016, 81–82; Pamuk 2015, 272–273). Following his role as undersecretary to the prime minister in the Demirel government, Özal was appointed by the generals as the deputy prime minister, tasked specifically with organizing economic affairs. Later, Özal became the prime minister as the head of his center-right Motherland Party (*Anavatan Partisi*), when the Party came to power after the military junta in 1983. In his various capacities, Özal was careful to personally direct liberalization policies, which led to a haphazard transition out of the import substitution experience, and opened up the political and economic sphere for corruption, Mafioso backdoor deals between government representatives, state officials, and 'entrepreneurs', and get-rich-quick type of schemes (Kazgan 2002; 2013; Tekeli 1984). According to Kazgan:

> Policies aiming to gradually liberalize the economy were implemented not consistently, but by trial and error. Sometimes a final stage policy suddenly got on the agenda (as in the unpegging of interest rates between July 1980 and July 1983); if it worked, it was let be; if it didn't, it was repealed, and the regulations were reinstituted. Sometimes (as in imports), regulations were slowly minimized. At other times, when most of the regulations were in place, specific regulations for a specific item were removed (for example, the liberalization of foreign currency deposit accounts in 1985, while audits continued in the foreign currency markets). In other words, the liberalization process was executed haphazardly, with an outlook of 'maybe it will work'. It was as if someone, when getting up in the morning, would decide on a policy while putting on his/her slippers, execute it during the day, and if they didn't like the way it was unfolding, repeal it by night, as s/he was putting on his/her pajamas (2002, 128; author's translation).

to the Decisions, the signs of de-agrarianization[9] (Keyder and Yenal 2014a) were already visible. Although relatively slow at first, the process gradually picked up, as more and more farmers quit agriculture throughout the 1990s and 2000s. Meanwhile, Turkey – let alone Istanbul – was fast becoming unable to feed itself.

But what if the farmers do quit? Trade liberalization in the 1980s (followed by international trade agreements in the 1990s) had expanded imports, particularly of food. Now, once again, the world could – and was going to – feed Istanbul. In about 100 years, the city had come full circle.

2   The 1990s: A Decade of Crises

The long 1990s started with widely supported strikes in 1988–1989, that forced the central authority to intervene and to raise real wages and base prices for agricultural commodities. These strikes were important in that they signaled a possibility of a return to the populism of earlier decades. However, impeded as the implementation of the Decisions were, the 'structural adjustments'[10] continued. In fact, two important processes shaped the decade: Internationalization, and financialization. Following the liberalization of trade, capital markets were also liberalized, which led to money (capital, more specifically) to be more easily moved, not just between borders and bank accounts, but between different sectors. As a result, the domestic economy became much more concentrated, so to say, with more and more sectors becoming tied up with each other and with the financial sector. Meanwhile, integration with the global market increased. The flow of commodities (information and technology included) between borders and regions became faster and smoother, and prices came to

---

9   Bryceson defines de-agrarianization as "a long-term process of occupational adjustment, income-earning reorientation, social identification and spatial relocation of rural dwellers away from strictly agricultural-based modes of livelihood" (Bryceson 2002, 726).

10   With structural adjustments, I mean the implementation of policies that would *ideally* enable

> the removal of price intervention [which] would create efficiency in the allocation of resources and trade liberalization would lead to increases in foreign trade – and therefore in production – on the basis of comparative advantages. Direct and indirect foreign investments would enable both a productive capacity increase and support current deficit financing. Also, via the privatization of public enterprises, services would be provided more effectively and efficiently (and importantly, they would not be a burden to the budget). The combined effects of the new measures (...) would benefit all sections of society (...) (Öztürk 2012, 166).

be determined globally. As a result, it became almost impossible to contain crises to regions, markets, or sectors. The spillover effects of an economic crisis in a specific sector in one country moved like wildfire to different countries, triggering cascading effects in other sectors and markets. Thus, domestically, long-established agrarian structures, and rural and urban networks, came undone; wages and purchasing power suffered. Frequent economic crises and political instability shaped the decade all around the world. In Turkey too, the end of the long 1990s was unsurprisingly marked by the 2001–2002 economic crisis.

Throughout the 1990s, politically established checks and balances on the economy were removed, in tandem with increasing privatization, internationalization, and financialization, in all sectors, including agriculture and urban provisioning. In a matter of a decade, capital markets were liberalized, free-floating interest rates were endorsed, foreign exchange deposit accounts were legalized, stock markets were established, and public guarantees for private debts were set (Kazgan 2006).[11] While these shifts led to some amount of liquidity for lenders, they also began to tie various economic agents together. For example, after the unpegging of the Turkish Lira and promises of public guarantees, Turkish public and private banks could borrow more freely, both domestically and internationally. Yet, many of these private banks were a part of large conglomerates that had investments in other sectors; and due to trade liberalizations, they had begun to show losses, even going bankrupt in some cases (Kazgan 2006; 2013). To offset their losses, conglomerates began to borrow heavily from their own banks; and when they could not pay back, they asked the public banks to save them[12] (Kazgan 2013), leading to the failure of the public banks.

The banking sector thus crashed multiple times, costing millions to the national budget (Kazgan 2006; 2013). Plus, from dairy processing facilities to orange orchards, public banks ended up with a bunch of investments, that they did not possess the know-how to manage (Kazgan 2013). While these collaterals were transferred to various public enterprises to make up for some of the public banks' losses, they also caused the expansion of public enterprises, by way of having to incorporate operations and/or facilities that had – one way or another – gone bankrupt (ibid.). As a result, right before their privatization,

---

11   For more on capital market liberalization and the economic, legal, and political problems it has triggered, see Kazgan (2002; 2013; 2006).

12   Of course, this also worked as an efficient scheme for those who wanted to siphon off public funds; and as the economic history literature clearly demonstrates, such schemes were more the rule than the exception (Kazgan 2006; 2013; Boratav 2016; 2007; Oral 2015; Pamuk, 2012; 2015).

for example, certain public enterprises[13] began to show losses, operational difficulties, higher than before costs, etc. – which conveniently decreased their prices while strengthening the arguments for their privatization.

Another way in which privatization, internationalization, and financialization worked in tandem became evident at times of crisis. Multiple crashes of the banking sector on the one hand, bankruptcies in the private sector (due to dumping of cheaper goods by multinationals, following trade liberalization) on the other, had made the economy very fragile. When a large-enough economic agent began to go under, there was a domino effect, causing multifarious failures and even wholescale economic crises. At these times, foreign capital, drawn to Turkey due to high interest rates, would also threaten to leave, inadvertently coercing the public to raise interest rates and offer more bailout guarantees to the lenders. However, this would cost the budget billions and exacerbate the deficit. To offset it, the central authority would borrow from international monetary organizations – the IMF and the World Bank (WB) – which, of course, came with certain conditions: More cuts in public spending, more comprehensive privatization of public assets, more liberalization of commodities and capital markets (Kazgan 2006; 2013; Boratav 2016; 2007). As a result, not only were the crisis-inducing tendencies of privatization, internationalization, and financialization exacerbated (Aydın 2010; Öztürk 2012;

---

13   Most of these public enterprises served as public intervention mechanisms, as also as intermediaries and as processors. For example, they produced, sold, and distributed various agricultural inputs; they instituted base prices and made bulk purchases; they worked as processing plants for certain agricultural commodities and acted as suppliers for other institutions that would buy the processed commodities in bulk. More critically, especially in certain sectors like infrastructure and energy, public enterprises constituted 'natural monopolies'; that is, they required high startup capital, but costs of production decreased over time (Kazgan 2013, 240). Thus, privatizing these public enterprises not only did not make economic sense, but also, in some cases, constituted a national security risk for the country (ibid, 242). With a return to populist politics, and mass resistance to privatization and implementation of the Decisions, on the one hand, and evident imprudence and lack of economic logic, on the other, how did the privatization of public enterprises become possible? Boratav points to a convincing yet troubling answer: Wage and price increases between 1989 and 1993 had increased costs of operation (Boratav 2007, 178). Yet, adhering to the Decisions, supports for public enterprises were either removed completely or significantly reduced. Thus, public enterprises began to declare losses and to look for private loans domestically, and with the liberalization of capital markets, internationally. Soon after, however, they became unable to pay back their debts. In these cases, bankruptcy provided a sufficient reason for privatization. In other cases, where the revenue generated was barely paying the interest of debts, they could not invest more and expand their operation, nor improve their technological capacity, nor diversify. As such, once imports began to flood the domestic market, they were quickly outcompeted.

Keyder and Yenal 2014a), but dependency on foreign capital grew. Constantly spiraling thus, the 2001–2002 crash was anything but unexpected for the political community and the central authority alike.

Finally, in the 1990s, Turkey became a party to several international treaties, which generated new venues for privatization, internationalization, and financialization. The most important of these was the GATT in 1994, which concluded the Uruguay Round, and the Customs Union agreement with the European Union in 1995. While both initiated new liberalization policies, the former came with strong punitive measures if not abided by and the latter implied tacit consent to customs policies that Turkey did not participate directly in developing, either in the drawing up of plans or in the negotiating process. Moreover, the intellectual property rights the GATT put forth enabled international and/or multinational companies to have, in effect, a monopoly in their sectors of operation (Kazgan 2006, 154; Keyder and Yenal 2014a, 59; Yenal 2014) by preventing domestic competitors from transferring technology and/or interim products that may be used to produce final products.

It is noteworthy that these trade treaties were coming in the footsteps of the privatization efforts of the previous decade. In the 1980s, multinationals had already entered the Turkish markets and outcompeted many of the domestic companies. For the few remaining, that had managed to withstand international competition, mergers and acquisitions seemed a good option. Public enterprises were among these lucky few. Given that they were effectively monopolies with extensive distribution networks, they already seemed like appealing investments for multinationals looking to expand into the Turkish markets (Kazgan 2013; Gönenç and Rehber 2007; Yenal 2014, 108). Plus, they had become significantly cheaper for buy-ins, as they were declaring losses or bankruptcy. Indeed, many were bought by international and/or multinational corporations (Kazgan 2013)[14]. Using both the intellectual property laws, punitive measures, and privatization, thus, multinational corporations essentially eliminated the remaining domestic competition (Kazgan 2013; 2006; Oral 2015; Öztürk 2012, 90) and initiated a wave of de-industrialization, the effects of which are felt even today.

For Istanbul's provisioning, all these changes signaled a chronic precarity. The privatization of the public enterprises shocked both the producers and the consumers, who now had to rely exclusively on the market. However, the

---

14   And as the economic history literature indicates, these public enterprises never went back into production. Facilities were not upgraded nor put back into operation (as the propagators of privatization claimed they would). Instead, facilities were dismantled, and production was outsourced (Kazgan 2013; 2006; Oral 2015; Gönenç and Rehber 2007).

global market with which Turkey was now well-integrated, was unstable and
prone to crises. Worse, domestic production was no longer sufficient to feed
the country nor to offset the negative effects of crises. In fact, in a crisis situation, it made more sense for producers to direct their production to exports.
Even if food prices would rise as the value of Turkish Lira fell, the cheapening
Lira would generate a finer competitive edge for exporters. Thus, rather than
redirect their production to the domestic market, they would use the currency
crisis to their advantage and increase exports.

The picture did not look good for consumers either. Frequent crises were
constantly eroding the middle class and swelling the numbers of the urban
and rural poor. Meanwhile, real wages and base prices for agricultural goods
did not increase until 1989. Multiple devaluations and terrible inflation – at
times going up to triple digits – wreaked havoc on middle and working class
incomes. Even after the gradual return to populism in the 1990s, conditions did
not improve. While layoffs followed wage increases, informal employment[15]
rose drastically (Boratav 2007, 177). In the countryside, high inflation and
devaluations led to significant income inequality (Kazgan 2003): small farmers, in particular, were unable to absorb the increases in their costs, due to high
inflation. Thus, they either quit farming altogether, or turned to subsistence
farming, while family members looked for income through different means,
usually somehow tied to the urban economy. Mid-size farmers, on the other
hand, had to take significant cuts in their profit margins and gradually shifted –
some tried to adapt by diversifying their produce (Keyder and Yenal 2014a),
some shifted their focus almost entirely from fruits and vegetables to grains
(which require less investment and maintenance), others borrowed heavily
from local moneylenders to expand their production. Unfortunately, many
of these borrowers could not maintain their farms nor pay back their loans
and lost their land. Others had to switched to contract farming[16]. Finally, even

---

15   As Kazgan points out, most of this informal employment was in the export-oriented man-
      ufacturing sector (Kazgan 2006, 160–161). Moreover, the flexibility of these sectors, par-
      ticularly the 'disposability' of the informally employed workers, leaves them incredibly
      susceptible to global macroeconomic fluctuations. Even the hint of a crisis may lead to
      mass layoffs. While present in older economic centers like Istanbul, these export-oriented
      manufacturers are even more common in parts (of the country) that picked up after the
      1980s, with the integration into the global economy. Known as "the Anatolian tigers", their
      success has been noticeable but limited (For more on these, please see Pamuk 2012, 307–
      310; 2015, 273–282).

16   Contract farming involves farmers making a deal with intermediaries (either traders,
      shop owners at the wholesale ports and/or the supermarkets), usually before the planting
      season, for a certain quantity and quality of produce, in return for price and purchase
      guarantees after the harvest. For the farmers, contract farming enables an easy cash flow

in households profiting from agriculture, some members of the family had to look for non-agricultural work to increase their household income (Keyder and Yenal 2014a, 93; 2014c; 2014d).[17] Gradually, more and more farmers left farming and migrated out of the countryside.

The 1990s was also the last decade of rural-to-urban migrations. As I have discussed in previous chapters, the rural push – urban pull has been a consistent political-economic dynamic throughout the import substitution period, and Istanbul has been one of the urban centers that received the majority of these migrants. Following fundamental changes that the Decisions triggered in agrarian structures, these migrations briefly intensified, but then slowed down. This was primarily because by the end of the 1990s, it had become clear that migration to the city no longer increased the chance of employment nor did it necessarily bring in higher income (Keyder and Yenal 2014d; 2014c). More crucially, living conditions in the countryside began to improve (Keyder and Yenal 2014c, 179): Notwithstanding the cuts in public spending, public-private partnerships had invested in the electricity, telecommunication, and transportation infrastructures and services.[18] Private sector investments into education and health facilities also made these services somewhat accessible to the rural populations – of course, only to those who could afford them. In other words, by the end of the decade, both the rural push and the urban pull were weakening, even though neither de-agrarianization nor Istanbul's expansion had halted. Istanbul continued to grow, farming communities continued to dwindle, and Istanbul became even more dependent on imports to feed itself, as the remaining farmers increasingly turned toward production for export.

Finally, privatization-internationalization-financialization has qualitatively and quantitatively altered the (nature, role, composition of) intermediaries. Intermediaries are those who buy from the farmers and sell to the final

---

and provides them a degree of certainty for recovering their costs, in case global prices fall. For the intermediaries, it guarantees a smooth flow of commodities, better transportation, and sales planning, so as to mitigate their costs. For more on how contract farming became a part of Turkish agriculture post-Decisions, see Keyder and Yenal 2014c; 2014a; 2014b.

17   While this change in the demographics is significant in and of itself, it is not unique to Turkey. We see similar trends all across the Global South, following the structural adjustments in the 1980s and 1990s. What was unique to Turkey, however, was the shock-absorber capacity of agriculture, which also diminished, in parallel to the gradual decrease in the numbers of small and mid-size farmers and farming communities (Keyder and Yenal 2014d). As such, whenever a crisis hit, both the urban and rural population alike felt its life-threatening effects.

18   Most of these public investments were later privatized – either in whole, or in parts.

consumers. As such, they can be retailers, like the grocery chain Migros, and/ or wholesalers, like the global grocery giant Metro Cash & Carry, or any of the trading companies that operate in Istanbul's wholesale ports. During the import substitution era, public enterprises were the primary intermediaries for certain food items – meat, dairy, fish, and sugar, for example. Following the privatization of these, various multinational retail and wholesale companies began to enter the grocery retail and wholesale sector in Turkey as the new intermediaries.

Multiple factors played a role in the transformation of the intermediaries: Most centrally, the liberalization of capital markets had made it easier to invest. International investors could come in relatively easily, without having to jump through a lot of legal hoops. High interest rates made investing in Turkey appealing, while public guarantees against bank failures instilled trust. For those who wanted to the invest in specific sectors, however, partnerships with the local big bourgeois were preferable (Yenal 2014). Promising high returns, the grocery sector seemed like a profitable sector for early global investors. Plus, the dismantling of price control mechanisms had increased profit margins. Without the public enterprises to set prices through bulk purchases, profit margins for farmers had reduced rapidly, while consumers had gotten used to high prices due to inflation and price hikes.[19] As such, regardless of improvements in agricultural production or increases in efficiency, intermediaries could maintain their expanding profit margins.

In addition, transportation costs were declining. Throughout the 1980s and the 1990s, public investments into the transportation and the telecommunication infrastructures had resulted in significant improvements in both sectors.

---

19   This was true for some foods more than others. As Kazgan points out, prices for those goods that the public enterprises purchased in bulk (cereals, pulses, sugar, tobacco, hazelnut, for example) increased more rapidly than vegetables and fruits, for which there had been no public enterprises to set prices during the import substitution era (Kazgan 2003, 381–385). Thus, prices for vegetables and fruits usually followed global price trends – although various mechanisms (especially in-city production) helped mediate high prices. Plus, farmers could still rely on state-subsidized fertilizers and fixed prices for the diesel for their tractors. In the 1990s, bananas were an exception to major price hikes. In Turkey, the local variety was produced in the coastal Mediterranean region, especially around the Anamur area. In the 1990s, after pressure from the United Fruit Company (present-day Chiquita Brands International), Turkey 'had to' open up for banana imports (Kazgan 2002, 144). United Fruits' initial strategy involved dumping: That is, import a lot of bananas to Turkey, lower the prices to an unsustainable low, and decimate local production (ibid.). Unfortunately, United Fruit succeeded, and the local variety was almost completely eradicated. But even then, Turkey did not – or could not – institute proper anti-dumping legislation. That would have to wait until after the Customs Union agreement.

Not only were the rural peripheries and the urban centers better connected to each other, transporting goods between them had become easier, faster, and cheaper. The only missing element, so to say, was refrigeration – particularly, refrigerated trucks and storage facilities were lacking. During the import substitution era, those public enterprises that had such storage facilities, would rent some of their extra capacity to private intermediaries. After they were privatized, however, this practice was abolished, thus pushing intermediaries effectively into a bottleneck: On the one hand, there were the small to mid-size intermediaries, who continued to transport grocery items through 'traditional', flatbed (open carrier) trucks. This was at a comparatively lower cost, but it was also an unsanitary and a relatively unsafe method of transportation. The quality of the produce declined rapidly and visibly during transportation. Plus, not everything could be transported thus – which, in turn, limited the items these capital-scarce intermediaries could carry. Still, their low costs kept them competitive. On the other hand, there were the large intermediaries that came about through the domestic-foreign partnerships, and slightly smaller, domestic entrepreneurs who utilized their local networks and raised enough capital to invest in refrigerated trucks and storage facilities. Fewer in number, regionally concentrated, and fiercely competitive, these intermediaries usually supplied specific supermarkets. In fact, often specific supermarkets expanded into logistics, establishing their own cold chains and distribution networks, setting up shops in Istanbul's wholesale ports, and signing contracts with big farmers for exclusive production.[20].

For the residents of the city, these qualitative and quantitative changes in the intermediaries implied a diversification of food exchange sites. In addition to the neighborhood periodic markets (bazaars) and the few and far in-between public-private ventures of the import substitution era (like Migros), a number of different sites began to open, where Istanbulites could now purchase FFVs as well as other food items. Metro Cash & Carry, the global wholesale giant, is one such example. Even Migros, after complete privatization, began to diversify its operation through both mergers and acquisitions and operational expansion: They bought some of their competitors, but also opened up more specialized shops, targeting neighborhood-specific demographics. On the flip side, this diversification and relative abundancy of sites did not necessarily indicate an easier access to fresh fruits and vegetables for the residents of the

---

20   Today, these domestic and joint-capital supermarkets comprise about 35–40% of the country's retail sector; and they expect a market growth of 20% over the next few years, thus aiming for a 60% market share by 2020 (interview with Migros 2015; interview with TPF Istanbul 2015).

city. In fact, the almost-complete eradication of in-city and hinterland FFV production, in addition to the decoupling of producers and sellers, had radically
increased Istanbul's provisioning precarity. Not only was the city fed globally,
but the provisioning actors themselves had become global players, thanks to
the internationalization and financialization that shaped the 1990s.

3   The 2000s: A World City? Globalization and Istanbul

Other than juridical and economic transformations, the Decisions also initiated a discursive shift, that redefined many of the economic demands the
urban working classes and farming communities had been voicing over the
decades. These demands included the right to food and the right to subsistence,
though they did venture beyond those to include the right to free education, to
express one's religious conviction (always a contested issue under secularism),
to free speech, to protest and to assemble, to education in one's native tongue
as well as to free healthcare, a reliable pension, and a secure job that would
pay enough to live – in short, civic, as well as economic and social demands.
The 1980 coup that reinforced the Decisions had muzzled these demands –
not just by outright banning them, but also by physically removing anyone
and/or group who had voiced them. Thus, throughout the 1980s (even after
the move back to electoral politics in 1983), these demands remained muffled.
When the muzzle was finally somewhat lifted in the late 1980s, strikes followed
(Boratav 2007, 177), showing that, despite the literal blood loss, demands for
these rights remained strong. At the same time, in the context of the coup and
the structural adjustments, a more robust return to radical left politics seemed
difficult at best and life-threatening at worst. Plus, "[the] distribution policies
[following the Decisions] had been dominated by a strategy that followed a
stringent and hardline approach against class-based economic demands, that
is, union-organizing, wage struggle, peasants' support demands" (ibid, 155). In
other words, it had become necessary to rearticulate these demands and to
provide a new vocabulary – if not a new set of associations and imageries – for
the urban working classes and the farming communities to identify with.

The governing party at the time[21] was able to do precisely that. Rather than
responding to the class-based demands of the urban working classes, it managed to rebrand not only the demands, but also the populations who made
those demand. Thus, for example, instead of urban working classes, they

---

21   *Anavatan Partisi* (Motherland Party).

became 'poor', 'urbane', 'consumers', stuck in informally-built makeshift apartments in the city's shantytowns (Boratav 2007, 155). Peasants, on the other hand, were completely shut out of the discussions – unless, of course, they were large landowners and/or export-oriented producers. Squeezed between falling rates of profit, global competitors, and rising land prices (particularly if they were situated on the peripheries of metropolitan centers, like Istanbul), farming communities thus lost their voice and ability to shape policy decisions. In the long run, with the introduction of global food movements like Slow Food and the rise in demand for organic and sustainably-produced alternatives, farming communities became more vocal once again. However, at the time of writing, small farmers still do not command much political respect, nor do they have a significant political support base. Urban working classes, in contrast, remain torn between political actors on the left, who continue to articulate most of the class-based economic and social demands through the language of rights (as I have mentioned above), and those on the right, who have increasingly coopted the language of oppression and poverty, without any references to class. Indeed, among this now-rebranded population of urban working classes in Istanbul, ethnic and regional references play a much stronger role for ideational association than class.

Further, following the 2001–2002 economic crisis, globalization initiated another discursive shift in the ways in which class-based economic demands were articulated. Roughly defined as the "intensification of global networks [that] penetrate and restructure the [domestic] economy, introducing new types of employment and levels of income commensurate with the wealthier areas of the world, resulting in new levels of differentiation between those who become part of the networks and those who are left out" (Keyder 2005, 124), globalization was highly effective in restructuring both production and consumption patterns all around the world, including in Istanbul. Not only were the same, similar, or equivalent commodities being produced in different parts of the world (or sometimes, different parts of the same commodity being produced in different countries, only to be assembled as the final product in yet another), but also, consumption trends, fashions, habits, and practices were now crossing borders, seeping into localities and generating new demands for previously unarticulated needs.

For Istanbul in particular, globalization brought in both an expansion of the cityscape (vertically and horizontally) and an increase in urban density. Although more traditional rural-to-urban migrations had slowed down by the end of 1990s, two new movements continued to feed the city's expansion. One was internal displacement, which was one of the results of the violent ethnic conflict engulfing primarily the eastern and southeastern regions of the country, and the other was international immigration, that brought in white-collar working classes and the global managerial class, respectively, to Istanbul. While the former swelled the numbers of Istanbul's shantytowns, the latter concentrated in the city's prosperous neighborhoods. Both, however, added to an ongoing housing crisis and created a new spurt of demand for housing (Keyder 1999b). Unable to appropriately accommodate as quickly, the numbers of semi-legal and illegal houses in the city continued to grow consistently. According to official statistics, the numbers of semi-formal/informal houses (*gecekondu*) increased from 8,239 in 1950 to roughly 61,400 in 1959 and 120,000 in 1963 (Ekinci 2010a, 413–414). A more significant jump came later, though: Whereas in the 1960s, only about 35% of Istanbul's population – or 1 in 3 – lived in a *gecekondu*, by the 2000s, this had climbed up to 65% (ibid.). In other words, by the 2000s, at least 6 out of 10 Istanbulites lived in a semi-formal or informal building.

Moreover, in many of the older neighborhoods, traditional-style houses (at most 3-storied), catered towards either a few tenants or one large family, had begun to be replaced by multistoried apartment blocks that could house more families (Keyder 1999b; 1999a). This meant a sudden increase in urban density in many parts of the city, and more importantly, a much heavier load on the city's infrastructure and public services. Indeed, Istanbul of the 1990s and 2000s was plagued by traffic congestions, electricity and water shortages, explosions at garbage disposal sites,[22] air pollution, and overcrowded public schools and hospitals. Finally, in many cases, these new and taller apartment blocks along the Bosporus were in clear violation of the *Boğaziçi Yasası* (Bosporus Code), which declared the Bosporus and the historic neighborhoods along the Bosporus as a protected zone, requiring special permits for construction (Ekinci 1993). Yet, more significant than the corruption scandals that were unearthed in the context of violation of this law, was the ways in which these buildings altered the defining architectural characteristics of the city's historic neighborhoods, and destroyed the historic in-city locations of agricultural production (*bostans*).

The increasing urban density and the expansion of the city also worked in tandem. The spread of semi-legal and illegal housing triggered by the housing crisis was not limited to poor and/or working class neighborhoods. The neighborhoods of the upper and middle classes were similarly impacted by the *gecekondus*. In the posh neighborhoods of Nişantaşı, Levent, Ulus, and Etiler – on the European side; and Kalamış, Moda, Suadiye, and Fenerbahçe – on the

---

22   For more on Istanbul's garbage disposal and sanitation problems, see Budak (1993).

Asian side, *gecekondu*s sometimes came up right alongside expensive apartment blocks or single-family houses (Ekinci 2010b; Tanyeli 2010). Following the gradual return to populism in the late 1980s, most of these *gecekondu*s received legal permits and could convert from an informal housing unit to a formal apartment block (Ekinci 2010b; Tanyeli 2010), thus giving rise to a class of people who became rich overnight through real estate. While this created an incentive for more *gecekondu*s in well-chosen spots in prosperous neighborhoods, it also caused many of the upper and upper middle class residents of the city to move to the newly built suburbs (Ekinci 2010b; Tanyeli 2010)[23]. This new suburban expansion, in turn, was particularly brutal for the northeastern (Asian side) and northwestern (European side) region of the city, both originally covered in woods extending into the Northern Anatolian conifer forests (Çubuk 1993; Çakır et al. 2008). In the southeastern and southwestern directions, in turn, the city took over what used to be the peripheral farmlands – which constituted the final blow to food production in and around the city.

The construction of new transportation infrastructures also contributed to the city's expansion and the intensification of urban density. The coastal roads along the Bosporus finally connected (what used to be) self-contained fishing villages to one another and unified them with the larger city (İstanbul 1993c; Çubuk 1993). As such, in the decades after 1980, these villages became neighborhoods of the city proper for the first time in their history (Kuban 1994). At the same time, coastal roads triggered an expansion of these villages and led them to somewhat merge into one another. Consequently, settlements along the Bosporus became almost continuous. Moreover, the completion of the Hacı Osman-Maslak-Taksim axis of the subway line on the European side, the opening of the Kartal-Kadıköy subway line on the Asian side, and the expansion of both into their respective hinterlands, as well as their connection with each other through the underwater Marmaray line, eased transportation between different sides of the city and significantly decreased travel times. Yet, so far as these public investments provided some relief from problems caused by high urban density, they did not offer solutions to overcrowding, pollution, and traffic congestions (İstanbul 1993c). In fact, capitalizing on the convenience this new transportation network offered, settlements along the major axes intensified (such as the bridges over the Bosporus and their connecting roads, for example, and the Hacı Osman-Maslak-Taksim and Kartal-Kadıköy lines). In this respect, the urban planning authorities were also influential, since they

---

23   See, for example Keyder (2005; 1999a; 2010; 1999b; 1999c); Keyder and Öncü (1994; 1993); Öncü (1999; 1997; 1993); Robins and Aksoy (1995).

designated several neighborhoods along these axes as central business districts (such as Maslak) and encouraged the horizontal and vertical expansion of the city in these directions (Eruzun 1993).

Another factor that contributed to Istanbul's expansion and the intensification of its urban density in the 1990s and the 2000s was the stark increase in the numbers of skyscrapers and malls across the city. While tall buildings and 'towers' were not necessarily alien to Istanbul,[24] the skyscrapers and malls of the post-1980s were different – and differently purposed – from what the city was used to. If anything, they were symbols of globalization and the diverse, multicolored, consumption-oriented lifestyle globalization represented (Ekinci 2010b, 428). In this imaginary, Istanbul would become an international financial hub, acting as a regional center for the movement of global capital. Thus, it was necessary, argued the proponents of globalization, for Istanbul to gain a new identity as a 'world city'; and skyscrapers were going to be its architectural representation. Plus, this new vision was already a part of Turkey's new political-economic order: Indeed, 2 years after the 1980 coup, as leftist activists were disappearing into prisons, strikes were banned and the Decisions were put into law, an executive order titled *Turizmi Teşvik Yasası* (Decree to Encourage Tourism) gave major land, construction, credit, and tax incentives to encourage investments – including real estate – in the tourism sector (ibid, 429). Many of the skyscrapers that fill Istanbul's skyline today have made use of this decree to both access subsidies and to get land rights for construction.

Even with *Turizmi Teşvik Yasası* at hand, however, where these skyscrapers and malls were going to be built remained a polarizing issue. The ongoing housing crisis aside, the lack of space in the already densely settled city posed a problem. Relatively few options presented themselves. First was a possible expansion into the peripheries, particularly along the new, major transportation axes. For example, the neighborhoods of Ümraniye and Gülsuyu on the Asian side are results of such an expansion. Second, space could be 'freed up' by the forced removal of large-scale manufacturing facilities from what had become central locations of Istanbul, to either the outskirts of the city or to altogether different towns or cities (Küçükerman 2010, 797). Zeytinburnu on the European side, which housed leather workshops since the time of Mehmed II, for example, underwent such a 'clearing' in the 1990s, and was subsequently rebuilt to house various apartment blocks and malls. A third option was expansion into the already few public parks, woods, and gardens

---

24   From Galata Tower in Pera, to Fire Tower in Süleymaniye, to the slightly shorter clock tower in Dolmabahçe, as well as the minarets of the Fatih, Hagia Sophia, and Blue Mosques, Ottoman Istanbul contained many towers and tall buildings.

scattered across the city, usually attached to historical sites or buildings. Although this option consistently proved more arduous due to various laws protecting the historical sites and buildings, it has also proven to be extremely profitable whenever construction has been successful. The best option, however, was an opportunity that presented itself on a hot, ordinary August night in 1999 when a 7.6 scale earthquake hit the nearby town of İzmit at around 3.02 AM. The earthquake killed and injured thousands of people and left many practically homeless. While whole neighborhoods descended into the Marmara Sea in the İzmit area, many more in the region were condemned for demolition because they were assessed as structurally weak. Thus, in the decade following the earthquake, the central authority, in tandem with private real estate and construction sectors, began a new wave of urban transformation across the region. Selected neighborhoods were emptied, buildings were demolished, and new ones were built. In Istanbul, this process focused primarily on centrally located *gecekondu* neighborhoods, such as Fikirtepe, Kuştepe, Dolapdere, Sulukule, Tarlabaşı, Zeytinburnu, neighborhoods overlooking the Bosporus, and middle to lower class neighborhoods on major transportation axes (Ekinci 2010b). Not only did many of these poor and working class neighborhoods, and the remaining mixed-income neighborhoods near these 'regenerated' areas, become gentrified (Keyder 2010; Uzun 2003), but also, whatever greenery in the form of a *bostan*, park, or garden that had remained, was completely obliterated, to build ever-higher towers of concrete and steel.

In terms of Istanbul's provisioning, urban expansion and intensification signaled, first, the end of the few remaining in-city locations of production, and second, a major transformation in the consumption patterns and practices of the city's residents. Vis-à-vis the former, suffice it to say that by the 2000s, whatever in-city and peripheral production there was in Istanbul, it was limited primarily to private gardens of *gecekondu* dwellers (İstanbul 1993a; 1993b; Yaltırık 1993; Yurt Ansiklopedisi 1981). Traditional, regularly cultivated fields (*bostan*s) and vineyards (*bağ*s) numbered less than 10; and their production was not enough to sustain the FFV needs of the neighborhoods they were in – let alone the city (Kaldijan 2004). Similarly, production at the peripheries kept falling, as farmers quit farming due to rising land prices.

Changes in the consumption patterns and practices followed in the footsteps of globalization. With malls and skyscrapers mushrooming across the city, new and spatially distinct places of consumption had been generated. In addition, the immigration of international managerial and white-collar working classes had introduced new, globally-sanctioned consumption patterns and practices (Keyder 2005; 2010). These coincided with the increasing prevalence of credit cards, which provided greater purchasing power for many[25], regular availability of previously unavailable, imported foods, and increasing segmentation and diversification within retail and wholesale locations. Credit cards did not increase real incomes; but they did provide greater purchasing power for middle- and lower-income households. Thus, on the consumer side at least, previously inaccessible goods began to be/seem more accessible. In terms of urban provisioning, this heightened purchasing power translated to both increased demand and a diversification of tastes and preferences. Bananas, for example, earlier considered to be expensive enough to be gifts, became a part of daily household consumption in many middle class homes[26]. In addition,

---

25   The increasing prevalence of credit cards was an indirect consequence of two seemingly unrelated processes: Financialization and the expansion of the telecommunications infrastructure. Regarding the former, as I have discussed in the previous section, the Turkish economy was vertically and horizontally integrated into global financial markets during the long 1990s. That is, connections between the financial and manufacturing sectors, for example, increased, while Turkish banks got accredited, merged, and/or partnered with foreign banks. Meanwhile, amidst economic crises and devaluations, the liquidity of the Turkish Lira increased, and credit became an available resource for more people. Credit cards managed to tap into this resource, making credit accessible for personal consumption, and thus, increased purchasing power – albeit by projecting costs and risks onto consumers through exorbitant interest rates. The story of the latter is somewhat more convoluted. In effect, the 24 January Decisions were unsupportive of – if not directly against – such public investments. It was argued that public investments on this scale would widen the budget deficit and increase public debt. Nevertheless, the condition of the country's telecommunication infrastructure was dire enough to warrant national security concerns. Plus, reliable, high-speed, and secure telecommunication was necessary to draw foreign direct investment and to encourage financial market activity (Keyder 1999c, Keyder and Öncü 1994; 1993). Thus, beginning with the extension of telephone and electric lines to villages, Turkey upgraded its basic telecommunication infrastructure throughout the 1980s (İçöz 2003, 47–54; Soyak 1996, 87–100). By the 1990s, all villages were provided with land lines, and at least one home in each village was equipped with a telephone machine (İçöz 2003, 47–54). In urban areas, line memberships increased from pre-1980 levels of 5%, to 20% and above in less than a decade, while almost all switchboards across the country were upgraded to automatic (ibid). Still, before each household could get a telephone machine and a subscription to the national service provider (PTT, short for Posta, Telefon, Telgraf or Post, Telephone, Telegraph), mobile phones and dial-up internet began to make an appearance (ibid). They quickly gained subscribers, especially in the urban centers where coverage was already widespread, and replaced mail and fax services, which were, by then, in widespread use in most businesses. Credit cards became available in the 1990s following these infrastructural developments. They were relatively accessible and quite widespread among consumers of almost all income levels by the mid-2000s.
26   In this, the political-economic pressures of (erstwhile) United Fruit to liberalize the Turkish banana market in the 1980s were also effective (Kazgan 2002, 144). Because of these pressures, banana supplies increased, and prices went down; at the same time,

following import liberalization in the 1980s, FFVs which were previously not available for consumption in the country, had begun to be sold. Initially, they were priced slightly higher and oriented to high-income, luxury consumption. However, throughout the 1990s, their prices went down, and with the heightened purchasing power credit cards enabled, residents of the city had a chance to taste these foreign foods: Kiwis, pineapples, coconuts, avocados, mangos, papayas, cashews, and broccoli were among those newly introduced to Istanbulites' palates. While some of these became highly preferred FFVs (kiwis and broccoli, for example) and began to be produced domestically, others remained relatively less consumed (Yenal 2014, 116–117). Moreover, new varieties of domestically produced FFVs began to show up. Thus, Istanbulites learned about limes, Chinese garlic, mandarins, nectarines, jalapeños, daikon radishes, in addition to various types of grapes, apples, eggplants, melons, walnuts, and pears, from east Asia and South America[27]. Their consumption depended largely on pricing. If the local varieties were expensive, consumers preferred the import; and if the import was expensive, consumers tended towards the domestic produce. Some of these, however, could not find a more permanent place on Istanbulites' palates. Daikon radish, for example, disappeared relatively quickly; it could not compete against strongly preferred local varieties. Finally, diversity increased in certain foods that have always been imported, like coffee and dates. Dates are a particularly interesting example as they are usually wrapped in religious symbolism. In the pre-1980 period, only two types of dates were available; and they would be sold exclusively during the month of Ramadan. Moreover, due to their relatively high prices, they would show up primarily on the *iftar* feasts of the well-off. Today, in the aftermath of import liberalization, dates are available year-round; however, they are still quite expensive. Yet, in another example of the heightened purchasing power credit cards enable, they are more widely consumed, though credit and

---

many banana producers on the Mediterranean coast of Turkey went out of business (ibid.). More importantly, the local banana variety, *Anamur muzu* (Anamur banana), almost completely disappeared. It only came back very recently (in the second decade of the 2000s), after the government implemented specific policies to protect the variety and encourage its propagation.

27 I should note that in terms of cuisine, these decades were also a time of rediscovery. Istanbulites relearned and remembered some of the FFVs, nuts, and herbs Ottoman Istanbulites regularly consumed. Today, fresh coriander (cilantro), for example, is making a comeback in some kitchens. Limes, spices, and sauces (pomegranate and plum syrups, rosewater, zahter, for example) are also showing up more frequently in middle class kitchens.

interest – practices that enable that consumption – continue to be contested in Islam.

In terms of diversification of consumer tastes and preferences, wider access to mass media was as much a contributing factor as the regular availability of previously unavailable, imported FFVs. Especially the television, but more so the internet, enabled consumers to learn about the cuisines of different cultures, new food trends, and cooking techniques (interview with Mutfak Sanatları Akademisi (MSA) 2015). Cooking and recipe exchanges, which were traditionally associated with 'homemaker women' and significantly undervalued, were rebranded and elevated to high culture (ibid). Celebrity chefs and cooking shows took over airtime, introducing trendy restaurants, exotic cuisines, and fusion foods (ibid). Similarly, new magazines in print, devoted to cooking, cuisine, food culture and history, began to pop up in bookstores (ibid). Because of this media attention, the 2000s saw an influx in luxury food consumption (ibid). Middle class consumers in particular seemed much more interested and willing to experiment with new foods. Coupled, again, with the heightened purchasing power enabled by credit cards, tastes and preferences began to expand and diversify.

Such expansion and diversification also required outlets to supply the demand. Indeed, beginning in the 1990s, but more so in the 2000s, restaurant businesses boomed in the city. While Istanbul had never lacked restaurants, street vendors, and food joints for various income groups, media attention to food and foodways and heightened purchasing power led to a major surge in all types of restaurants. From traditional street food carts (and boats) to American fast food chains, high-end bars and steak houses, the number of restaurants increased drastically. Not only were the middle and upper class residents spending more money on food in general, they were spending more money on eating out.

This increase in numbers, however, should not be read as an 'invasion' of the city's food scene by the multinationals or a forced westernization of the cuisine. Although fast food chains like McDonald's, Burger King, KFC, and etc. did open up multiple branches across the city and did alter food consumption habits (see the discussions in Chase 1994; Keyder and Yenal 2014b; Yenal 2014), the transformation in the restaurants in particular and the city's foodscape in general was much more comprehensive and complicated than a unidirectional change an 'invasion' or 'westernization' may suggest. As incoming investors, these multinationals had to compete with not only familiar and cheaper local delicacies (*tükürük köftesi, nohutlu pilav, kokoreç, kelle paça, dürüm döner, midye dolma, midye tava, balık ekmek*[28]), but also the domestic versions of

---

28   Respectively: Grilled meatballs, rice with chickpeas, grilled spicy intestines, head and trot soup, gyro rolls, steamed mussels filled with rice and spices, fried mussels, fish sandwich.

the foods they offered that had already begun to pop up once multinationals became somewhat established in Istanbul[29].

Plus, regional foods began to find eager consumers in the city. While immigrant populations of all classes and incomes had always shown a tendency to continue consuming foods and cuisines of their origins, the movement toward 'localization' and 'regionalization' in Istanbul of the 1990s and the 2000s was of a different kind. It was a direct reaction to globalization and everything associated with it (job insecurity, precarity, privatization, internationalization, and financialization), that had swept the country since the Decisions and reflected an attitude of fighting back, while at the same time, of preserving and of rediscovering[30] what belonged 'here'. The most unequivocal example of this was the high-end *kebapçıs* or *ocakbaşıs* opening in the poshest neighborhoods and malls in the city, sometimes exactly across the street from or right next to a Western-style steak house. Previously considered passé if not outright inferior, these high-end kebab shops and grills served to show that 'local culture' could be also be a treasure trove waiting to be 'rediscovered', that local delicacies required as much knowledge and skill, and one could become a connoisseur of kebab as much as they could be of sushi or whiskey. Incoming multinationals thus found themselves in the middle of a bitter culture war and steep competition that spanned across class lines.

The increasing segmentation and diversification within sites of food exchange was the final factor contributing to the diversification and segmentation in consumer tastes and preferences. With segmentation and diversification within sites of food exchange, I mean a two-level transformation within the grocery retail and wholesale sector: First, an overall increase in types of food exchange sites; and second, a differentiation within these sites based on customer profile. In the pre-1980 period, for example, bazaars had been the primary sites of grocery retail for many, followed by the neighborhood greengrocers (*manavs*) and delis (*bakkals*). The store model of grocery retailing – what we today think of as supermarkets – was more of an exception, represented almost singularly by Migros. In the 1990s, when a number of multinationals entered the grocery retail and wholesale sector through either direct

---

29 For similar trends in different parts of the world, please see Caldwell (2008); Lozada (2008).

30 For a more comprehensive discussion of these very important debates between proponents of globalization and reactionaries, see the larger debates on Istanbul's municipal elections, and specifically, the urban transformation discussion around Beyoğlu and Tarlabaşı districts, in: Bora (1997; 1999); Bartu (2001; 1999); Çakır (1997); Keyder (2005; 2010; 1999c); Robins and Aksoy (1995; 2012).

FIGURE 12   *Manav*s are still operational in most Istanbul neighborhoods; however, their
prices are usually higher than supermarkets and bazaars. The *manav* pictured
here is located at Kadiköy
PHOTO BY ALPEREN BUĞRA YILMAZ

investments or private partnerships, this store model became the dominant model. In addition, the technology and knowhow these multinational chains imported have been critical for upgrading provisioning practices across the retail and wholesale sector. While neither bazaar vendors nor neighborhood greengrocers willingly adopted these better practices, the clear advantage the chains had in managing their costs, plus their ability to draw a wide breadth of consumers (thanks to, for example, accepting payments through credit cards, offering home delivery, having uniform prices across shops) pushed these traditional provisioning agents to expand their supply networks and update their business conduct as well as the technologies they used.

Diversification in the sector increased in the 2000s as several domestic entrepreneurs entered the grocery sector and opened stores like the multinationals'. Alike in shelving, interior design, lighting, variety of items sold, and use of technology[31], these domestic supermarkets were as aggressive

---

31   Cold chain during transportation, barcode systems for tracking, standardized labelling, and hygienic packing practices, for example.

FIGURE 13   Domestic supermarkets today are practically indistinguishable from their
             multinational counterparts
             PHOTO BY ALPEREN BUĞRA YILMAZ

as competitors towards the multinationals, as the multinationals had been
towards the bazaars and other traditional provisioning agents. They targeted
poor, lower middle and working class residents of the city as their primary
customer base – groups largely ignored by the multinationals (at least in their
earlier years). Capitalizing on the culture wars around globalization, these
domestic supermarkets branded themselves by their local roots and the domestic source of their capital, focused on a wide range of regional food items and
regionally famous brands, and emphasized their role as entrepreneurs who
brought together traditional tastes, the convenience of supermarket shopping,
and state-of-the-art hygiene practices (interview with Türkiye Perakendeciler
Federasyonu (TPF) Istanbul 2015). Like the kebab house right across the street
from the steak house, these domestic supermarkets stressed 'traditionality'
(geleneksellik), 'locality' (yerellik), and 'domesticity' (yerlilik) (Turkkan 2016,
2018). However, unlike the kebab shops that rebranded the open grill (ocak-
başı) for upper class Istanbulites, these domestic supermarkets targeted primarily (and at least, initially) the lower middle and working class residents of
the city.

It should be noted that domestic and multinational supermarkets are
further diversified among customer lines. Today, it is possible to find 'hard

discount'-style supermarkets targeting the lower-income and poor population, and 'specialty stores' targeting high-income and upper middle class Istanbulites, under the same domestic and multinational grocery chain. In fact, as my informants made it clear, it is impossible to survive in the sector today unless a grocery chain diversifies and caters to different customer segments (interview with CarrefourSA 2015; interview with MSA 2015; interview with Metro Cash & Carry 2015; interview with Migros 2015; interview with TazeDirekt 2015; interview with TPF Istanbul 2015). Because tastes and preferences change across class lines, and because different classes of consumers prefer different retailers, many in the sector diversify their operations based on customer segments in specific neighborhoods of the city (interview with CarrefourSA 2015). In such cases, although prices across branches do not vary, the availability of space for parking, for example, may; similarly, depending on how conservative a neighborhood is, alcoholic drinks may be present or absent. Furthermore, retailers and wholesalers may open different grocery chains, under different names, catering to different customer segments and selling different kinds of grocery items. However, these decisions are not made based on pure market (and marketing) strategy. Instead, such diversification and segmentation usually results from mergers and acquisitions in the sector (Yenal 2014; Koç, Boluk, and Kovacı 2009; Franz, Appel, and Hassler 2013; Atasoy 2013).

While grocery retail chains (domestic and multinational) were increasing, expanding, and diversifying, more traditional sites of food exchange like bazaars and provisioning agents like *bakkal*s and *manav*s were shrinking. This was primarily because domestic and multinational supermarkets kept claiming more of the grocery retail market share; and through effective lobbying efforts[32], they managed to have pass urban planning laws that either outright prohibited or undercut the operational capacities of the neighborhood bazaars (interviews with Bazaar Vendors Associations 2015; Öz and Eder 2012; Ünsal 2010). Plus, unlike neighborhood *bakkal*s and *manav*s or vendors who operated in the bazaars, domestic and multinational supermarkets commanded a heftier capital and had higher chances of withstanding the frequent economic crises. Indeed, the number of *bakkal*s in Istanbul went down from 16,527 in 1987 to 11,800 in 1992 (Akçura 1993, 5). *Manav*s closed at even more drastic rates. Traditionally, they had been the primary exchange sites for fresh fruits and vegetables grown in the neighborhood *bostan*s (fields), *bahçe*s (gardens), and *bağ*s

---

[32]   The owners of some of the domestic supermarket chains have been consistently elected as members of parliament from the *Adalet ve Kalkınma Partisi* (AKP; Justice and Development Party), ever since the 2002 general elections that first carried the AKP to power.

FIGURE 14   Multinational supermarkets are rapidly outcompeting all other provisioning
             agents. They are able to offer diversity, not just in types of products but also in
             quality
             PHOTO BY THE AUTHOR

(vineyards, orchards). Once these in-city locations of production disappeared,
so did the *manavs*[33].

4   The Contemporary Provisioning Apparatus

For groceries, a resident of Istanbul has a range of options, that are largely
neighborhood- dependent. To begin with, there is the neighborhood bazaar,

---

33   Traditionally, *manavs* would buy fresh fruits and vegetables grown in the neighborhood
      bostans (fields), *bahçes* (gardens), and *bağs* (vineyards, orchards) and sell them to resi-
      dents of the neighborhood. On occasion, the *manavs* themselves would tend to the *bos-
      tans*, *bahçes*, and *bağs*. This set-up has completely disappeared from Istanbul. The stores
      that remain, which still look like the traditional *manavs*, purchase their stock from the
      wholesale ports. They are essentially vendors, not very different from those in the neigh-
      borhood bazaars/periodic markets.

FIGURE 15   With consolidated supply chains, multinationals are strong competitors against
             other provisioning agents
             PHOTO BY ALPEREN BUĞRA YILMAZ

either in the neighborhood itself or in a close vicinity. These are complemented
by permanent, neighborhood-based stores: *manav*s and *bakkal*s. People usually frequent these stores if they want to purchase certain foods (say, cheese)
in quantities smaller than would be available in a supermarket, or if these are
the shops closest to their homes, or if they need to make purchases on informal credit. Bazaars, on the other hand, are primarily for their FFV needs. The
most significant competitor for either has been the hard discount supermarkets (currently: A101, Bim, and Şok). They are the fastest growing actors in the
provisioning apparatus today. Their expansion has intensified primarily in the
lower-income neighborhoods[34] and fueled the decline of *manav*s and *bakkal*s,
as well as bazaars.

In addition to the hard discount supermarkets, they can go to one of the
many branches of domestic and multinational grocery retailers that are in the

---

34   The availability of a diverse array of commodities (convenience), consistently low prices
      (affordability), and the relatively depersonalized nature of interactions on the shop floor,
      as opposed to the all-too-personal and communal interactions in the neighborhood
      stores, were mentioned as the 3 primary reasons why lower-income residents, in particu-
      lar, prefer the hard-discount stores (interview with Şok Süpermarketler 2015).

neighborhood. These compete bitterly against each other, but they have been on the same page about outcompeting the bazaars, and if possible, eliminating them from the grocery retailscape of the city all together. Whereas the multinationals see the bazaars – or as they put it, 'fragmented supply chains' – as inefficient, ill-planned, and public health and safety hazards (interview with Migros 2015; interview with Metro Cash & Carry 2015; interview with CarrefourSA 2015), domestic supermarkets consider them as unfair competitors, because the costs associated with vending, including taxes and registration fees, are much lesser than running a proper retail operation (interview with TPF Istanbul 2015). Thus, both domestic and multinational grocery retailers have been advocating for more strict laws and regulations regarding public health and safety and zoning, to make vending in the bazaars more expensive and difficult. And they have been relatively successful. Indeed, by the end of the 2000s, the neighborhood bazaars in Istanbul were only barely drawing more people than the domestic and multinational grocery retailers (supermarkets). In fact, for most food items – cereals, legumes and nuts, processed (pasta, oils, pastes) and canned foods, dairy products (milk, yoghurt, cheeses), meat (processed and raw) and eggs, tea and coffee, spices, and snacks – Istanbulites had already switched to the supermarkets. Bazaars catered almost exclusively for their FFV needs. Perhaps, in a matter of a few decades, they will completely disappear, thus crowning the supermarkets as the primary sites of grocery retail in the city.

However, this is not the first-time periodic markets have been shaken by looming change. Traditionally, bazaars were of two kinds: Permanent markets and periodic markets. Permanent markets were, as their name suggests, permanent; they were mostly spaces where traders sold their commodities. Periodic markets were different. They provided opportunities for farmers to come into the city and sell their produce once or twice a week. As such, in every neighborhood, periodic markets were established at different times, with different frequency, containing different vendors and regionally produced items. They were also usually set up in less dense parts of the city, close to the peripheries where the farmers would come from. Permanent markets, in contrast, were in more populated parts of the city; and they provided access to residents who lived in neighborhoods where they weren't any *bostan*s (fields), *bahçe*s (gardens), and *bağ*s (vineyards, orchards), or where the production from the *bostan*s, *bahçe*s, and *bağ*s was not enough to feed the residents. Traditionally, the produce in the vendors or shops in the permanent markets would come from longer distances and would be less fresh. As such, it wasn't uncommon for many residents to go to the periodic markets on the peripheries, even if that meant traversing some distance via public transportation. Gradually, however,

FIGURE 16   Periodic markets continue to be the primary locations for FFV provisioning for
most residents, though competition with the supermarkets is quite tight
PHOTO BY THE AUTHOR

permanent markets disappeared, and periodic markets multiplied, spreading all over to the city, to neighborhoods dense and sparse alike. They have also changed in many ways. With in-city and peripheral locations of production decreasing sharply, all the produce sold in periodic markets (bazaars) began to come from longer distances. Today, the supply chains supplying the bazaars tend to be quite long, extending into the furthest regions of the country and sometimes across the globe.

4.1   In the Day of a Bazaar Vendor

For a family vending in one of Istanbul's 393 bazaars today[35], the day starts relatively early: Around midnight or 1 AM, they have to be in one of the 2 wholesale ports of the city. If they are going to be vending on the European side, they will go to the Bayrampaşa *Hali* (Port of Bayrampaşa – not actually a

35   For a full list of contemporary bazaars in the city, see İstanbul Umum Pazarcılar Esnaf Odası (2020).

FIGURE 17   Periodic markets no longer sell local products. Almost all the FFVs sold come
             from elsewhere in the country and sometimes, from across the globe
             PHOTO BY THE AUTHOR

port anymore, but still referred to as such, following the Ottoman provisioning apparatus I discussed in Chapter 2), and if they will be vending on the Asian side, they will be at the İçerenköy *Hali* (Port of İçerenköy). They will have to know one of the many shop owners in the *Hal*; otherwise, it will be difficult for them to guarantee a good supply. This shop owner may be someone they have known and have been working with for years; he might even be part of the extended family or an acquaintance from back in the village or town they all migrated from some years ago. In any case, they will have to purchase the items at night – and most certainly before the shop runs out. Friends or family, cash is what gets business done at the *Hal*; and if they don't have it, they will come out of the *Hal* empty-handed.

3–4 AM is going to be the busiest time. They will have to bargain, pay, unload the produce from the shop's stock, load it up in their trucks, and head out. If the different members of the family are operating at different bazaars around the city, they will have to share the purchase at this time: Whoever has put in more for the bulk payment, will get more of the share, and at the end of the day, they will have more revenue – a perfect opportunity for all sorts of family

FIGURE 18   Assemble/disassemble the bazaar: This is an everyday, twice a day, task for the
vendors
PHOTO BY ALPEREN BUĞRA YILMAZ

drama. Thus, after much shouting, bargaining, unloading, and loading, they
will head to their bazaar locations by 6.30 AM, before the morning rush sets in.
If they are lucky, they even will get a couple hours of shut-eye, before they have
to start assembling the bazaar at around 8–8.30 AM. When I say, 'assembling
the bazaar', I mean literally putting together the bazaar: setting up the poles,
tying the tarps up top to make cover, setting up the stalls, unloading the produce from trucks, cleaning it and putting it out for display. All of these will have
to be done before the bazaar opens up by 9 AM.

When the bazaar opens, the streets (it is located on) are closed to traffic.
The night before, the municipal cleaning crew does extra work, sweeping away
whatever litter there may be. Cars parked on the street will also have to move
by the morning or they will be towed – or worse, they will be stuck amidst
the vendors, their trucks, and customers, throughout the day, unable to move.
After the bazaar opens at around 9 AM, the municipal police will go around
checking that all the vendors are registered with the Chamber of Bazaar and
Mobile Vendors, have valid licenses to vend, and are actually at the spot they
have rented and not taking over extra space or hijacking someone else's space.
If there are any violations, the municipal police will warn the vendor and let
the Chamber know. After 3 such warnings, the vendor is out, and his space

FIGURE 19   A bazaar vendor having hot soup for breakfast on a chilly Istanbul morning
PHOTO BY ALPEREN BUĞRA YILMAZ

becomes available for rent. Such cases, however, are rare in Istanbul – though much more common in smaller cities and towns.

During the day, bazaars tend to be calm. Elderly, retired, and non-working people make up the primary customer base at this time. An hour or two before closing (around 6.30 PM), however, crowds suddenly increase. People who have just left work as well as lower-income residents come to get their groceries. Vendors, unwilling to shoulder the costs of taking the remaining produce back, and lacking a storage space, may decrease their prices by as much as 30%. Most of the produce will sell during these two hours. Whatever remains will be carefully sorted, and bruised, rotten, and wilted pieces will be discarded. The rest will be loaded back onto the truck; poles and tarps will be disassembled; and the road will be open for traffic latest by 7 PM. The municipal cleaning crew will be back shortly after, to do multiple rounds of street cleaning, removing any sign that there was a periodic market on that very street just a few hours ago. By 9 PM, cars will be parked where the vendors were in the afternoon. Meanwhile, vendors will be heading home to take a few hours of much-needed rest. But they don't have much time to do so. The same cycle will start by midnight that night – and it will go on every night of the week, with no breaks throughout the year. And that is why it is a family business. Because the hours are so long, profits so low, and the work itself so heavy, only

FIGURE 20   On the day of the bazaar, the streets (it is located on) are closed, cars are moved, and a new, quasi-covered public space is created. Space, time, people, and foods seem to be in flux – particularly in the winter, when days are short, and darkness descends early on the streets
PHOTO BY ALPEREN BUĞRA YILMAZ

family members are willing to collectively take it up. Even with such ruthless self-exploitation, however, there are no guarantees that revenues are going to be enough to live on.

4.2   *At the* Hal

In contrast to vending in the bazaars, owning a shop in a *Hal* in Istanbul is a supremely profitable business. The shop owners are, in fact, traders: They buy the produce from other wholesale ports all around the country, bring it to Istanbul, and sell it to bazaar vendors, greengrocers, and/or anyone else (hospitals, catering companies, schools, restaurants, etc.)[36] who wants to buy wholesale to either process it (say, make paste out of tomatoes) or sell for retail. As such, from an operational point of view, their primary task is logistics (getting the produce to Istanbul) and storage (until the produce is sold). In effect,

---

36   According to Edict 28135, anyone who buys wholesale and sells directly to consumers, even after processing or cooking, must register at the *Hal*, though they do not need to own a shop in the *Hal*.

however, the system is slightly more complicated. According to the regulations, unless bought directly from the producers at a farm or at a farmers' market or via a farmers' cooperative, every fresh fruit and vegetable sold directly to consumers has to come out from one of the two wholesale ports in the city.[37] While the prices of each item – imports included – are determined by the free market, the Istanbul Metropolitan Municipality (*İstanbul Büyükşehir Belediyesi*; IBB), under which the wholesale ports operate, declares the lowest and the highest prices for all items, including the imported ones, every day. These prices are suggestions; to convey a sense of the market. Customers are thus expected to go around the *Hal*, looking for the best product at the best price. However, as I mentioned above, it is a customer's access to cash that determines whether or not a transaction is going to happen. If they have cash, then they can indeed go around looking for the best product at the best price. In most cases, however, customers are cash-strapped, and if a shop owner is willing to open a line of credit for them or trade via bonds, for example, they will buy regardless of the quality or price of the produce. This is one of the primary methods through which shop owners can increase their rate of profit.

That being said, my informants claimed that the profits at the *Hal* average between 8 to 12% (interview with the Directorate of Bayrampaşa Wholesale Port 2015). It may not seem much, but the shop owners generate other opportunities to raise rates as well. They can, for example, accumulate more, if they can consolidate their operation. Let me explain: Because Istanbul cannot feed itself, most of its food comes from elsewhere. Thus, before the produce gets into the storage facility of one of the shops in Istanbul's Bayrampaşa or İçerenköy wholesale ports, it has to leave yet another shop's storage facility at another city's wholesale port. Of course, the same regulations apply there as well: the municipality declares the lowest and the highest prices, and the profits shop owners can add on are also about the same (8 to 12%). So a shop owner in Bayrampaşa has a rough idea about how much it will cost to buy, say, tomatoes from a shop in Antalya *Hali* or Bolu *Hali*, and it is in his self-interest to call around every day to his connections across the country to find the best prices (i.e. cheapest) for tomatoes. It is even better if his connection at the other wholesale port is part of his extended family – it will be a win-win as they will work together to adjust the prices for maximum profit on both ends of the line. Finally, if they also have a few trucks and some other cousins or brothers to drive them, they can accumulate even more capital!

---

37   See Statuary Decree 769. There is a similar regulation for fish as well, though no such
      regulations exist for dried fruits and vegetables, legumes, cereals, meat, dairy or eggs.

FIGURE 21   Shops at İçerenköy *Hali* displaying their produce
PHOTO BY ALPEREN BUĞRA YILMAZ

Another way shop owners can increase their profit is to declare a loss. Trucks transporting produce are weighed when they are leaving the wholesale port at their location of origin, and when they arrive at the wholesale port of their destination. Because most of these trucks are still the traditional flatbed trucks, some of the transported produce is expected to perish – though the amount is unclear. Shop owners can thus declare high losses and artificially increase their prices. They can also sell the loss they have declared on the side, away from the prying eyes of the tax authorities. Alternatively, they can declare the produce to be of lower quality, and on paper, decrease its prices. They will then sell the produce at the market price, pocketing the handsome difference.

One action shop owners at a *Hal* are exclusively prohibited from, is to sell directly to the supermarkets. Instead, supermarkets – domestic and multinational – are encouraged to open a shop at a *Hal* and establish their own supply lines. Alternatively, shops at a *Hal* can expand into retailing. While both are intended to fuel competition in the hope of lowering prices for urban consumers, they unfortunately have the exact opposite effect. Such consolidation across the supply chain tends to bring in a higher rate of profit and triggers higher prices.

Finally, how does the produce get to the wholesale ports in the first place? Here, the availability of cash is, again, key. By the time the harvest comes in,

FIGURE 22 Bottlenecks for global capital (high-rises) and global commodities (food)
PHOTO BY ALPEREN BUĞRA YILMAZ

FIGURE 23 Shops at the *Hal* are also active loading and offloading locations
PHOTO BY ALPEREN BUĞRA YILMAZ

most farmers are strapped for cash – so much so that, in some cases, if they
cannot find it, they will not be able to rent the machinery necessary to harvest
their crops. Traders (*aracıs*), aware of this dire need, offer ready cash in return
for low prices. For most small and mid-size farmers, they have no other option
but to accept. Going around the villages, thus, traders collect as much produce
as they can, and then sell it off to shop owners at the wholesale ports for a
profit. Lately, it is more often the case that the shop owners and the traders are
the same – that is, they are either from the same company, or family, or both.
In other words, the provisioning actors between the farmers and consumers
have consolidated along supply lines. Concentrating their profits thus, these
in-between provisioning actors generate the highest rate of profit by pressur-
ing farmers to sell as cheaply as possible, cutting the costs of transportation,
and sorting and selling to the consumers as expensively as possible.

For produce that is imported, the supply lines are not very different. The
customs port that the produce is unloaded from – whether airfreight, ship,
rail, or truck – is legally considered its wholesale port of origin. The rest of the
process is pretty much the same: From the shop at the port, it is transported
to another shop at one of Istanbul's two wholesale ports, where it is sold to
retailers. Like domestic produce, its suggested lowest and highest prices are
also declared by the Istanbul Metropolitan Municipality (*İstanbul Büyükşehir
Belediyesi*; IBB), though its market prices are much more directly affected by
exchange rate fluctuations.

By the time the produce gets to consumers, prices have increased drastically.
At times of crisis, this increase can be more than 600%; but even in normal
times, 200% is not uncommon. Looking at tables 3 and 4, the profit margins
may look as high for the bazaar vendors as they are for the supermarkets. But
remember that supermarkets have consolidated their supply lines, and thus
appropriate more of these price increases than bazaar vendors, who are still, at
the end of the day, only retailers. In either case though, the residents of the city
suffer – the poor, of course, more so than the rich.

5   A Precarious Sovereignty or the Sovereignty of Precarity?

The changes triggered by the 24 January Decisions removed the central authority from its position of organizing, controlling, supervising – in short, *governing* – Istanbul's provisioning. However, it did not necessarily replace it with the
market. The changes were much more exhaustive and intricate than replacing
one actor (the central authority) with a mechanism (the market). Moreover,
when the central authority was removed from its position of governance, not

TABLE 3   Farm-to-table price increases in April 2017 (TZMOB 2017)

Product	Producer Price (TL/Kg)	Wholesale port (WP) Price (TL/Kg)	Bazaar Price (TL/Kg)	Supermarket Price (TL/Kg)	WP/Producer Price difference (%)	Bazaar/Producer Price difference (%)	Supermarket/Producer Price difference (%)
Onion	0,15	0,52	1,05	1,12	246,67	600	646,67
Apple	0,67	1,83	2,75	3,94	172,39	310,45	488,43
Dried apricot	6,5	-	25	29,9	-	284,62	360
Cabbage	0,37	0,51	1,13	1,61	39,09	206,82	339,64
Eggplant	0,63	1,01	1,67	2,72	60,9	165,96	334,75
Parsley (Unit)	0,25	0,37	0,75	1,02	47,2	200	308
Dried fig	6,5	-	25	24,26	-	284,62	273,21
Zucchini	0,61	0,9	1,71	2,21	48,35	181,59	264,84
Leek	0,88	1,39	2,1	3,19	58,14	117,8	262,5
Cucumber	0,53	0,77	1,58	1,92	43,75	196,88	260,83
Raisins	3,75	-	12	13,26	-	220	253,69
Cauliflower	0,89	1,14	1,8	2,61	28,09	102,25	192,7
Lettuce (Unit)	0,83	1,28	1,58	2,39	54,55	91,92	189,62
Carrot	1	1,33	2	2,77	32,5	100	177
Hazelnuts	19,96	-	45	51,63	-	125,45	158,68
Red lentil	2,77	3,6	6,83	6,97	29,96	146,69	151,54

TABLE 3   Farm-to-table price increases in April 2017 (TZMOB 2017) (cont.)

Product	Producer Price (TL/Kg)	Wholesale port (WP) Price (TL/Kg)	Bazaar Price (TL/Kg)	Supermarket Price (TL/Kg)	WP/ Producer Price difference (%)	Bazaar/ Producer Price difference (%)	Supermarket /Producer Price difference (%)
Green pepper	1,16	1,58	2,42	2,83	35,78	108,33	143,75
Lentils	3,48	6,2	7,33	8,41	78,16	110,73	141,67
Spinach	1,15	1,36	1,92	2,74	18,26	66,67	138,12
Rice	2,4	3,6	5,5	5,69	50	129,17	137,28
Chickpeas	4,79	8,2	9,67	11,23	71,19	101,81	134,5
Scallions	1,33	1,9	2,67	3,11	42,86	100,5	133,83
Lemon	1,99	2,47	3,38	4,63	23,95	70,02	132,5
Dried beans	4,08	5	8	8,9	22,55	96,08	118,22
Potato	1,01	1,38	1,67	2,2	37,3	65,43	118,03
Pistachio	29	-	50	55,64	-	72,41	91,88
Tomato	2,97	3,75	4,5	5,5	26,26	51,52	85,22
Strawberry	3	3,88	4,4	4,74	29,17	46,67	58,13

TABLE 4   Farm-to-table price increases in November 2019 (TZMOB 2019)

Products	Producer Price (TL/Kg)	Wholesale port (WP) Price (TL/Kg)	Bazaar Price (TL/Kg)	Supermarket Price (TL/Kg)	WP/Producer Price difference (%)	Bazaar/Producer Price difference (%)	Supermarket/Producer Price difference (%)
Dried fig	13	-	45	59,97	-	246,15	361,28
Dried apricot	10	-	28	44,88	-	180	348,83
Carrot	0,8	1,4	2,12	3,17	75	164,58	296,33
Mandarin	0,98	1,96	2,72	3,63	99,32	176,27	268,75
Chickpeas	2,89	5	10,25	10,32	73,01	254,67	256,92
Leek	1,19	1,35	2,6	4,11	13,68	118,95	245,82
Orange	1,15	2,26	3,17	3,94	96,52	175,36	242,32
Cabbage	0,5	0,84	1,17	1,68	68	133,33	236,22
Spinach	1,13	1,43	2,6	3,65	27,11	131,11	224,44
Lentils	2,95	4,5	7,5	9,49	52,54	154,24	221,61
Potato	0,65	1,23	1,88	2,01	89,23	188,46	209,36
Onion	0,63	1,02	1,75	1,86	63,2	180	197,6
Eggplant	1,17	1,66	2,8	3,37	42,29	140	189,14
Cauliflower	1,38	1,91	2,7	3,64	38,91	96,36	164,61
Green pepper	2,23	3,24	4,38	5,89	45,07	95,9	163,66
Lettuce (unit)	1,22	1,65	2,75	3,16	35,62	126,03	159,32
Pistachios	45,05	-	80	114,23	-	77,58	153,57

TABLE 4 Farm-to-table price increases in November 2019 (TZMOB 2019) (cont.)

Products	Producer Price (TL/Kg)	Wholesale port (WP) Price (TL/Kg)	Bazaar Price (TL/Kg)	Supermarket Price (TL/Kg)	WP/ Producer Price difference (%)	Bazaar/ Producer Price difference (%)	Supermarket/ Producer Price difference (%)
Red lentils	3,29	6,2	7,5	8,14	88,45	127,96	147,47
Hazelnuts (shelled)	36	-	55	87,4	-	52,78	142,78
Apple	2,06	3,1	3,58	4,96	50,49	73,95	140,65
Scallions	2,56	3,63	4,83	5,98	41,46	88,62	133,5
Tomato	2,03	2,99	3,9	4,66	47,05	91,8	129,23
Parsley (unit)	0,6	0,73	1,25	1,36	20,83	108,33	126,67
Lemon	2,6	3,24	4,45	5,65	24,62	71,15	117,18
Cucumber	2,38	3,2	4,3	5,16	34,27	80,42	116,39
Dried beans	6,1	8	11	12,96	31,15	80,33	112,46
Raisins	9,83	-	16	20,78	-	62,77	111,43
Zucchini	2,32	3,02	3,75	4,84	30,36	61,87	108,83
Rice	4,8	6	6,75	7,71	25	40,63	60,68

only did the provisioning mechanisms, practices, and networks that were tied directly to the central authority disappear, but also, the idea that Istanbul, or any city – or any constituency for that matter – needed to be provisioned, faded from public discourse.

More interestingly perhaps, Istanbul's provisioning became an accidental outcome. In previous food regimes, the central authority, through direct or indirect interventions, had governed the production, distribution, exchange, and consumption of food in the city. This 'government' had involved the regulation of production and exchange, inspection of quality, quantity, and price, supervision of distribution, among others. The market, however, is neither an actor capable of such actions, nor does it have any authority to govern. Rather, it is a network of actors, decisions, and practices, that emphasizes non-governance as its primary principle of conduct: People participate in the market, not because they are directed to do so by the central authority, but because they can profit by doing so. As such, in the new food regime, Istanbul is provisioned because each provisioning actor used the market to make – and if possible, maximize – a profit.

However, this begs another question: If, in a market-mediated food regime, 'provisioning the city' is more of an accidental outcome of provisioning actors wanting to profit, than a meticulously-organized, minutely-directed and closely-supervised effort by a central authority wanting to feed its constituency; and as such, the market indeed does not replace the central authority, but rather pushes the central authority out of its position of governance; then, what does the central authority do? In other words, if on the one hand, economic power and sovereign power are differentiated such that the extraction and appropriation of surplus labor takes place through purely economic means (Meiksins Wood 2016, 28–31), and on the other hand, people rely singularly on commodity exchange through the market to satisfy their needs (ibid.), then what is left for the sovereign to do? For what is the sovereign power useful?

The short answer is that in the *urban food supply chain* food regime, the primary task of the central authority is to inflict violence, to make sure that the market functions as efficiently and as unhindered as possible. This is one of the ways in which, as Ellen Meiksins Wood describes it, economic power "rest[ing] firmly on the political" (Meiksins Wood 2016, 30–33); and in this specific case, it takes three specific forms – all of which significantly alter the relationship between the central authority and the political community. First, the central authority actively eliminates non-competitive and less competitive market agents, and thus, renders the market an efficient way of ordering the provisioning apparatus and the political community at large. Second, it eradicates venues, mechanisms, and networks through which alternative "social rationalit[ies] could be defined and formed in such a way as to nullify economic irrationality" (Foucault 2008, 106), and thus, consolidates market rationality and prevents competing rationalities from arising and/or to taking hold in the public discourse. And third, it catalyzes expropriation from living spaces and aids their re-appropriation as resources, thus constantly opening new spaces and new relations for the market to penetrate. In some of these cases, the violence the central authority inflicts is quite blatant (as in the 1980 coup, for example, or as in the ongoing war in the eastern and the southeastern parts of the country); but more often, the violence remains concealed, permeating and ingrained in the everyday practices of provisioning agents. It thus both feeds, and feeds from, the market-based precarity widespread in the political community.

Out of the three specific ways in which the central authority inflicts violence, the first one – the elimination of non-competitive and less competitive market agents – relies primarily on techniques of government inherited from the previous *codependent provisioning* food regime. However, unlike in *codependent provisioning*, where *friends* and *enemies* were decided on the basis of non-market rationales and concerns, in the *urban food supply chain*, they are decided on the basis of each agent's market competitiveness. That is, if a market agent is competitive, the central authority pools in more resources to support it: For example, large farmers who produce for export are supported by various incentives; vertical and horizontal integration along the supply chain is allowed, even encouraged; local and global partnerships are fostered to create and to nurture market agents with enough capital to withstand crises; agents who develop competitive practices in alternative food networks are emboldened as sector leaders. In contrast, if a market agent is not competitive, the central authority works through various channels to eliminate, or depending on the agent, to eradicate it. Direct income subsidies, for example, incentivize some small and mid-size farmers to quit agriculture; the removal of price protections, quotas, and privatization of public enterprises and farmers' cooperatives contribute to de-peasantization; new urban planning regulations led to the shrinking of bazaars; cold chain regulations push those with less capital out of the perishable sector. In other words, through various policies, the central authority segregates those who are already competitive as its *friends* and regards those who cannot compete as its *enemies*.

The elimination of the non-competitive and less competitive economic agents, or *enemies*, serves a three-fold purpose: First, it ensures that the market functions and remains functional, and that wealth is generated. As such, any comparison with the pre-1980 period, for example, ends up redeeming the 24 January Decisions and the violent military junta that enforced them. By the same token, critiques that target the Decisions and point out the corruption, crises, and sense of subservience to global market agents, are reformulated as the failures of the central authority – not the market. Second, it orders the political community in line with market imperatives and renders the resources of the political community (human, financial, territorial, and/or otherwise) legible and accessible to the global market and its dynamics. As I discussed in the section 'The 2000s: A World City?', this rendering manifests not only in the attempts to make Istanbul a 'global city' (hence the construction-friendly legislations, infrastructural investments, skyscrapers, malls, urban transformation projects), but also in new migration patterns, changes in consumption patterns and practices, and the treatment of rural and urban populations and living spaces as resources. Third, it provides the central authority with a new role, function, and source of legitimacy: By eliminating the less/non-competitive market agents, the central authority does indeed make sure that everyone can access the market without hindrance and use their advantages to the best of their capabilities (Keyder 2014, 216; Keyder and Yenal 2014a, 60).

There are, however, also certain caveats: To begin with, the wealth that is generated is appropriated by specific market agents; it does not belong to the whole political community – nor is it used for the welfare of the whole political community. As the central authority uses public resources to support certain populations (more competitive ones) over others (less/non-competitive ones), income inequality becomes an entrenched problem that entails, among others, the inability to access sufficient and nutritious food, and in the worst cases, the inability to access food at all. Conceptually, this implies a transition from vulnerability to precarity, where the imminence of death, shifting of limits of one's mortality and endurance due to external or internal infringements, breaking down of one's bodily order, harmony, constitution, and/or balance, are imminent, if not already in progress. Contingencies that arise from being eliminated from the market become additional feedback loops. For example, in order to counter the effects of wage depreciation in the urban economy, lower-income households tend to maintain some level of connection to the rural economy – a process Keyder and Yenal describe as "semi-proletarianization" (2014d, 139–144). The overall effect, however, is the exact opposite, in that self-exploitation makes it possible for one to survive on wages below subsistence levels in the urban centers (ibid). This implies, for these members of the political community, an exacerbation of their vulnerabilities due to increased contingency (Keyder and Yenal 2014a, 71; 2014d, 164; 2014b, 20–34), so much so that death due to hunger is imminent.

More crucially, as Keyder and Yenal's analysis of semi-proletarianization also shows, the central authority does not necessarily have to actively kill certain

(less/non-competitive as market agents) members of the political community.
The elimination of the less/non-competitive can take the form of forsaking or
separating, grouping, and containing variously less/non-competitive agents,
so that they share a resource pool different from their competitive counterparts. Still, there is an irksome resemblance to what Foucault describes as the
state's right to kill. For Foucault, the state's right to kill is attached to biopower's ingrained link to the sovereign right to life and death (Foucault 2003, 254–
256). However, biopower's "objective is essentially to make live" (ibid, 254);
whereas, the sovereign right to life and death is "a political power to kill, to call
for deaths, to demand deaths, to give the order to kill, and to expose not only
enemies but its own citizens to the risk of death" (ibid, 254). As such, to be able
to kill, to demand deaths, etc., the power to make live must become racist (ibid,
254). That is, it needs

> a way of introducing a break into the domain of life that is under power's
> control: the break between what must live and what must die. (....) a way
> of separating out the groups that exist within a population (...) a way of
> establishing a biological-type caesura within a population that appears
> to be a biological domain. (...) to create caesuras within the biological
> continuum addressed by biopower (Foucault 2003, 255).

However, in Foucault's account, "the enemies who have to be done away with
are not adversaries in the political sense of the term; they are threats, either
external or internal, to the population and for the population" (Foucault 2003,
256). In other words, biopower that deploys the sovereign right to kill, treats
its enemies as private problems, not public ones (*inimicus*, not *hostis* (Schmitt
1976, 27–28)). In the Turkish case, in contrast, once the central authority des-
ignates certain members of the political community as less competitive or
non-competitive market agents, they become public enemies (*hostis*, not
inimicus)[38]. Thus, even if they are not actively killed, but forsaken, or grouped
and contained, there is very little recourse for them to contest the decision
that led them there, or to work their way out of precarity. A recourse that may
be available to them is to stay at the margins – by way of participating either
in the formal economy (though, by denouncing the market dynamics and the

---

38   Note that the difference here is between the Turkish case and Foucault's account, and not
      between the *codependent provisioning* and the *urban food supply chain* food regimes. In
      other words, in both food regimes, *enemies* are designated as 'public enemies' (*hostis*, not
      inimicus), though as I have noted above, how that designation occurs is very different in
      the two food regimes.

profit motive[39]), or move almost completely to the informal economy – or resist, rebel or fight back, and exit the political community.

To sum up, then, in the *urban food supply chain* food regime, the central authority's primary task is to inflict violence so as to ensure that the market functions as efficiently as possible. It, thus, eliminates the less/non-competitive market actors and pools public resources to support those who are already competitive. This makes it seem like the market works smoothly and efficiently, that relying on provisioning actors to take actions and make decisions to maximize their profit and to minimize their costs, is the most cost-effective method of provisioning the city. At the same time, the central authority eradicates venues, mechanisms, and networks that may give rise to rationalities alternative to market rationality. As such, for all those who question and criticize the current method of provisioning the city, and attempt to look for other venues, practices, relations to provision the city, not only are there no alternatives, but the market and the market rationality seem as 'natural' as they seem functional.[40] Finally, by declaring the less/non-competitive actors as 'public *enemies*', the central authority effectively blocks conversations about why they are or have become less/non-competitive, the disadvantages they might have (which are usually structural – as in the case of small- to mid-scale farmers, for example), and the sorts of critiques they offer, with regard to practices and mechanisms of support (direct income subsidies, for example) that are there to eliminate them, one way or another. As a result, from constructive criticisms, to on-the-ground practices, as well as challenges and alternatives to market rationality – all become inaudible.

The relation between economic power and sovereign power, then, goes beyond one (economic power) resting on the other (sovereign power) (Meiksins Wood 2016, 30–33). Sovereign power not only enables economic power (that is, the extraction and appropriation of surplus labor through purely economic means), it subjugates itself to the imperatives of economic power: Government of the political community now entails a differentiation of *friends* and *enemies* based on market competitiveness; and a deployment of the sovereign power's coercive forces for the elimination of both the relations, and the alternative to the *mentalité* of "the imperatives of competition,

---

39   Quite a few alternative food networks or initiatives (AFNs) that attempt to denounce the profit motive, have a small number of participants, and make a low impact in the provisioning sector, could be recounted here (though how successful they are in their attempts is debatable). I will be discussing these in the next chapter.

40   In other words, the market is no longer a site of verification (*a la* Foucault 2008); it rather becomes a teleology that only verifies itself.

accumulation, and profit-maximization, and hence a constant systemic need to develop productive forces" (Meiksins Wood 2017, 97). However, this is not merely the sovereign power drilling the market imperative into the political community and disciplining the members. It is that, in addition to the politicization of the processes of life and death for the market: Just as the members of the political community are now compelled to access the commodities they need for subsistence through the market, they can also be left to die through the market by the sovereign power, which has abdicated its duty to protect them against their vulnerabilities. In other words, like the 'making live of the *friends*', the 'letting die of the *enemies*' is through the market as it is for the market.

For Istanbulites of the post-Decisions era, the hegemony of the market in the provisioning apparatus entailed, one, an increase in diversification and (for those who could afford it) abundance of food items and, two, a decrease in the rural-to-urban population rate. While the former was due to the global interdependency of the provisioning apparatus (see the section 'The 2000s: A World City?'), the latter was largely a product of the restructuring of agriculture, initiated by the Decisions. By the late 2000s, even with rural-to-urban migration slowing down and reversing, the labor-to-land ratio in the countryside remained low. This meant either employing more wage-labor in agriculture during the planting and harvesting seasons and as such, treating agriculture, agricultural work, and rural life spaces as derivatives of the labor market; or increasing capital investment in the form of technology, machinery, and inputs (seeds, pesticides, fertilizers, etc.) to increase agricultural outputs. In either case, everyone directly and indirectly connected to the agricultural sector experienced various degrees of precarity: Local seasonal wage laborers had to compete with quasi-formalized immigrant- and later refugee- labor for below subsistence-level wages; price fluctuations made exports unpredictable for large producers; and the volatility of the currency was enough to bankrupt many small and mid-size farms. Yet, from the point of view of urban dwellers, food items in the city seemed more diverse, and more abundant. While Istanbulites of an older generation fondly remember the days of the *manav*s from which they could buy the (now-disappearing) local FFV varieties, freshly picked from the neighborhood *bostan*s (interview with Aylin Öney Tan 2015; interview with Gastronomika 2015)[41], the Decisions have undoubtedly

41   The remaining few *bostan*s, *bağ*s, and *bahçe*s are predominantly on the outskirts of the city, and they can supply only a small portion of the city's population. In upper class suburbs, they are the preferred alternatives to supermarkets, and are treated as foundational constituents of alternative food networks. Even in the absence of certification, they may

encouraged imports and introduced Istanbulites to new FFVs from around the world. Food today undeniably travels longer distances even domestically; however, the competition among domestic and multinational supermarkets and the bazaars does guarantee at least some level of freshness and quality.

This is, then, the ideal set-up that the proponents of the Decisions argued for: For its FFV needs, a growing urban population relies on a diminishing rural population, who must treat their lands as a resource, employ (regularly) temporary work force, continuously make capital investments (machinery, know-how) and innovate (grow new FFV varieties, adopt better farming practices, find high-yielding seed varieties, etc.). Whenever domestic agricultural production is inadequate, competitive provisioning actors (supermarkets) step in to supply urban demand by way of imports, thus keeping prices low and enabling more Istanbulites to access food. Inefficient producers (who sell their produce for too high a price) and low-quality products are also weeded out through competition, and wide-ranging foodstuffs can be continuously supplied to the city. Plus, because of competition among various provisioning actors, different quality foods are supplied to the city at different prices, which enables access to food for different income groups. In this set-up, then, the market functions perfectly through competition; and the provisioning actors who want to remain in the market are constantly pushed to invest and innovate. Thus, not only are resources utilized to the best of everyone's abilities, but also, the city is provisioned efficiently and smoothly. Moreover, constant investment and innovation creates vigorous rural communities, from which people would be less likely to leave and cause overcrowding in the cities. Finally, all of this is done through the market, and because of the market, without the central authority directly intervening in the decisions and/or actions of the provisioning actors.

Yet, even if we assume that the provisioning actors, guided through competition and working to maximize their profits, do perfect the supply chain, this food system still requires Istanbulites to buy the FFVs. In other words, this ostensibly ideal set-up is equally contingent on Istanbulites having enough purchasing power – which, in turn, is dependent on the wages, the labor market,

---

be considered 'organic', 'natural', and 'healthy', and collectively sought-after (interview with TazeDirekt 2015; interview with Beyhan Uzunçarşılı 2015). In lower class *gecekondu* neighborhoods, in contrast, home gardens are common (especially if the neighborhood is on the city's outskirts), not because they are preferred alternatives, but because they help supply the household with certain fundamental FFVs. However, once the city expands and *gecekondu* neighborhoods become more integrated into the city, these gardens are quickly replaced by apartment buildings, which the owners can then rent out. Many prefer the cash income generated from rent, so that they can buy FFVs from the provisioning actors, rather than growing them for self-consumption.

and the value of the Turkish Lira, among other factors. There are no guarantees, support mechanisms, solidarity networks to make sure that people are provisioned; nor – unlike in the *urban food provisioning* food regime – does the central authority have an interest in, vested or otherwise, keeping the subject-citizens provisioned. Rather, it is assumed that Istanbulites – also out of self-interest – will buy whatever the provisioning apparatus has to offer. If they do not, either they have some alternative way of procuring food (private gardens, for example) or they would be starving themselves. In short, then: Either buy what is delivered through the supply chain or starve.

In the *urban food supply chain* food regime then, Istanbulites are made increasingly precarious – not just by the lack of options, except for what is made available by the provisioning apparatus, but also by the instability in their own global interdependencies. Yet, the central authority focuses only on making the market work; unlike in other food regimes, it has no consideration for the bodily maintenance of the members of the political community. It assumes that people are going to maintain their own bodies and bodily needs, that this is their private responsibility[42]. What is critical for the central authority is the economic potential of the bodies and the bodily – as labor power, as consumers, as resources, etc. It is this potential that the central authority needs to govern, to make sure that it remains competitive in the market, and if or when it is not, to eliminate it so that the market remains functional and competitive.

What this construction of the relationship between the central authority and the political community ultimately posits to the members of the political community is the precarity of their present – corporeal and political – condition. They can be eliminated (as market agents) or starved (as residents of the city); but worse, they are utterly unable to exert control over global forces that shape the market, and by the same token, the provisioning apparatus and their purchasing power. As individuals (or families or communities), they may perhaps move from group to group: Yesterday's highly competitive market agents may be on the road to elimination tomorrow, due to a global dive in prices; booming towns may bust, as purchasing power declines in relation to exchange rates. Whatever the case, in this food regime, everyone, every relation, arguably even every operation, is precarious – that is, susceptible to contingencies that arise from the possibility of elimination from the market – which, in turn, exacerbates everyone's vulnerabilities so much so that

---

42   This is also why obesity and malnutrition are considered personal failures and not the
      failures of the food system, or for that matter, of the food regime.

the breakdown of their bodily order, harmony, constitution, and/or balance
is imminent.

As in the *codependent provisioning* food regime, then, *necroeconomics*
(Montag 2005) serves *necropolitics* (Mbembe 2003). That is, without having to
generate exceptions, the central authority eliminates the *enemy* populations
by making it difficult and/or impossible for them to engage in the productive
and reproductive labor necessary for subsistence. But unlike in *codependent
provisioning*, in the *urban food supply chain* food regime, everyone can become
an *enemy*, if they fail to compete effectively in the market. No one population –
by virtue of ethnicity, religious group or sect, class or gender – is permanently
sheltered, nor is there any arbitrariness to the designation: If they are unable
to compete, they become *enemies*. Yet, amidst currency fluctuations and global
interdependencies, the possibility is always there, lurking, that one will go
under, if not in this currency crisis, then definitely in the next one, and thus,
no longer have the support of the central authority; or fail to innovate and/or
invest and as such, become unable to draw from the pool of resources the central authority allocates to competitive market actors; or not have a sufficiently
high purchasing power so as to access what the provisioning apparatus has to
offer, and as a result, slowly but surely starve...

Necropolitics thus becomes the only form of politics available to the political community. As precarity becomes the new norm, hunger, scarcity and/or
malnutrition – through either the fist of the central authority or the invisible
hand of the market – are regularized, and death remains as a yet unactualized
potential. Worse still, the members have no recourse to contest this set-up nor
to resist it. Resisting implies challenging the hegemony of the market and the
profit motive and as such, draws the unwanted attention of the central authority. Whatever practices, relations, and networks that attempt to confront the
food regime, must make do with challenging the food system; and even then,
they cannot – they are not allowed to – expand and develop unless they are
integrated somehow into the market or they somehow integrate the profit
motive into their relations of production. As such, most alternatives remain
within the comfort zone of the food regime, confined to familiar discussions of
ethical consumerism[43] and/or "neoliberal sustainabilities" (Goodman, DuPuis,
and Goodman 2012, 235).

Finally, and I think most importantly, in the *urban food supply chain* food
regime, the protection-obedience relation between the political community

---

43   See, for example, Besky's critique of Fair Trade (2015) and Pilcher's critique of the Slow
      Food movement (2008).

and the central authority remains intact. Roles, however, are changed: Now, the market singlehandedly delivers what the members of the political community need in order to subsist and thus enables them to exercise their right to subsistence. It is the responsibility of the members to take advantage of what the market has to offer and as such, to exercise their right to subsistence. The central authority contributes, by eliminating the non-competitive market agents and making sure that the market remains functional. As such, the members are still protected, and the central authority can still demand their obedience. This is, then, a perfect union: While the central authority works to maintain the market (by "deliberate[ly] refraining or withdrawal from action – not simply the inertia of non-action, but a strategically conceived retreat, a leaving alone or an abandonment" (Hill and Montag 2015, 263–264)), the market works to maintain sovereign power by enabling the rights of the members of the political community to be exercised – even if, at the end of the day, the political community looks more like an aggregation of consumers with specific tastes and preferences; and their rights, including the right to subsistence, are reduced to commodities and services that merely need to be delivered.

6   The *Urban Food Supply Chain* Food Regime

This chapter focused on Istanbul's provisioning after the 1980s, when the country went through an extensive liberalization of its capital and commodities markets. Change started with the 24 January Decisions and the military coup, continued with increasing privatization and financialization in the 1990s, and then with internationalization in almost all sectors of the economy, including agriculture, manufacturing and finance in the 2000s. Within this 30-year period, consumption – like production – also changed: Following trade liberalizations, Istanbulites began to access imported goods more easily. The mushrooming of new spaces of recreation and entertainment spaces, in-flow of new trends, as well as new classes of immigrants, led to a diversification of consumption patterns and preferences. While upper and upper middle class residents adhered to global trends, working class and lower middle class Istanbulites enjoyed a revival of regional cultures, practices, and products. Yet, the unpegging of the currency often ate away at purchasing powers, and in conjunction, the city's recreational and entertainment spaces began to segregate more strictly along class lines.

The provisioning apparatus also changed rapidly. Urban transformation and expansion led to the disappearance of the city's historic gardens, orchards, and fields, and in parallel, traditional neighborhood retailers (*bakkal*s and *manav*s).

While Istanbulites continue to frequent the bazaars, the multinationals entering the grocery retail sector in the 1990s expanded rapidly and aggressively. Domestic retailers responded by bringing in more region-specific goods to their chains and diversifying their prices, products, and services across class lines. These transformations also fueled (and were fueled by) structural transformations in agriculture. Although the number of farmers who abandoned farming increased drastically, overall, the rural-to-urban migration slowed down by the 2000s (after a continuous increase into the 1990s). The removal of agricultural subsidies, cheap insurance for farmers, and dissolution of farmers' cooperatives, exposed farmers to the waxing and waning of the global market. To achieve some stability, more farmers began to engage in contract farming – which, in turn, helped both domestic and multinational supermarkets to consolidate their supply lines and become more competitive.

In addition, the provisioning apparatus has become increasingly global. Some of the provisioning actors who now feed the city are literally halfway across the planet, and others who may seem local (that is, territorially located in the country), might have foreign capital to fund them or foreign laborers working for them, or use inputs imported from elsewhere to grow the 'local produce' sold in the city's supermarkets and the bazaars. Indeed, from the rennet to ferment the cheese to the hay to feed the cattle, Turkey imports a diverse array of agricultural products and inputs; and, as such, it is increasingly dependent on the rest of the world to feed itself. And this is not unique in any way. Such dependencies have sprung up all across the world, so much so that following things from their locations of consumption to production (or vice-versa) has become a productive method of scholarly analysis for mapping out global connections, and understanding how global capital penetrates into local relations of production (and consumption) (Cook and Harrison 2007; Cook et al. 2004; 2006; Benson and Fischer 2007; Kaplan 2007).

Whether this dependency is 'good' is a different question and an ongoing discussion. Proponents of globalization point out that globalization is not dependency; it is rather interdependency: Turkey is dependent on others for its food and agriculture needs, and others are dependent on Turkey. As such, it is neither bad for the country nor it is a weakness – and if it is, then it downgrades everyone. Plus, proponents suggest, globalization has brought in different flavors, ingredients, cooking techniques, new meanings to food, and new rituals, practices, consumption habits and patterns that generate those new meanings. What used to be foreign – not just alien, but also unknown – today, is just 'new'. And it is 'new' only for so long. As in the case of kiwi, it can become familiar and domestic all too quickly. Thanks to globalization, we don't have to shirk with fear from the sight – or rather, the taste – of the unknown anymore.

Instead, we can get to know each other and perhaps gradually learn to enjoy each other's foods and foodways. In fact, such [inter]dependencies may even foster peace. Since everyone needs each other to feed themselves, no one can afford to fight.

Opponents, in contrast, highlight the fragility of the entire system. Globalization means that everything is tied to one another; so no matter how big or small a crisis is, or whether it is far away or right here next door, or in finance or manufacturing, it can have cataclysmic effects for everyone involved – not just the residents of a metropolitan center like Istanbul, but also the farmers who have to live with, say, the ecological consequences of conventional monoculture farming practices with which they supply those centers. Plus, thanks to globalization and the interdependency it fosters, no one now produces enough to sustain themselves. Indeed, populations stricken with hunger and scarcity, amidst political communities of abundance, have become all too common, as also cases of *en masse* hunger and scarcity – not only because food simply cannot make it into the country, but also because even if it does make it in, it may be too expensive for many to purchase. In other words, interdependency has made global both the successes (feeding large populations with diverse foodstuffs) as well as the failures (depriving large populations of clean, nutritious, and culturally appropriate foodstuffs) of the current food system. And if this is how peace is going to be fostered, then it will be a fragile peace, one in which many will be hungry and/or malnourished.

What defines the *urban food supply chain* food system and its provisioning apparatus is the primacy of the profit motive, more so than the system's global interdependencies. From farmers to retailers, each actor gets the food items to the next one without the coercion of an overseer (as was the case in the *urban food provisioning* food system I discussed in Chapter 2, for example) simply because they would like to make as much profit as possible. Profit is also the reason why such a disjointed and a fragile system works – albeit tenuously. Particularly in the fragmented supply lines, where there isn't much planning and actors are not consolidated across the nodes, food gets from one actor to another on time, in the right quantity and quality, only because by doing so, it acts as a commodity; and as a commodity, it enables the generation of capital. Once an actor has enough capital, they then work to eliminate competition and expand horizontally and vertically to consolidate their control over supply lines. More consolidation leads to more streamlined capital generation through the supply chain. For the city, however, this does not necessarily mean cheaper prices, more abundance or diversity, or for that matter, higher likelihood of access to food. In effect, the more consolidated the supply lines are, the higher the tendency for Type 2 failures, since the consolidated intermediaries will likely use whatever tools, mechanisms, and strategies they can to push the prices up.

This is a major change from the *urban food provisioning* food system: In this system, Type 1 failures were systemically more possible, and indeed, historically frequent (Karademir 2017). In the *urban food supply chain* food system, in contrast, Type 2 failures are much more common, and hunger and malnourishment are chronic conditions for particularly the lower-income sector and the marginalized. Moreover, in *urban food provisioning*, Type 1 failures usually involved all or most food items (though, surely, depending on the context, some items may be more available than others); whereas in the *urban food supply chain* food system, Type 2 failures are usually item- specific – certain populations may not have enough protein, for example, or they might be stuck in areas without access to FFVs (areas that are commonly known as food deserts, though the term is beginning to be contested (see Eplett 2016; Brones 2018; Byrne 2019). Finally, in *urban food provisioning*, Type 1 failures affect the entirety of the political community one way or another (though the poor may experience it much more fatally); whereas in the *urban food supply chain* food system, Type 2 failures remains contained to specific populations, to such an extent that sometimes, other populations within the same political community may be completely unaware of each other's experiences.

Yet the failure of the food system is different from the failure of the food regime. The *urban food supply chain* food system is set-up such that food is not withheld from any one or any specific region or population (unless, of course, by a clear act of international belligerence and/or foreign policy decision). If anything, by providing a diverse range of foods from across the world and almost all the time, the food system seems to make exercising the right to food more convenient for the subject-citizens. The condition, of course, is that they pay, and that they not rely on any authority, including the central authority, to intervene when/if they cannot. In other words, having the money to be able to pay for what the provisioning apparatus has to offer, at whatever price, is considered the subject-citizens' responsibility; the provisioning actors are neither coerced to sell at affordable prices, nor does the central authority have the right to coerce them to. Provisioning is a private business, transacted between members of the political community, without the interference of the central authority, to the extent possible. The central authority only has to guarantee that the market works smoothly and efficiently (for which it eliminates, directly and indirectly, those market agents who cannot compete), that the subject-citizens have market access (as both buyers and sellers), and that legal tools and mechanisms exist to arbitrate between market actors when necessary. Thus, if any member suffers from hunger, food scarcity and/

or malnutrition, it is not the failure of the provisioning actors, or of the food system, or of the central authority, but of the members themselves.

I would have loved to finish the chapter on an uplifting note; however, neither the 2010s, nor my current research on alternative food initiatives and provisioning networks in Istanbul have given me much reason to be hopeful. The *urban food supply chain* food system and food regime seem here to stay. Though there is resistance, and some are indeed trying to come up with alternatives, under the threat of (direct and indirect) violence from the central authority, they are barely making a dent in the food system. Worse still, is what seems to be our collective inability to imagine a different set-up between the political community and the central authority. The profit motive and the market-mediated provisioning apparatus have become so hegemonic that the central authority is expected to both shield them and eliminate alternatives that might challenge them in the future. Plus, market competitiveness has become the sole yardstick to measure whether one can (or, perhaps 'deserves to') access resources that the central authority now so 'frugally' (Foucault 2008, 28–29) governs. More than access, however, 'inaccess' is the key: By diverting resources away from those who are not competitive, the central authority eliminates these new *enemies*. Yet, the market remains unpredictable, which means precarity is now a given pretty much for everyone. Indeed, just like having a job does not mean having enough purchasing power to feed oneself, abundance today does not guarantee abundance tomorrow.

What hope amidst such despair?

CHAPTER 6

Diverging Paths

With a vague collusion between supply and demand, *seduction becomes nothing more than an exchange value*, serving the circulation of exchanges and the lubrication of social relations.

JEAN BAUDRILLARD[1]

∴

Coffee is a drink that Istanbulites have been familiar with for at least 2 centuries. Not only is there a specific – local – way of making coffee (I don't want to say Turkish, because every people in the region claim it as their own), but there are traditions interlocked with it[2]. Tea, in contrast, is relatively new. In the climate of tight currency controls in the 1940s, the government spurred farmers to grow it in the suitable microclimate along the Black Sea coast. It then helped increase tea consumption by opening a processing facility that bought it in bulk and sold it cheap to urban and rural consumers alike. If tea is considered a national drink today, it is because of consistent government efforts since then.

Coffee, however, is making a comeback – not in its local variety, but as an imported and highly globalized item from the Global North (though it is still produced in the Global South and has a much longer history there). If there are any clear beginnings to such comeback stories, this one's in the early 2000s, with Starbucks gently creeping into the hot beverages sector in Turkey via one of the many malls mushrooming in Istanbul at the time. Slowly but steadily, Starbucks got a foothold and today, it has more than 480 branches across the country – second only to the UK in Europe (Çavuşoğlu 2018). With a cup of regular filter coffee priced at more than 10 TL (at the time of writing), it is a taste only the well-off can afford. A regular cup of Turkish tea, meanwhile, is

---

1   Baudrillard, Jean. 1990. *Seduction*. Brian Singer (trans.) New York, NY: St. Martin's Press, 176; emphasis in the original.

2   For example, the first meeting of the parents before a marriage cannot be without coffee. My Grandma remembers that even during the "Great War", when coffee was in very short supply, people used to mix roasted chickpea flour with chicory and serve it as coffee to make sure that the pre-marriage rituals were properly completed.

50 kuruş (0.5 Lira) – not only much more affordable, but also much easier to find. It is, in fact, offered for free, with as many refills as one can drink, during visits to friends and relatives or while one waits for their appointment at a doctor's waiting room, pops into a neighborhood store for a quick, last minute purchase, or is about to ask for the check just after finishing off a meal at a restaurant.

Yet, with new Starbucks branches and now third-wave coffee shops sprouting up all across the city, coffee – not tea – seems to be the beverage of the future. Today, it is not surprising to see people sipping their coffees as they run from the bus to the subway, sporting expensive thermoses or single-use cups. Multinational as well as local coffee chains and third-wave coffee shops can be found in more university campuses today than 20 or 10 years ago. Even in sleepy little Anatolian towns, new branches are opening up and unlike the traditional coffeeshops of old, where primarily men hung out and socialized, women and men, old and young, are now enjoying their cups of coffee together. As such, it isn't surprising that conservatives condemn the 'café culture' severely, claiming that they are destroying the 'local' culture, transgressing the violently policed boundaries of gendered spaces and, making 'us' dependent on the multinational 'others'. Progressives, in contrast, laud the new cafes, endorsing their inclusiveness and courage to change the 'old' for the 'new' and for chipping away at the regressive gender norms and traditional *lifeworlds*.

As I mentioned in the previous chapter, the 2000s witnessed the transformation of consumer preferences, with the penetration of global trends into local consumer cultures, in conjunction with the liberalization of commodities markets across the globe. As such, neither the comeback nor the discussions over it are unique to coffee or to Turkey. What is unique is the ways in which this penetration has gotten entangled with local identity politics – class in particular – and, as Tulasi Srinivas puts it, "how the relations among people are shaped by relations between people and things" (Srinivas 2008, 355). In the case at hand, the coffee that Starbucks and other multinational coffee retailers brought to Istanbul – supposedly – is not the coffee that Istanbulites had drunk, were drinking, and are drinking. It is something else: more the cup showing off the brand than the coffee, more on-the-go and fast than slow and ritualistic, more milky, chocolaty, at times rainbow-y than simple and dark, or in short, a simulation of the 4th order really ... (Wolters 2014). More importantly, the coffee that has been here seems to have never left. Even as wars and then the import restrictions of the ISI were devastating the supply lines, Istanbulites held on to their coffee. Its consumption remained a significant component of the city's cosmopolitan culture even as the city's demographics got a major do-over. In other words, there was no going out of fashion to require a comeback.

This chapter picks up where I left off in Chapter 5, starting with a discussion of the transformations in Istanbul's provisioning apparatus in the 2010s, where through various mechanisms and strategies, certain provisioning actors have increasingly come to dominate the city's provisioning apparatus. The following section, 'The Future of Istanbul's Provisioning Apparatus', underlines the three fault lines this domination has unearthed within the provisioning apparatus: the effects of changes in the population; the continuing expansion of supermarkets and their increasing consolidation within the food supply chains; and the increasing prevalence of alternative food networks (AFN s) and other counter-movements that challenge both the expansion and the consolidation. The next section, 'The Promise of a Different Future', parses out this last fault line more and introduces some of the alternative food networks. The section also evaluates whether the alternatives are really alternatives and whether they can offer a different provisioning apparatus for the city in the future. The section after, 'Of the Sovereignty, Political Community and the Central Authority', focuses on the kind of relationship between the central authority and the (subject-)citizens imagined in the alternative food networks, taking the idea of 'food sovereignty' these networks espouse as its reference point. Finally, 'The Global and the Local' takes up the issue of generalizability, inquiring how common the transformations that have brought about the *urban food supply chain* food system and food regime are, as also the challenges and the resistances directed against them.

Before moving on, let me note a few details about my ongoing research project on which I rely for the discussions in the sections, 'The Future of Istanbul's Provisioning Apparatus', 'The Promise of a Different Future' and 'Of the Sovereignty, Political Community and the Central Authority'. The aim of this project is, primarily, to understand the criticisms and concerns the alternative food networks raise against the conventional urban food supply chain, and second, to assess whether they are able to transform consumption and production practices, market mechanisms, and discourses around urban provisioning. To do so, along with some very capable research assistants, I began to contact various organizations in and around the city that describe themselves as AFN s and conducted semi-structured interviews with their representatives/ members. Though I tried to uncover how the representatives/members define what AFN s are (as in, what they think to be the constitutive characteristics of AFN s), my focus was more on the priorities of each specific organization, and as such, how each organization saw itself, its operational principles, and practices to be challenging the conventional provisioning agents. In my early research cluster, most of these organizations were consumer cooperatives; and my research assistants followed up on the topics and points that came up during the interviews by joining in on their members' meetings and listening in on the discussions there. I then expanded my research cluster to local small farmers (as in, those operating within the administrative limits of the city), who were not working with these consumer cooperatives, but were selling their produce at the farmers' markets. I wanted to understand how – or if – the farmers' markets were AFN s, particularly from the farmers' point of view, and assess whether they could be a feasible alternative to the food supply chains of the conventional provisioning agents. During the interviews, however, I noticed that there were also quite a few farmers (the remaining vast majority, to be fair), who were outside of all of these AFN discussions and who were surprisingly unorganized (in that, they were neither members of, nor wanted to be members of, a farmers' cooperative, nor did they want to work with consumers' cooperatives). Wanting to understand how these small farmers and their concerns as farmers were similar to or different from the previous interviewees', I expanded my interview cluster yet again. This meant interviewing small farmers who farmed not only conventionally, but also operated greenhouses and sold their produce directly to the shops at the wholesale ports. At the time of writing, the fieldwork is ongoing (the COVID-19 pandemic, notwithstanding). So far, we have conducted 23 interviews in total, using primarily snowball sampling. Though the focus remains on the first two clusters, I have also gained valuable insights from farmers in the third cluster. Indeed, tensions between different groups of farmers who use different production techniques and sales venues, for example, and practical and political differences between consumer and producer cooperatives, which I will discuss below, are the preliminary findings of this research.

1   The 2010s: From Consolidation to Domination

By the end of the 2000s, most in-city locations of production had disappeared, taking with them some of the traditional sites of food exchange – like *bakkal*s and *manav*s. Bazaars, although still preferred sites of food exchange, were losing their market share to domestic and multinational grocery retailers (Öz and Eder 2012). In some neighborhoods, bazaars had resisted the competition coming from the domestic and multinational supermarkets, by bringing in more regional products, and fine-tuning their product quality, range, and prices to their customer demographic. However, the fragmented supply chain of the bazaars and the high profit margins intermediaries attached to the products, decreased the bazaars' competitive advantage (Bignebat, Koç, and Lemeilleur 2009, Öz and Eder 2012). Plus, vendors were notoriously difficult to organize. For example, two professional associations of the bazaar vendors, *Istanbul Umum Pazarcılar Esnaf Odası* (Istanbul Bazaar Vendors Association) and *Anadolu Yakası Pazarcılar ve Seyyar Esnaf Odası* (Anatolian Side Bazaar Vendors and Mobile Vendors Association) functioned more as permit boards[3] rather than non-governmental advocacy organizations that could organize collective action or lobby for pro-bazaar urban planning laws, zoning regulations, and public health policies. In bazaars, fights were relatively common and often brutal, to the extent that they damaged bazaars' reputation as functional sites of food retail. While infringements on each other's vending space was a common cause for fights, ethnic differences between the vendors also contributed to the tensions – thus further inhibiting their collective action capabilities. In contrast, both domestic and multinational supermarkets, which had entered the grocery retail sector in the 1990s, kept on expanding into more cities and towns across Turkey, increased their market share, and diversified their products to cater to different customer segments (Atasoy 2013; Franz, Appel, and Hassler 2013). Nonetheless, the fragmented state of their supply lines also affected them (particularly the domestic ones), hindering their growth, and reducing their capability to respond to price, quality, and demand fluctuations (interview with Migros 2015, interview with Metro Cash & Carry 2015). Unlike bazaars, however, both domestic and multinational supermarkets had the financial and technological capital to develop various practices, mechanisms, and networks, either to decrease the fragmentation of their supply lines or to contain the effects of fragmentation.

To reiterate, by a fragmented supply line, I mean multiple producers, intermediaries, and sellers (either in retail or in wholesale) working not always in tandem with each other. As my informants at the *Hal* put it,

> in the old system, intermediaries would buy from multiple small to mid-size farmers, compile and mix the produce at their 'home city' Ports, add their markup, and then truck it over to their partners in the Istanbul Ports. In Istanbul, the partners would register the produce, add their markup, and then sell to the retailers. Sometimes, even truckers would act as intermediaries and add a markup. By the time produce reached the final consumers, prices would be significantly inflated. And there was no way of

3   To operate in bazaars, vendors need permits stating that they are certified (legally recognized) vendors and are assigned specific places in the bazaar. A vendor requires this certificate, which costs a hefty sum, for each bazaar he operates in.

FIGURE 24   One of many Migros branches in Kadiköy today
PHOTO BY ALPEREN BUĞRA YILMAZ

auditing the intermediaries. They would add crazy markups, not declare
the right amount [of produce they have in their shops] and do anything
to not pay taxes. We had very little capacity [to audit their activities]
(interview with the Directorate of Bayrampaşa Wholesale Port 2015).

In other words, the intermediaries would dictate a maximum price to the farmers; and the retailers would dictate another maximum price to the consumers.
Whatever lay in between, minus the costs of transportation, processing (which
may involve cleaning, sorting, and packing) and taxes, would be the profits for
the intermediaries and the retailers – who, as I have discussed in the previous
chapter, are increasingly the same provisioning agents. As such, an increase in
the profits of the intermediaries often implied a clear transfer of capital and
resources away from the rural economy (agriculture) to the urban economy
(trade), thus hurting farmers and consumers alike.

Supermarkets had entered the provisioning network as retailers; and until
they could get their own supply lines going, they had to rely on similarly fragmented supply lines. As such, like bazaar vendors and *manav*s, they were
adversely affected by the intermediaries' markups. Thus their first intervention into the provisioning apparatus was to set up their own shops in various ports across the country. They were then able to control markups and

appropriate more profit across the chain. Second, they began to more actively invest in and use cold storage and transportation technologies. These technologies decreased transportation time (though they certainly increased the costs) and enabled produce to last longer and look fresher when it arrived at the stores. Moreover, cold storage and transportation technologies inadvertently pushed the supermarkets to alter their storage practices. Because 'cold chain' is costlier to maintain, it requires the supermarkets to store as few days' worth of produce as possible and "to keep things moving as quickly as possible across the chain" (interview with Metro Cash & Carry 2015). Third, then, the supermarkets intervened in the provisioning apparatus by changing transportation logistics and introducing a "quick response [to demand] – no storage model" (interview with Migros 2015) into retail practices.

Finally, the supermarkets adopted contract farming into their operations. Large farmers had already shifted to contract farming following the Decisions; but they were mainly producing for export. After supermarkets integrated contract farming into their operations, it became quite a common practice among commercial producers of all sizes. In this practice, farmers would make deals with a specific intermediary before the planting season, to sell their produce in toto at a set price after the harvest. The farmer would guarantee an agreed-upon quality and quantity; and the intermediaries would provide capital for inputs, and purchase and price guarantees for the produce. As such, contract farming would work as a credit source for the farmer, with the added benefit of a sales guarantee and no interest payment. The farmer would fall at a disadvantage, however, when/if the global prices for the commodity they are producing rose higher than the contract price; and/or when/if produce would not fit the agreed quality and quantity. Still, as Keyder and Yenal clearly document, many farmers are stifled by the volatility of the global market, a lack of adequate cheap credit sources and/or purchasing guarantees, and internationally imposed standards (which are drawn and adopted without their involvement). For these farmers, contract farming is indeed a relief, since it offers some sort of price stability and purchase guarantee (Keyder and Yenal 2014a). For the supermarkets, in turn, contract farming provides a sure source of produce, at quality and prices they determine and reinforce. Moreover, through clauses that give supermarkets the capability to determine delivery dates, contract farming enables supermarkets to optimize storage and transportation costs (interview with Migros 2015).

Contract farming came on the heels of two other important changes: First, the implementation of electronic registration and recordkeeping systems for farmers, and more importantly, for intermediaries at the Ports. While the *Çiftçi Kayıt Sistemi* (Farmer Registration System) aims to "audit production capacity of the country more accurately and to enforce taxation", according to my informants, the *Hal Kayıt Sistemi* (Ports Registration System) aims to audit sales and purchases, to enforce taxes, to assess markups and prices, and to supervise the city's provisioning apparatus so as "to be able to quickly intervene at times of crisis" (interview with the Directorate of Bayrampaşa Wholesale Port 2015). Composed of standardized barcodes to track produce, automated scales for incoming and outgoing trucks, and an online identification system for buyers and sellers, the Ports Registration System is designed to record every transaction that happens at the wholesale ports (ibid.). Through the system, consumers can access online records of each registered shop in the ports as well as the daily suggested base and ceiling prices of each imported and domestically produced item (ibid.). Furthermore, the central authority is planning to connect the Farmer Registration System and the Ports Registration System which would enable customers, producers, and the central authority itself to track each item of produce from its location of production to consumption (ibid.).

The second important change pertained to subsidies provided to farmers, specifically the adoption of *Doğrudan Gelir Desteği* (Direct Income Subsidy; DIS). As I mentioned in Chapter 5, the 24 January Decisions had significantly cut – if not eliminated altogether – input subsidies for farmers, and initiated the privatization of what used to be public sources of credit and insurance, in addition to many other public institutions that made bulk purchases, processed agricultural commodities, and offered set prices. Among these public sources, farmers' cooperatives were the most effective ones since they tended to be organized locally and responded quickly and directly to farmers' needs (Aydın 2010). With their conversion to private enterprises, and subsequently, the removal of any state support from them, these cooperatives became defunct in the early 2000s (ibid.); and farmers were left to deal with global price fluctuations, increasing concentration and internationalization of intermediaries, and frequent economic crises caused by financialization on their own. Indeed, between 1999 and 2002, the agricultural sector experienced a 16% income loss, of which 80% was due to the elimination of subsidies (Keyder 2014, 202). Yet, by the 2000s, farmers still made up 35% of the workforce, and the agricultural sectors continued to generate 13% of the gross domestic income (Pamuk 2012, 215). Moreover, rural constituents were decisive for general elections; and as such, none of the political parties and governments could afford to alienate them (Keyder 2014, 197). Thus, governments kept making promises to the WB and the IMF for structural adjustment reforms and nominating the WB- and the IMF-approved officials for budgetary supervisory positions. They have even adopted the WB's Agricultural Reform Implementation Project (ARIP) and approved the Uruguay Round of the GATT (Keyder 2014; Öztürk 2012;

Aydın 2010). At the same time, they were quite slow to implement the reforms. Following the 2002 general elections and the 2004 municipal elections, purchase guarantees and input subsidies even made a comeback (Keyder 2014, 202–203). Plus, some of the debts and interest payments of farmers were forgiven (ibid.).

DIS was adopted as a mechanism to support farmers in this context and as such, it contained opposing tendencies and intentions in itself: On the one hand, it "was intended to 'cushion the blow' felt by farmers due to the withdrawal of other supports, to 'compensate for the drop in intervention prices'" (Öztürk 2012, 96). On the other hand, it did not aim to resist, reverse, or combat de-agrarianization and/or rising rural poverty (Bağımsız Sosyal Bilimciler 2007, 114). Because it was based on land ownership, DIS encouraged small and mid-size farmers to quit cultivation and thus, contributed to an ongoing trend of de-agrarianization (Öztürk 2012, 96–99; Oyan 2015, 121–125; Bağımsız Sosyal Bilimciler 2007, 114–118). Similarly, DIS has not been enough to help farmers to make profit or to accumulate capital, as farmers used the DIS payments primarily to pay off their debts or the interest on their loans (Öztürk 2012, 96–99). At the same time, none of these 'failures' were necessarily unexpected, since the WB and the IMF reforms intended to lower "the number of people directly dependent on agriculture (...) [and to reduce] the number of smallholdings" (ibid, 74) anyway.

More noteworthy perhaps, "the number of people directly dependent on agriculture" (Öztürk 2012, 96–99) that the WB and the IMF aimed to reduce were primarily small farmers, who were also disproportionally FFV cultivators (Öztürk 2012, 84; Oyan 2015, 123). As such, the DIS had a direct effect on the FFV sector and Istanbul's FFV provisioning. Most fundamentally, by reducing the number of small farmers, the DIS contributed to the lessening of the fragmentation of the supply lines and helped achieve greater vertical integration along the supply chain (Keyder and Yenal 2014a, 62). That is, once the small FFV producers were out of the way, intermediaries who had enough capital expanded into the production node by way of contract farming. They lent money to large producers by way of contracts, and thus, consolidated their supply lines from production to retail. Indeed, as my informants pointed out, even further consolidation was underway: intermediaries were now preferring to work with land-owning companies that employed seasonal laborers or local farmers to work the land, rather than work directly with land-owning farmers who lived on or near their lands (interview with Board of Agricultural Engineers Istanbul 2015). They could thus reduce their costs further, but more importantly, either through working with a company that owns land, or through corporatizing their land ownership, the intermediaries could expand into production. Thus, as owners of one of the fundamental means of production in agriculture – land – they could concentrate even more capital.[4]

Meanwhile, both FFV exports and domestic demand for FFVs increased substantially throughout the 2000s and the 2010s. Yet, rather than open more land to cultivation, farmers worked to get better yields out of the lands they were already cultivating. This implied not only an increase in agricultural labor productivity, but also, once again, a concentration of capital – in the form, specifically, of higher yielding seeds, more biochemical inputs (pesticides, fertilizers, etc.), and more efficient technology. However, not everyone could move from a model of extensive agriculture to intensive agriculture; and those who couldn't, had very few options: They could either stop cultivating, sell the land, and look for other sources of income – in other words, move out of agriculture; or, by sticking to the extensive agriculture model, open up more land for cultivation and try to increase their yields through more labor (yet, less labor productivity – which would also slow down their capital accumulation); or, diversify their produce range and even take up commercial husbandry (interview with Board of Agricultural Engineers Istanbul 2015; Keyder and Yenal 2014d). Alternatively, they could supplement their income from farming by taking up other jobs; or even work on someone else's field while continuing to cultivate their own (Keyder and Yenal 2014d). Indeed, in the 2000s and the early 2010s, it was possible to see all of these alternatives being deployed by small- to mid-scale farmers, who could not transition to intensive farming (interview with Board of Agricultural Engineers Istanbul 2015). Some quit and moved to the cities; others went into laboring elsewhere – either on a different farm, or in a different sector all together, to supplement their incomes, and others switched to what they thought were niche produce (stevia, tarragon, arugula, cilantro, ginger, etc.) and/or value-added, processed products (vinegar, vegetable pastes and dried fruit snacks, honey and pollen products, etc.).

In addition to the mechanisms and technologies like the registration systems, DIS, and contract farming, these structural transformations in agriculture have thus led Turkey to become completely interdependent on the global market for provisioning (Köymen 1999, 28). The need to import food arose not only because population growth outpaced agricultural productivity (even as more farmers shifted to intensive agriculture), but also because market mechanisms – with which farming was now thoroughly integrated – pushed some out while enabling others to accumulate more capital and expand their

---

4   Note that the literature on store brands, and their effects on supply chains and retail from all around the world, highlights similar conclusions and observations (see, for example Gönenç and Rehber 2007; Yenal 2014; Barrett et al. 1999; Burch and Goss 1999).

production. As a result, supply lines consolidated even further, such that a single company, along with its subsidiaries, might be producing, processing (sorting and cleaning), transporting, and selling the produce, both as a wholesaler and a retailer. In tandem, rural and urban living spaces became resources that needed to be utilized in the most cost-effective and profit-driven manner possible. For example, with a decree in 2012, all the villages remaining on the peripheries of metropolitan cities were converted to neighborhoods, thus increasing the market pressures on the peripheral farmers to sell their lands[5]. Meanwhile, with more efficient infrastructural connections between rural and urban areas, rural populations were expected to cushion crises in the urban economy, absorb effects of urban unemployment, and supply an army of (semi-proletarianized) laborers when needed, as they tried to supplement their incomes from farming and agriculture. Equally importantly, the rural and urban populations began to be considered solely as customers. However, unlike the urban populations whose diversity in consumption preferences and habits were at least taken into account in provisioning (due, no doubt, to their higher purchasing power), rural populations were assumed to be a homogenous group with no specific preferences – until, at least, the supermarkets, particularly the hard discount supermarkets (A101, BIM, and Şok), began to expand into the countryside.

2   The Future of Istanbul's Provisioning Apparatus

Going forward, three fault lines will be pivotal in shaping Istanbul's provisioning apparatus: Changes in population and demographics; continuing expansion of the supermarkets within the grocery retail sector and increasing consolidation among the intermediaries; and finally, the increasing prevalence of alternative food networks and other counter-movements that aim to halt supermarkets' expansion, prevent consolidation, and shorten the supply chain. Exactly how these fault lines are going to shape the provisioning apparatus remains open; there are, however, certain trajectories worth pointing out.

    In terms of changes in population and demographics, the most important factor has been the rural push – urban pull dynamic. As I discussed in chapters 4 and 5, it has given rise to a consistent population increase in Istanbul since the early 1950s. Beginning in the 1990s, however, with the slowing down of growth

---

5   28489 On Dört İlde Büyükşehir Belediyesi ve Yirmi Yedi İlçe Kurulması ile Bazı Kanun ve Kanun Hükmünde Kararnamelerde Değişiklik Yapılmasına Dair Kanun (2012, 12 06). Ankara: Resmi Gazete.

in manufacturing, and a shift towards services in the urban economy, this factor gradually became less effective (Keyder and Yenal 2014c, 184–187, Keyder 2014, 210–214). By the 2000s, the dynamic itself was changing in the opposite direction (urban push – rural pull) as the markets for high-value-added, niche agricultural commodities were expanding and thus, drawing wealthy urbanites to invest in farms and farming. In the 2010s, it had become possible to identify these new agricultural investors, who I call 'neo-peasants', in various rural localities across Turkey. Their numbers remain small; however, their success stories strike a chord with many. As one of my informants put it,

> when I was young, everyone's dream was to quit their jobs and to open a small, cozy café somewhere. Today, the dream is different. People are tired of [Istanbul]'s chaos. They want to leave the city and set up a farm. They dream of the simple, modest peasant life, in sync with nature.

Whether this shift is just the latest lifestyle fad, sure to go away in a decade, or a sign of a fundamental, bottom-up transformation in the agrarian structure, is yet unclear. Plus, as I will discuss in the following section, it contains major fault lines in itself that are quite hard to reconcile with each other (most notably, between its for-profit orientation and its counter-culture orientation). As such, at least for now, it is difficult to see how the 'neo-peasant' trajectory is going to shape the future of the city's provisioning apparatus.

Note that in the 1990s, population increase did not stop or slow down; rather, the rural push – urban pull dynamic was supplemented by the migration of displaced populations from the east and the southeast regions of the country, as well as the immigration of global, managerial, and white-collar working classes into the city (Keyder 2010, Keyder and Öncü 1993). Going forward, the latter trend is not expected to continue. In fact, immigration patterns have already shifted (Yükseker 2004; Erder 2010). Today, Turkey gets its immigrants from the former Soviet Republics in Eastern Europe and Central Asia, as well as others sharing a border, like Syria, Iraq, Azerbaijan, Georgia, and Armenia. The Syrian conflict has obviously contributed to new migration patterns, but it has been neither the dominating event nor the dominating factor. This becomes clear when one traces the changes in the demographics of agricultural and farm labor. As one of the farmers on the peripheries of the city, producing salad greens destined for Istanbul's bazaar, remarked, "Afghans and Uzbeks are doing the farm labor" that involves value-adding processing, whereas "the Syrians do the seasonal, basic harvest and planting work for the large landowners in the east and the southeast". Moreover, because of the kind of work they do, Afghans and Uzbeks tend to stay in the farms and blend in with the community; Syrians, in contrast, "are looking to leave as quickly as possible". As a result, non-Syrian workers have earned a good reputation among agricultural employers. Not only are they preferred by the farmer-employers, they are also provided with better (even if only incrementally) work conditions and wages compared to the Syrians. It is, again, unclear how this trend is going to continue; but it is clear that in the long run, farm labor is going to be supplied by immigrants – whether that will be legal or illegal, formal or informal, remains to be seen.

For the provisioning apparatus, both transformations signal towards the need to diversify, for increasingly cosmopolitan urban and rural demographics. Customer segmentation is also expected to increase in the foreseeable future. In other words, urban and rural populations are going to become more diverse, not only in terms of consumer habits and preferences, but also purchasing power and consumption patterns. Unlike before, when the rural populations were assumed to be non-segmented homogeneous blocks, with immigrants increasingly going into farm labor on the one hand and with wealthy urbanites transforming themselves into 'neo-peasants' on the other, the provisioning apparatus will have to respond to a lot more segmented diversity.

The second fault line is the supermarkets' expansion within the grocery retail sector and increasing consolidation among the intermediaries. Although I am pointing out two different tendencies here – expansion (that is, supermarkets outcompeting other provisioning actors within the retail node, most notably the bazaars) and consolidation (that is, intermediaries merging vertically throughout the supply chain), the two are actually converging. That is, among all the intermediaries in the provisioning apparatus (traders, shop owners in the *Hal*, bazaar vendors, supermarkets, greengrocers, etc.), the supermarkets are the ones expanding both vertically and horizontally, either outcompeting every other provisioning agent or acquiring and merging with them. As I mentioned in the previous section and in Chapter 5, in the post-Decisions era, a tendency toward consolidation had already manifested among the intermediaries, so much so that particularly after the 2000s, a single company with its subsidiaries could be provisioning the residents literally from farm to table. During the 2010s, it became blatantly clear that such companies were increasingly one of a handful of domestic and multinational grocery retailers. Transferring the wealth, expertise, and connections they generated from the grocery retailing sector to farming, logistics, and even to food processing, they have come to bottleneck and dominate the provisioning apparatus. Equally importantly, they have been hugely successful in preventing any sort of law and regulation to be passed that would affect them adversely. Regardless of consumers' rights associations, protests, or pro-competition laws and regulations, the oligopolistic tendencies of the grocery retailers (Koç, Boluk, and Kovacı 2009; Franz, Appel, and Hassler 2013; Yenal 2014) could not be curtailed. Indeed, the vertical and horizontal expansion of the supermarkets is expected to continue. Within the next 15 to 20 years, bazaars are expected to lose their market share almost completely and the provisioning apparatus is expected to be fully dominated by the supermarkets.

Istanbulites, however, are not surrendering without a fight. The third fault line, the increasing prevalence of alternative food networks and other counter-movements that aim to halt supermarkets' expansion, hinder consolidation, and shorten the supply chain, is there to prove it. When I say counter-movements, I have in mind both the more-organized, globally-connected, and well-publicized movements, like Slow Food and La Via Campesina, and the more fragmented, local movements, like *Bombalar Değil Sofralar* (Food, Not Bombs), *BÜKOOP* (Bosporus University Cooperative), *Buğday Ekolojik Yaşam Destekleme Derneği* (Wheat: Association to Support Ecological Living), and *Yeryüzü Derneği* (The Earth Association). While some of these organizations have been around in one form or another since the late 1970s, others were started in the 1990s and the 2000s, when intensive agriculture, expansion of the supermarkets, and consolidation of the supply lines, were increasingly visible. On a personal level, almost all of my informants involved with these counter-movements have stressed that these were also the decades when the flavors of FFVs were becoming blander and standardized, when local varieties were disappearing, and most importantly, the humanitarian and ecological consequences of the so-called Green Revolution and export-oriented growth were visibly acute. At stake, according to my informants, is "socio-ecological justice" and the health and the prosperity of future generations.

Through these associations, consumer cooperatives, and other organizations, concerned Istanbulites lobby for better practices in agriculture, reach out to inform and educate the public on nutrition, organic farming, and sustainable provisioning, and most importantly, organize alternative food networks (AFNs) and farmers' markets to provision the city. These networks and markets primarily aim to shorten the supply chain and lessen the carbon footprint of FFVs consumed in the city. Secondarily, they aim to raise awareness and emphasize direct action; and, at the time of writing, they seem to be quite successful: Today, the number of Istanbulites joining or starting such organizations and consumer cooperatives is increasing; there is more emphasis on nutrition, sustainable farming, and organic agriculture in the public discourse; and I think most importantly, more people today are thinking and talking about themselves as both consumers and producers, or in the AFN-lingo, *türetici* (*tüketici-üretici*; producer-consumer).

FIGURE 25   Interior of a consumer cooperative. Though some sell FFVs, most goods tend to
             be packaged, bottled, and/or canned
             PHOTO BY ELIF BIRBIRI

It is highly likely that the AFNs and *türeticis* will play a more central role in shaping the city's provisioning apparatus. In fact, they are already doing their part: Supermarkets (domestic and multinational), noticing the appeal of the AFNs, have begun to draw up ecologically-conscious 'best practices' and integrate them into their supply chains. Plus, they have started to carry organic and local produce regularly in their stores. Going forward, they expect consumer demand for ethically-sourced produce and 'eco-conscious' agricultural goods (including textiles, canned, frozen, and processed foods) to increase. As such, albeit slowly, they are emphasizing sustainable production methods and resource use in their supply chains.

Activists from the counter-movements, however, emphasize that there can be neither socio-economic nor ecological justice in the supermarkets' supply chain model. Even if 'best practices' are drawn and ethical sourcing and eco-conscious production methods are adopted, "there could be no social justice because the whole system is based on workers', (im)migrants', women's exploitation" (interview with BÜKOOP 2015). For socio-economic and ecological justice, "it is necessary to talk about a 'network' than a 'supply chain', where the [consumers] know the farmers and the farmers know the [consumers]" (ibid.). Plus, it is essential that the profit motive is removed and the " 'people'

FIGURE 26   Carefully-labeled products from selected producers at one of Istanbul's many
            consumer cooperatives
            PHOTO BY ALPEREN BUĞRA YILMAZ

and 'feeding the people' are brought back into the focus of the provisioning"
(interview with Yeryüzü Derneği 2015). In other words, "there could be no justice unless [social, economic, political, ecological] exploitation is removed,"
(interview with Buğday Derneği 2015); and that, according to the activists, is
clearly not in the interest of supermarkets (interview with BÜKOOP 2015).

   Again, it remains to be seen how long the push that the counter-movements
and the AFNs have generated is going to last and how effective it will be in
changing the supply chain model. In any case, the criticisms the activists are
directing towards the supermarkets are gaining further traction in the public
discourse and the call for direct action seems to be paying off – in perhaps
unexpected ways. Most notably, the in-city locations of production – *bostan*s
(fields), *bağ*s (vineyards, orchards), and *bahçe*s (gardens) – that disappeared,
are coming back. While some of the concerned Istanbulites are organizing to
protect the very few remaining *bostan*s in the city, others are starting up new
ones. Time will tell how effective these organizations and actions will be in
reintroducing local production into the city's provisioning apparatus.

   Meanwhile, investors with an eye for social entrepreneurship are already
procuring competitive, 'sustainable' alternatives to the short supply chains
(for example, *TazeDirekt* and *İpek Hanımın Çiftliği*). They advertise and sell

FIGURE 27   Carefully-labeled products from selected producers at one of Istanbul's many
consumer cooperatives
PHOTO BY ALPEREN BUĞRA YILMAZ

primarily online; some are quite exclusive, working only with members
recruited on a referral basis via WhatsApp chat groups. As such, their clientele
remains limited and are usually high-income. Their locations of production are
outside the city (some are quite far away); the produce they sell is sustainably
produced or certified organic; their processing, sorting, and packaging strictly
follow the food codex and their supply lines are subject to the regulations for
cold chain. If there are any items supplied from another farm, the parent com-
pany/farm makes sure that the quality of the produce is at par and the production practices are sustainable. The whole network thus works on the basis of
trust: The members trust that the production practices are sustainable, that
the produce is high-quality and organic; and the company/farm trusts that it
will be able to justify the costs of production and turn enough profits to keep
going. Again, time will tell how successful these 'eco-conscious farms' are as
businesses and business models. So far, however, their numbers are growing.
More interestingly, their customer reach, product quality and adherence to
organic certification, cold chain regulations, and sustainable production principles, in parallel with their prices, mirror the conventional supply chains that
they are supposed to be countering. Since no 'industry standard' is yet set for
these online AFN s, perhaps there will be more of this mirroring, if not on the

ground cooperation with conventional supply chains and provisioning agents, going ahead.

3   The Promise of a Different Future

In 2019, I started a new research project aiming to uncover the difficulties faced by farmers operating on the peripheries of Istanbul. I was curious to know what these farmers were doing to survive under market pressures and being in such close proximity to the most populous marketplace of the country, and whether it was easier for them to reach the city's residents. In conjunction, I was wondering how effective the farm-to-table idea was in practice. As I mentioned in the previous section, the number of AFN s (consumer cooperatives, online stores for organic company-farms, farmers' markets organized by concerned consumers and producers) have been increasing and more people are subscribing to AFN s. One of the fundamental aims of these AFN s is to shorten the food supply chain by first, directly linking the consumers and the producers; second, initiating local production (hence the comeback of the *bostan*s); and third, preventing consolidation within the existing food supply chains (usually by way of redirecting the farmers from intermediaries to farmers' cooperatives and buying from the farmers' cooperatives to support the farmers). Working with these AFN s, then, could the farmers really generate enough profit? Was there a substantive difference between farmers who work with the AFN s and those who don't? Would the former, for example, be willing to not sell their lands even if the land prices were rising, to leave an operational farm to their kids and actually want their kids to go into farming (and support them when they do so)? In other words, AFN s seem to be working for the consumers, but were they also working for the farmers?

As I was conducting field interviews for the project, I came upon another realization: Discursively, there was quite a bit of support for small farmers, particularly for those who were on the peripheries of Istanbul. However, these farmers were neither included in the online AFN s nor were they receiving much interest from the many consumer cooperatives operating in the city. Consumer cooperatives were sharing a macro, country-wide list of producers among themselves and they were all buying from the same producers in this list. As a result, some of the producers had morphed into monopolies within the 'alternative provisioning' sector; so much so that they had become 'parent producers' that employed other farmers, dairy farmers, and secondary producers (processors) in their regions, and were selling their products – under the 'parent' name, with a markup, of course – to the consumer cooperatives. More

FIGURE 28   It is relatively common to see consumer cooperatives selling products of farmers'
cooperatives
PHOTO BY ELIF BIRBIRI

interestingly, not only were the members of the consumer cooperatives not
marking this as a problem, they were in fact quite grateful for the consolidation as it made their job somewhat easier: They could work with one producer
who would then find other producers and supervise and manage them so that
they too adhered to similar principles of sustainable production and ecological, social, and economic justice that the consumer cooperatives and the
AFNS promote. Members of the consumer cooperatives were also not both-
ered by the Instagram-fame of some of these 'parent producers', their well-
oiled connections with celebrity chefs, and the prominent, mainstream food
and gastronomy media in the country that carried them into farmer-stardom.
Meanwhile, their not-so-famous counterparts on the peripheries, who lived
and toiled literally in the same city as the consumer cooperatives, were failing,
even as 'local food' and farmers' markets were becoming the next hype.

    To make matters even more complicated, the Istanbul Metropolitan
Municipality (İstanbul Büyükşehir Belediyesi; IBB) got involved in the 'alternative sector'. The municipality changed hands in the 2019 local elections; and
the newly elected progressive mayor, Ekrem İmamoğlu, wanted to address
the city's food and provisioning problems. Specifically, three problems were
identified: Consolidation within the provisioning apparatus and the resultant

high prices consumers pay; peripheral farmers' inability to reach consumers in Istanbul; and the pressures that the land and housing markets are imposing on the peripheral farmers. Yet, as İmamoğlu and his team were bringing together agricultural engineers, academics (myself included), and other interested parties (including farmers and representatives of various AFNs and consumer cooperatives) to brainstorm on these issues, a string of suicides wrecked the city: A family of 4 sisters, unable to pay back loans and put food on the table collectively killed themselves (Elden 2019); then a few months later, a university student, unable to afford the subsidized prices at her university's cafeteria took her own life (Hamsici 2020). Meanwhile, reports of suicides and suicide attempts, triggered by long-term unemployment, job insecurity, and high food prices, kept on coming from all over the country. The severity of the situation thus laid bare, the conversations at the IBB shifted: Was there a way to directly connect the farmers and consumers, so that farmers could earn more, while consumers could access food at affordable prices?

Yet this question also marked a major tension, one that the members of the AFNs usually refused to engage with: Their prices were relatively high (in some cases, as much as 40% higher than the supermarkets), especially for the lower-income residents of the city. When confronted, the AFN-members justified the high prices by arguing that these were fair prices – enough for the farmers to live on without having to work with intermediaries or taking up non-sustainable (meaning, conventional) production practices. The farmers I talked to, however, were not entirely on the same page with the AFN-members. Or rather, there was a significant divergence within the farming community: Farmers who had inherited farms from their families (farmers by birth, or 'older generation farmers') focused on profit-generating practices, whether that be opening up more land for farming and/or intensifying production by way of GMOs and the agro-chemical inputs of the Green Revolution. So long as they could profit, these older generation farmers did not care whether their production practices were sustainable or not. The calculation they were making was thus relatively 'simple': If they were convinced that they could make money by switching to organic methods, they would; otherwise, they would not. Farmers who had migrated to the country and picked up farming after a life in the city ('neo-peasants', or 'new generation farmers') staunchly stood against focusing solely on profit. While being able to subsist as farmers was surely important, they saw farming and life on the land as a lifestyle and conceptualized farming as a way of living that produces what is consumed and consumes what is produced. For these farmers, non-sustainable production practices did not make sense at all. Their calculation was thus also relatively 'simple': They were willing to live a 'simple' life, making less money, so long as they could lead socio-economically just and eco-conscious lives.

I saw these two stances clash, somewhat loudly, at a meeting the IBB held with farmers' cooperatives from all around the country in early February 2020. Led by Abdullah Aysu, the former head of the Farmers' Union (*Çiftçi-Sen*), and Ahmet Atalık, the former head of the Istanbul Branch of the Board of Agricultural Engineers (*Ziraat Mühendisleri Odası*), the meeting was convened to inform the cooperatives of the new mayor's plans to address the above-mentioned problems, ask for their input, and invite them to cooperate. Aysu and Atalık told the participants that the Municipality was going to establish first, a *Halk Market* (People's Supermarket) – a line of supermarkets that would buy directly from the farmers and sell with very low profit margins to Istanbulites. So far, 22 branches were planned for the *Halk Market*, and in compliance with the regulations, a shop in the Bayrampaşa *Hali* has already been rented to supply the branches. Plus, in each *Halk Market* location, there would be a *Halk Lokantası* (People's Canteen), where people could buy hot meals at affordable prices. Finally, one of the major bazaar locations within the Kadıköy district would be the new site for a permanent farmers' market. Farmers' cooperatives would be able to sell their produce here without having to pay any rent or vending dues to the Municipality. The Municipality would also provide free storage spaces to the farmers and free transportation service between the storage spaces and the farmers' market. It was to these three interconnected projects that Aysu and Atalık were asking the meeting's participants to join in.

Yet to participate, the farmers' cooperatives had to guarantee that the produce they were going to sell at the farmers' market and via the *Halk Market* was going to be organic and sustainably produced, though certification was not a requisite. Rather, following the model consumer cooperatives and some online AFN s use, Aysu was suggesting that the participating farmers get what is called a *Katılımcı Onay Sertifikası* (Participatory Guarantee System or PGS certificate),[6] with the necessary testing and other regular inspections for the enforcement of organic and sustainable production practices done by a group of volunteers made up of concerned citizens and municipality officials, not a private company charging a high fee[7]. Moreover, unlike the private organic certification companies, PGS is shaped by community

---

6   For more on PGS, see Buğday Ekolojik Yaşamı Destekleme Derneği 2020; IFOAM 2007.

7   The numbers vary between 400 Euros and 650 Euros, plus the cost of soil testing – all of which is paid every year, every other year, or every three years. Though these rates might be acceptable for farmers in Europe, they are too high for small farmers in Turkey – a complaint I consistently heard from all the farmers I interviewed during fieldwork.

concerns, which, in this case, as Aysu pointed out, included absence of child and slave labor in production, equal pay for men and women, full social security for permanent and temporary agricultural laborers, and zero tolerance for domestic violence. All in all, instead of the profit motive, PGS would make better practices for ecological justice and socio-economic sustainability the basis for entry to the alternative provisioning apparatus the IBB was trying to establish.

In response, the representatives from the [older generation] farmers' cooperatives complained that the farmers' market was not going to provide them with the desired market access, that their revenue from the sales would not be enough to keep them in farming, and suggested that the Municipality should also set up a website through which they could sell their produce. More interestingly, certain representatives argued against shifting to organic agriculture. Pointing out that their yields would dip for at least a couple of years, they stated that they were unsure if the higher prices they would be charging at the farmers' market would make up the difference. On top of it all, wasn't the mayor intending for lower prices to provision the lower-income Istanbulites? If they were to switch to a value-added product – that is, organic – they would have to charge more, not less. So, how were these two divergent aims supposed to come together?

Neo-peasants, in turn, rejected outright the profit-oriented approach the Municipality and other farmers were taking. Declaring that farming, which derives life from land, is essentially a lifestyle, they condemned conventional ("toxic") agricultural practices and the profit motive that pushed people and the environment to their limits. They suggested instead a collective move to organic and sustainable farming and invited other farmers, farmers' cooperatives, and unions to come check out what they were doing, share know-how, establish, and expand networks of solidarity. The neo-peasants argued that because they were not there to profit, their prices were not going to be too high anyway; rather, they would be 'fair' – that is, just enough to help them keep living on and off of the land.

Tellingly, the meeting ended with no consensus. The IBB did not weigh in on the discussion, nor did the older generation farmers concede to the economic sustainability of switching to organic methods, nor the neo-peasants relent to the relevance of the profit motive. Plus, no one was convinced that the permanent farmers' market was enough to resolve or even offer an 'alternative' vision to the increasing consolidation in the supply chain or the domination that a handful of provisioning agents were establishing within the city's provisioning apparatus. Finally, while those attending the meeting admitted that the *Halk Market* would be able to reach a wider group of people, they were unconvinced that it would become a strong enough competitor to the supermarkets or generate pressure on the supermarkets to keep their profit margins somewhat in check. In short, everyone was as skeptical of the solutions as they were hopeful that there were (and there could be) indeed solutions to the problems on the table.

The AFN s do promise a different future to the residents of the city, in terms of both provisioning practices and the relation between the political community and the central authority. Yet, the disagreements within them, particularly vis-à-vis the profit motive, and the divergences in approach to farming and agriculture, are quite strong – so much so that, going forward, the possibilities for reconciliation seem slim. In fact, the schisms might even get worse. Indeed, during the meeting, when some of the [older generation] farmers who had switched to organic methods mentioned that they would not recommend doing so to others, the neo-peasants berated them, calling them out as traitors to the nation. Similarly, when suggestions for switching to more niche and value-added products came up, like saffron, stevia, tarragon, mulberry molasses, and carob flour, the FFV growing [older generation] farmers, in particular, complained that they were being excluded from the picture because the costs of switching would simply be too high for them. Whatever the topic of discussion, adherence to the profit motive stood between the two sides; and with neither side relenting or looking for a compromise, I am not convinced that the AFN s can fulfill their promise of a different future – at least for the majority of Istanbulites.

Nonetheless, this picture looks quite different if one is at either end of the income spectrum. If one can afford the higher prices the consumer cooperatives and the online AFN s are charging, then organic, sustainably produced, child- and slave- labor free, 'clean' foods are readily available. For those who really want to be involved, PGS certification is a mechanism they can directly participate in, to make sure that the food that they are buying does indeed comply with community priorities and the sustainable production practices the farmers say they indeed adhere to. Volunteering at the consumer coop is also an option – and in some coops, a requirement: assisting at the coop store, getting in touch with producers, checking in for supplies, arranging for the transportation, receiving and then distributing the deliveries are the nitty gritty work that needs to be done to get the ethically sourced food from farms to tables via the coop. Though some coops give discounts to the volunteers to encourage them to participate more actively, there is no compensation for all the time spent sitting through long meetings in which every decision (sometimes even to take a break or to end the meeting!) is taken only with full consensus.

FIGURE 29   Due to their prices, AFN s unfortunately fall out of range for most lower-income
             residents of the city
             PHOTO BY ALPEREN BUĞRA YILMAZ

At the other end of the income spectrum, AFN s are really not much of an
option due to their prices. Rather, people rely on what I call alternative provisioning networks, or APN s. As I mentioned in the previous chapter, rural-to-
urban migrations have not resulted in a complete disconnect between the city
and the country. In fact, recent migrants usually maintain close relations with
the members of their extended family who remained in the villages. At times
of harvest and planting, for example, those in the city go back to help; children are sent to the village to spend the summer vacation and to help out; and
during the religious holidays, the entire family gets together in the village to
celebrate and help. In return, if or when more members of the family want to
migrate out of the village, those who have already migrated out support them
by providing temporary shelter (and also, helping them out when building the
shelter), for example, and finding schools for kids and jobs for adults. Plus, for
those living in the city, the village is a source of nostalgia; it is the ancestral
land – always to be returned to (albeit never permanently, not at least until
one dies!), always to be maintained (yet never really lived in). The mores of
the village life, its foodways, dominant gender roles and norms, are considered
guiding principles that must be passed on to the children. As such, the 'village'
as an idea plays the role of a moral compass (or, is supposed to!). For those in

the village, in turn, the city and the urban life – even under the constraints of low income – are aspirational reference points: If someone migrates out and makes it in the city, it is considered a sign of success. More importantly, in cases of economic emergency, the extended family members in the city might be a source of help as they have access to a wider network of people and public services. The connection is thus beneficial for either side and is securely maintained as long as possible. On a day-to-day basis, food and provisioning are some of the ways in which such maintenance is practiced, as both are laden with symbolic meanings as well as biological functions. It is thus not uncommon to see bags and boxes of foods (fresh and self-processed) unloaded from cars and buses as the family comes back from visiting the elders in the village, for example, or when kids are returning from the summer vacation, etc.[8]

Yet for some, these bags and boxes of food are not merely nostalgic snacks from the ancestral lands. They are rather regular shipments of food that help them subsist in the city.[9] Hence the name, 'alternative provisioning networks': Particularly for lower-income families, these shipments are channels of provisioning that are alternatives to the conventional supply chains of the bazaars and the supermarkets, working at the intersections of the city and the country through the kinship networks. Unlike the AFNs, APNs are primarily support networks that tie the families living in urban and rural *lifeworlds* through foodways, subsistence economies, and provisioning. While one of the primary concerns for the AFNs is trust between the producers and the consumers that the food produced, sold, and consumed is 'clean' (produced without chemical inputs and non-GMO) and ethical (not produced with child and slave labor), for the APNs, the primary concern is subsistence and the maintenance of kin relations. Finally, most AFNs have an organic (pun intended!) relationship with the ecology movement; and AFN members tend to be highly aware and politicized citizens, very likely to be critical of the government's policies on agriculture, water use, energy, and environment. To put it succinctly, they are AFN members because they are concerned citizens and/or activists, taking a clear stance on a string of political (and increasingly, politicized and polarizing) issues. APN-users, in contrast, need not be politicized nor do they have to be critical of the government or its policies. They use APNs purely to subsist; and they do not perceive what they are doing as political or politicized – even

---

8   I think the prevalence and widespread of use of APNs is strictly related to the semi-proletarianization Keyder and Yenal (2014a) talk about. However, more expansive studies are necessary to understand exactly how and how intricately they are related.

9   For an interesting photo-documentary of these shipments, see Doğancayır and Kocagöz (2018).

if their subsistence, even with the help of the APN s, requires rampant self-exploitation for them as well as their relatives back in the village.

These differences between the APN s and the AFN s make clear the two divergent paths emerging around the supply chains of the conventional provisioning agents feeding the city: One for the affluent – or rather, those who can afford what the conventional provisioning agents offer but prefer not to buy them for concerns over the environment, health, and socio-economic justice; and another for the not-so affluent – or, those who need provisioning that is additional to what they have to get from the conventional provisioning agents. Going forward, it would not be surprising to see both of these networks multiply and expand. AFN s and the concerns they voice are already shaping the future of the city's provisioning apparatus – through the IBB, but more significantly because they have managed to raise awareness and shift the public discourse towards economically and socially just, eco-conscious production and consumption. Similarly, with worsening income inequality and deepening economic crisis (which started in mid-2018 and as of the time of writing, is ongoing), APN s will continue to be a fundamental 'alternative' to the supply chains of the conventional provisioning agents. Yet, I think their ability to shape the future of the provisioning apparatus and the public discourses on provisioning will be relatively limited – since most APN s function off-the-grid and have neither the financial power nor the socio-cultural capital or political acumen of the AFN s.

And what of the local farmers – those on the peripheries? Given Istanbul's urban expansion and redevelopment tendencies (and the profit-generation mechanisms attached to them), it is difficult to see them as functioning components of the city's provisioning apparatus. Perhaps, in the short term, they will be able to draw attention to their plight and attract concerned citizens who want to eat local. In the long run, however, their survival depends on the revenue they generate and whether that revenue is able to compete with the construction sector, which has been one of the primary growth-generating sectors of the economy and has shaped the cityscape as well as the urban economy, particularly since the 2000s. So far, my research has shown that unless the peripheral farmers are large landowners who do conventional farming, producing out-of-season FFVs and herbs in relatively capital-intensive greenhouses, or are working with the AFN s, they will not have much of a chance for survival against the pressures from the land and the housing markets. In other words, unfortunately, there does not seem to be much opportunity for the small, peripheral farmers to influence the future of the city's provisioning apparatus.

4   Of the Sovereignty, Political Community, and the Central Authority

I had concluded the previous chapter on a dark note, arguing that there does not seem to be much hope (yet) for a relationship between the central authority and the political community that is not entangled in *necroeconomics*, and by extension, *necropolitics*. In this section, I want to take up this argument again and reformulate it in the context of the diverging paths AFN s and APNs are spearheading: Can AFN s and APN s suggest and generate a different kind of relationship between the central authority and the subject-citizens? Are they, albeit differently, signs of new conceptualizations of the relationship between the central authority (the sovereign) and the subject-citizens?

APN s are a part of one of the many mechanisms that lower-income populations use to survive in the city. They have developed as a response to the central authority's deployment of *necroeconomy* to govern the political community, but unfortunately, not as a critique to it. Plus, as I mentioned in the previous section, APN users do not perceive what they are doing as a political practice, nor do they perceive the APN s (or for that matter, the conditions created by the [*necro*]economy that necessitate the APN s) as political organizations. Though there is politicization around food and food prices, unlike in AFN s, they do not translate into political action or activism. Finally, APN users rarely want to continue their reliance on these networks. Provisions coming from the village to supplement their incomes are literal representations of their inability to survive in the city on their own. Continuing reliance, thus, implies that they are still 'low-income', that they still have to maintain their peasant roots, that they have not been able to fully transition to urban lifestyles. As such, even if the foods provisioned through the APN s are 'clean', culturally appropriate (traditional) and healthy, neither the networks nor the relations they enact necessarily offer an alternative to the current formulation(s) of the relationship between the central authority and the political community. If anything, they hold a mirror to the implications of the current formulation, as experienced by the lower-income residents of the city.

AFN s, on the other hand, are highly politicized. Not only do the members consider food and provisioning as inherently political and contested issues, but they articulate alternative methods of procuring food in the city as a critical counter-movement of concerned (subject-)citizens. In conjunction, they emphasize 'food sovereignty' – that is, "the peoples', Countries' or State Unions' right to define their agricultural and food policy, without any dumping vis-à-vis third countries" (La Via Campesina 2003), and following the term's earlier formulation by the La Via Campesina movement, they emphasize:

- prioritizing local agricultural production in order to feed the people, access of peasants and landless people to land, water, seeds,
  and credit. Hence the need for land reforms, for fighting against
  Genetically Modified Organisms (GMOs), for free access to seeds, and
  for safeguarding water as a public good to be sustainably distributed.
- the right of farmers and peasants to produce food and the right of
  consumers to be able to decide what they consume, and how and by
  whom it is produced.
- the right of countries to protect themselves from agricultural and
  food imports priced at artificially low values.
- [linking of] agricultural prices [..] to production costs (...)
- the [peoples] taking part in the agricultural policy choices.
- [and,] the recognition of women farmers' rights, who play a major
  role in agricultural production and in food (La Via Campesina 2003)

The AFNs bring to the forefront the (subject-)citizens' right not just to food,
but to make decisions and to be involved in decisions with regards to food and
provisioning, thus challenging the current system at all levels. In this respect,
the AFNs definitely do contain the seeds for a new food regime.

Though it is a bit too early to tell what the relationship between the central
authority and the (subject-)citizens is going to be like in this new food regime,
there are some indicators. For example, given that food sovereignty is articulated through the framework of rights, we can assume that the central authority will maintain its position as the great discipliner – that is, the overseer and
the regulator of relations (through the force of law), provider of protections
(in return for obedience), and enforcer of permissions and prohibitions. At the
same time, given that "taking part in the agricultural policy choices" (La Via
Campesina 2003) is one of the major components, the (subject-)citizens will
be much more (directly) involved in the government of the urban provisioning apparatus. However, exactly what that direct involvement will be, remains
unclear. (Subject-)citizens might, for example, participate in the drawing up of
laws and regulations, but leave their enforcement to the central authority; alternatively, they might evaluate and rank 'best practices' for specific provisioning
actors; they might determine base and ceiling rates of profit; they might establish quotas for small farmers, minority and women producers, at every node
of the supply chain. Most importantly, the (subject-)citizens' participation in
the government of the provisioning apparatus and the food system writ large
may lead to *necroeconomic* practices of the food system and their *necropolitical*
implications to be contained, so that no member of the political community is
starved, goes hungry or remains malnourished. In other words, in conjunction

with the right to make decisions with respect to what foods one consumes, where those foods come from, how those foods are produced and who produces them, it may involve an aspiration for a political community-wide food security. Yet again, this is not only a matter of generating and guaranteeing access to 2000 to 3000 calories per person per day. Rather, it is making sure that structural inequalities – that make locally produced, culturally appropriate, clean (as in organic), fresh (as in not processed) and non-GMO foods unaffordable to the 'enemy' populations – are dismantled.

More radically perhaps, a shift in the *mentalité* of government can be expected. Although it is too early to tell what the new *mentalité* will be, some extrapolations from the case at hand are possible: For example, the method of government that is dividing the people into *friend* and *enemy* populations can be expected to remain, though perhaps the yardstick with which people are divided may change. Currently, that yardstick is market competitiveness: If they are competitive market actors, then they are categorized as *friends* and not only are they let live, they are supported by the central authority to make sure that they remain competitive and/or become more competitive. If they are not competitive, then they are categorized as *enemies* and gradually (or in some cases, quite suddenly) various supports – social, economic, and political – are removed so as to eliminate them from the market and eventually to starve them out. Based on the principles of food sovereignty I quoted above, the new yardstick may be belonging to the political community – that is, citizenship. The central authority can call all those non-citizen populations *enemies*, exclude them from the market, and leave them to starve. Citizens, meanwhile, can remain *friends* and be provided with various supports that enable them to live.

The seeds of such a *mentalité* of government are already widespread. Legally isolating the non-citizens, limiting their right to work, to move around, to own property, to trade, to send or receive money – all of which affect their capability to participate in the market and thus to subsist on their own – are and have been anything but extraordinary. Similarly, expulsion from the political community through restricting rights and/or criminalizing, for example, is and has been a punitive measure relatively common in justice systems all around the world. What is perhaps new is the ways in which these two are being put together: While globalization is fueling the movement of more people (that is, labor – which follows the movement of capital and commodities) across borders and for longer periods of time, restrictive immigration and citizenship policies are criminalizing immigration and immigrants, and declaring them – the 'illegals' – as the new 'enemies' of the political communities who are receiving them. Barred from working legally, immigrants are then pushed to work precariously and for below-subsistence wages. Though their labor helps maintain the rates of profit in almost all nodes of the food supply chain (particularly in agriculture and food processing), it is unfortunately not uncommon to see them go hungry, malnourished, or starve (Barndt 2008, Counihan 2005, Estabrook 2011, Pachirat 2013, Schlosser 2008).

Worse, these *necropolitical* implications are generally ignored by the vast majority of the members of the political community, as their subjects are the non-members, that is, the 'illegalized' *enemies*. The non-members, in turn, lack access to existing channels that would enable them to influence the policies, practices, and decisions of the central authority. In other words, the needs and preferences of the non-members rarely find a place on the political agenda; and the central authority undertakes the improvement of working conditions, the streamlining of immigration and neutralization processes, and the expansion of integrative social policies, only if there is an added benefit for the political community. To sum up, then, a 'locals'-oriented *mentalité* of government that prioritizes the members' right to "tak[e] part in the agricultural policy choices" (La Via Campesina 2003) is not going to remove the practices of the government that splits people into *friend* and *enemy* populations; it will, however, change the criteria by which *friend* and *enemy* populations are formulated. And it remains to be seen whether the AFNs and the food sovereignty movement will be influential enough to initiate such a shift in the *mentalité* in the first place.

To put it differently, neither the AFNs and the food sovereignty movement, nor the APNs, have the capacity to substantially challenge the capitalist imperatives (the imperatives of competition, accumulation, and profit-maximization, and hence a constant systemic need to develop productive forces" (Meiksins Wood 2017, 97)) or for that matter, the relationship between the economic and the sovereign power. At best, they can alter the deployment of extra-economic means of the state for the extraction and the appropriation of surplus labor. It is, however, unclear what that would lead to: Perhaps more marketization (in other words, further dependence on the commodity exchange in the market for life's necessities (Meiksins Wood 2016, 28–31)), or a more community-driven, more participant-regulated approach to managing the societal effects of enabling the extraction and appropriation of surplus labor purely through economic means, or, more radically, to a move away from the eradication of alternative *mentalité* and methods of commodity exchange and exclusive ownership of means of production. In either case, it is clear that the AFNs, the food sovereignty movement, and the APNs aim to resist the sovereign power (particularly its "right to let die" (Foucault 2003, 241)) rather than the economic power, which not only *compels* some subject-citizens to 'forego' their surplus labor to access means of production that are owned exclusively by other subject-citizens, but also to access "the most basic commodities and the implements of daily subsistence" (Meiksins Wood 2016, 29) through the market.

One aspect that the AFN s and the food sovereignty movement should be commended for is their *revaluation* of the political sphere and their emphasis on praxis. To reiterate, what sets capitalism apart is the extraction and appropriation of surplus labor purely through economic means. Those who do not own the means of production 'agree' to 'forego' their surplus labor in return for accessing means of production which are owned by others. As such, neither political rights of appropriation nor an entity that institutes, distributes, and polices such rights (Meiksins Wood 2005, 14–22) is necessary. With capitalism, then, civic status no longer correlates to a class position (or modifies class inequality (Meiksins Wood 2016, 213)). The political sphere is thus devalued (ibid, 211), even though political rights gradually expand to larger and larger groups of people. Arguably, the strong emphasis on participation in the decision-making vis-à-vis urban provisioning, agriculture, and consumption that the AFN s and the food sovereignty movement make, can contribute to the revaluation of the political sphere. Participation in decision-making would not only openly politicize food and provisioning, but also, by doing so, help civic status (which, as I pointed out above, seems to be the requirement for participation) modify, to some degree, class inequality – though to what extent remains unclear.

5   The Global and the Local

In many ways, the story I have told in this chapter, and the previous one, is not unique. The move from import substitution industrialization to export-oriented growth, and the liberalization of the capital and commodities markets, followed by frequent economic crises, plagued many throughout the 1980s, 1990s and 2000s, particularly in the Global South (Brown 2018; Pilcher 2008; Patel 2007). Yet if we look closely, we see that the transformations had started much earlier – notably, in the 1940s. While the newly independent countries of the Global South were making plans to 'develop' as fast as they could, through industrialization, in most cases (rather than agriculture or for that matter, commerce, service, or finance), the Marshall Fund and the PL 480 was redirecting the abundance generated by the well-subsidized US farmers to feed them (Patel 2007). Though farmers around the world protested against this global agri-food set up, they eventually had to accept it, albeit after much financial and military coercion. Thus, many in the Global South came to rely on food imports as they shifted their resources away from agriculture and rural economies to industry and urban economies. And slowly but surely, their food systems transformed from *codependent provisioning* to the *urban food supply chain.*

Yet not all farmers are created equal, and not all were – or are – against the transformation that was unfolding. Though dependent on oil and chemicals and overrun by the profit-drive of Big Ag, agricultural practices of the so-called 'Green Revolution' undeniably did benefit some and garnered their support – as farmers, landowners, and most influentially, as voters (Wise 2019). The foreign food aid and agricultural supports that kicked off the Green Revolution in the Global South were also effective in quieting the unrests over rising food prices and looming scarcities in the cities (Patel 2007). Instead of raising real wages and instituting redistributive land reforms, so that the urban working classes could buy food at prices that would enable the peasants to continue to be peasants, many a government could get away with policies that (in)advertently supported their domestic capitalists while dooming both their urban working classes and most of their peasants to below-subsistence incomes. In fact, with increasing mechanization in agriculture – also a byproduct of aid and the Green Revolution – these governments were able to solve two problems at once: Made redundant by the machinery, landless peasants, subsistence farmers, and small holders who supported their income with sharecropping, left the villages for the cities and joined the ever- expanding reserve army of labor. The pressures thus generated on the urban economy in the 1970s, were then relieved with the abundance and the diversity markets offered at the time, as a result of the liberalization of trade and globalization in the 1980s. Thus, the transformations that benefitted the large landowners and domestic bourgeois in the long run, were sold as abundance and diversity to the urban working classes in the short run.

The most important shift yet was in the way we think about the relationship between agriculture and urban provisioning, the village and the city, and most critically, abundance and scarcity. The *urban food supply chain* food system let us think that food is plentiful for everyone, that seasons don't exist (or don't matter), and that it isn't a big deal that produce from the four corners of the world can meet in our grocery aisles. And, so long as we can maintain this rosy image, we are happy to not think about the relations that make it possible or the transformations in agrarian structures that were necessary to make it happen. Indeed, while the Green Revolution convinced many that the era of food scarcity was now over, it was the convenience of accessing the global bounty provided by the *urban food supply chain* food system that drove home what abundance really looked like and aggregated support for the food system, not the public-private joint ventures nor the hegemonic discourses of national economy and the development of *codependent provisioning*. Today, confronted with income inequality threatening to make this promised abundance inaccessible yet again, we try to look for 'alternative networks', initiate 'sustainable solutions', and preserve whatever remains of the 'village', the 'peasant', and 'agriculture'. At the same time, we are not willing to give up the conveniences the *urban food supply chain* food system has provided for us. Hence, the contradictions: We want flexible supply chains to provision us on demand, yet we want the producers to respect the ecologies they are operating in. We want reduced costs and customized produce, yet we want them to be 'green', 'ethical', and 'sustainable'. We want 'our farmers' in 'our villages' producing 'our food', yet we refuse to move ourselves or our resources away from cities and urban communities to villages and rural communities. We want the idyllic *lifeworld* of family farms, yet we can neither stop our expanding cities nor give up on moving to the suburbs that have been built on the farmlands of those family farms we seem to want to preserve.

To add fuel to the fire, as recently as the 2008–2009 financial crisis, which started in the US and spread across the world like wildfire, the *urban food supply chain* food system proved to be quite fragile – for in a globalized world, seemingly unrelated sectors of the economy are connected to each other, not just producers and retailers, and a crisis in one part may trigger a crisis in the whole (Wise 2019, 163–174). Price increases that have nothing to do with agricultural supply and demand dynamics (ibid) can now strangle the provisioning apparatuses, causing Type 2 failures to shift between locales in the course of the crisis. Scarcity, in other words, is never far away, and hunger – now thought of as a thing of the past – can eat away our political communities from the inside. Worse still, protections are no longer what the central authorities offer. Price, we are told, is a sign from the market; and it is not meant to be intervened upon. If it is too expensive to produce, then may be the farmers should produce something else. So, no base and ceiling prices, no input subsidies, no bulk purchase guarantees. And, if it is too expensive to consume, well then, may be those who cannot afford it, should not eat it either. While our obedience is ever in demand, there is no protection on offer – at best, it is emergency food aid, provided primarily by private actors, and to get it, one has to jump through all sorts of hoops and end up feeling embarrassed anyway (Purdam, Garratt, and Esmail 2015; de Souza 2019).

This state of unprotectedness is perhaps the most pervasive consequence of the *urban food supply chain* food regime. In addition to varying levels of food insecurity, we see different rates of access to fresh and less processed foods that are low in salt, sugars, and fats even among those who are relatively food-secure. Scholars and activists have described this experience of 'want amid plenty' (Poppendieck 2013) as "food injustice" and studies have shown that it is prevalent across the world, in populations among both the wealthier nations of the Global North and the poorer nations of the Global South (Collier and DeKornfeld 2017; Jacobs and Richtel 2017a; 2017b; Searcey and Richtel 2017; Poppendieck 2013; Bradley and Harrera 2016). Nevertheless, as with most socio-political phenomena, food justice is also shaped by contextual dynamics –it does not manifest the same way everywhere, even if the indicators are similar (Alkon and Agyeman 2011). For example, a population experiencing food injustice might suffer from high rates of diet-related diseases (Nabhan 2013; Julier 2013), or it may be concentrated in neighborhoods that lack adequate sites from which the residents can purchase fresh and less-processed foods (Dutko, ver Ploeg, and Farrigan 2012), or they might lack access to foods necessary for a balanced diet (Anguelovski 2015a; 2015b). However, a balanced diet looks very different in Turkey, from one in Brazil, or Japan. Perhaps the nutrients that make a diet 'balanced' are the same or at least similar, but the food groups from which peoples prefer to (or are able to) get those nutrients differ. Plus, in most cases, all of the above indicators are usually present at varying degrees: People may rely on longer-lasting more processed foods because they might be living in neighborhoods that lack grocery retailers that carry fresh and less processed foods. And, because they consume more processed foods (in addition to having a relatively sedentary lifestyle), they are also more likely to be afflicted by diet-related diseases. Each indicator thus also signals a different underlying process that feeds (pun intended!) other indicators. This makes isolating a single factor or process difficult, as it is a constellation of practices, mechanisms, and discourses that work together to instigate food injustice in the first place.

That being said, scholars have convincingly showed that poverty and income inequality, interlaced with sexism, racism and xenophobia, are the primary causes of food injustice (Alkon and Agyeman 2011). Still, how these factors come together and generate specific cases thereof, remain context-dependent and are hard to generalize. Moreover, as I have shown in this and the previous chapters, the current *urban food supply chain* food system is not established on justice or fairness. It cannot *not* generate such localities of injustice. Food injustice is in fact a fundamental component of it, as are localities of injustice and hungry, malnourished, starving populations. The aim is not to lessen these and to feed everyone; rather, the aim is to feed those who can afford to be fed as efficiently, as copiously, and as diversely as possible, while making as much profit as possible. Food injustice thus is neither an exception nor a mistake. It is the outcome of a food system that is driven by the profit motive and a food regime keen on maintaining the *laissez mourir* that feeds the *laissez faire* (Hill and Montag 2015, 235–342).

So, where do we go from here? Should we stop talking of food justice and instead take on the gargantuan problems of poverty and income inequality? I would suggest, instead, that we look for particular solutions to particular problems in particular cases. At the end of the day, if global structures and relations (most notably, I think, capital) are able to penetrate into and change local structures and relations by relying on local histories, strategies, and techniques of domination and submission, then why not resist and speak back to the global through, yet again, local histories, strategies, and techniques? There will be quite a diversity of circumstances, and resistance in one context will not look like and may not be as effective elsewhere; but wouldn't that flexibility, which powers the current food system, also power our resistance to it?[10]

---

10   For really interesting examples of such resistance that deploys local histories, strategies, and techniques, see Trent Brown's rich discussion of three cases from India (Brown 2018, 80–166). Brown shows us where and how such resistance proliferates, as also where it stumbles and fails (for other examples, see Wise 2019; Patel 2007). In its early days, Slow Food tried to make use of such local histories, strategies, and techniques. However, I agree with Pilcher that "it will never represent a genuine revolution until it confronts the dilemmas of class that have been complicated but not obviated by increasing globalization" (2008, 426).

CHAPTER 7

Conclusion

> The democracy that socialism offers is one that is based on a
> reintegration of the 'economy' into the political life of the commu-
> nity, which begins with its subordination to the democratic self-
> determination of the producers themselves.
>
> ELLEN MEIKSINS WOOD[1]

∴

The (hi)story I have narrated here is not unique. It is what political communities all around the world lived through in the 19th, the 20th, and so far, the 21st
century. It has been analyzed as one of the core problems of political economy
circa the 17th century (Foucault 2007), theorized in reference to the shift to the
capitalist mode of production (Polanyi 2001), studied comparatively as (different models of) development (see, for example, Frank's (1966) and Rostow's
(1960) discussions of development as well as Wallerstein's world systems theory (1974)) – albeit with differing emphases – by political scientists, anthropol-
ogists, economists, geographers, and sociologists, to name a few. Though food
and provisioning feature substantially in early discussions, especially in the
political economy literature, contemporary scholars seem to have chosen to
focus more on agriculture and the role it plays in (global) capitalism, vis-à-vis
neoliberalism, or for development. My attempt to bring food and provisioning back into focus is not only to call back to these earlier discussions, but to
show – rather than tell – that food and provisioning were and are among the
foundational constituents in the relationship between political communities
and their central authorities, and that the politics and economics of food and
provisioning must be considered as functions and functionaries of power and
government.

The (hi)story is not intended just for demonstrative purposes, however.
In calling back to older political-economic discussions and the protection-
obedience dynamic in particular, I also intend to reopen the discussion of

---

1 Meiksins Wood, Ellen. 2016. *Democracy Against Capitalism: Renewing Historical Materialism.*
   New York, NY: Verso, 283.

(and to reignite the struggle for) the right to subsistence and the right to food. In the introduction, I have defined the right to subsistence as an individual subject-citizen's right to maintain his/her life in a dignified manner, with the caveat that what maintaining one's life in a dignified manner entails is always (necessarily) context-specific and cannot be fully defined in abstract. Perhaps clarifying what is included in the right to subsistence (shelter, clothing, healthcare?) and what is implied with the right to food (is it a positive or a negative right, for example) are good places to start. However, we can – and I think we should – go beyond that for, after all, positing subsistence and food as rights, regardless of how comprehensively they are defined, can be limiting, since 'rights' presume laws, lawmakers (or lawgivers!), and states. Why not recognize the desire for subsistence (self-preservation, or preservation, or conservation of one's self – however the self is defined) and food as inherent to the human condition and suggest that every social and political institution is established to guarantee and to maintain these? In other words, why not make subsistence and food the core of our political identities?

I am aware that such an approach may complicate some of the anthropocentric assumptions that we hold dear, and frequently use to distinguish ourselves from (and dare I say, declare ourselves superior to?) non-humans. If food and subsistence are at the core of our political identities, how different are we from animals, plants, or even fungi? Have we not formed communities, developed codes of conduct, instituted mechanisms to discipline ourselves and police each other's behavior so that we are not, in fact, 'just' animals? If we go back to situating our bodies and bodily needs at the core of politics, then are we not reverting to a conceptualization of ourselves, our political communities, and politics itself, that is primitive, impulsive, and violent? Plus, if we are going to take food and subsistence as the core of politics, why limit politics and society to humans? If, after all, we are no different from animals, plants, or fungi – in that we are all just trying to eat and survive, why not consider food and subsistence as the condition of the living – rather than simply 'the human condition' – and as such, why not have the primary distinction be between the living and the non-living rather than between the human and the non-human?

Such 'philosophizing' may seem out of place – in no small part because the (hi)story I have discussed in this book was of a political community that was established on genocidal political violence, and maintained by the constant regurgitation of new *friends* and *enemies*; a political community that does absolutely nothing, indeed actively refuses to – and in its refusal, tacitly endorses – the politics and economics of death that it is governed by and governed with. One might say that the priority should be to recognize the *necroeconomic* tendencies of the contemporary *mentalité* of government and to change it, or to come to terms with it. Why, instead, question the anthropocentric assumptions the members' sense of self is based on? When the political community cannot even refrain from declaring some of its members – those who are others' friends, neighbors, colleagues, relatives – as *enemies*, why 'philosophize' about a political community of the living?

In Chapter 5, *Feeding Global Istanbul*, I suggested that the central authority was displaced from its position of governing the provisioning apparatus, and the idea that the political community needed to be protected against hunger, food scarcity, and malnutrition – that the political community writ large or any specific population within it needed to be provisioned – disappeared with it. The task of provisioning instead was shifted entirely to provisioning actors, working through the market mechanism. Provisioning actors, however, were not doing whatever they were doing (farming, transporting, sorting, processing, cleaning, etc.) with the intent of provisioning the political community; they were doing it to make and to maximize profit. The provisioning of the political community was thus an accidental outcome of the provisioning actors engaging in profitable activity in the market. The central authority, meanwhile, set out to ensure that the market functioned efficiently and unhindered, by way of, among others, eliminating the new *enemies* – those members who were not competitive. Those not eliminated, in turn, were supported so that they could continue to be competitive and/or become even more competitive. These were the new *friends*; and they were protected until – for whatever reason – they lost their competitive edge. This protection, however, was neither a covert recognition of a right to food or a right to subsistence, nor an allotment of food or a ration. Protection was simply a temporary permission to continue to live, so long as they could afford to buy what the market had to offer. In other words, protection entailed neither a juridical nor a practical guarantee of food and/or provisioning. It was simply a temporary permission to let certain members of the political community continue to perform profitable market activity, so that they could access whatever resources they could afford to go on living.

The COVID-19 pandemic has shown us the fragility of this permission, when it got stretched even thinner. Even as (at the time of writing) the pandemic continues to rage, central authorities are prioritizing the markets, and they are working to make sure that business can go on as usual, even if that comes at the cost of lives lost (see, for example, Swonk et al. 2020). But the precarity of the members of the political community, even of those in the *friends* category, was already clear before the pandemic: In 'normal' times, the monthly income of a double-earning minimum wage household remains below the poverty line (Türk-İş 2018); the number of workers dying due to unsafe work conditions rises every year (Health and Safety Labour Watch (Turkey) 2020); working class parents unable to make ends meet kill themselves; more and more children require school lunches because they are food-insecure at home; meat becomes so expensive that people become vegetarians by compulsion; subsidized and sanctioned extractive industries trigger ever more catastrophic environmental destruction which, in turn, makes livelihoods based on farming and agriculture impossible... Meanwhile, the central authority claims that a family of 5 with double earners on minimum wage can not only feed themselves on the acclaimed Turkish staples of *simit* and *çay* for 3 meals a day, 7 days a week, but can even save for a rainy day (Sputnik News TR 2019)! As for the *enemies*, well, they can just "nibble at tree roots" (Erçakir and Çevikbaş 2016) – that is, if they don't disappear in prisons or are gunned down in the streets first.

I would argue that it is in these conditions, and in these conditions in particular, that we should be talking and thinking about a different form of political community: a political community of the living perhaps – or at least, one that does not discriminate so brazenly between humans – as well as between humans and non-human others who can be killed, starved, or left to perish due to their inability to access what they need to survive. By the same token, we have to start reformulating the relationship between our central authorities and our political communities. Today, the relationship is oddly shifted to favor the market -not us, nor the central authority. We have all become precarious (some more than others, surely); our lives reduced to our labor power, and our value as members of our political communities correlated to the profitability of our market activities. The central authority, in turn, is naught but a brutal, expansive, organized police force that cannot deliver even administrative justice. In reconstructing our political communities, then, we have to also reconstruct our central authorities and our relationships with them.

The case I have discussed here offers particularly rich food for thought on how these reformulations can unfold – though, unfortunately, not always in a progressive direction. For example, beginning in the early 2010s, the relationship between the market and the central authority in Turkey started to change. As I have pointed out before, in the post-1980 period, the central authority's primary task had been to ensure that the market works efficiently and unhindered, and to enable that, the central authority supported those who were already competitive in the market and eliminated others who were not or who were less so. Yet, in the early 2010s, rather than directing public resources to those who were competitive, the central authority began to support specific populations even if they were not particularly competitive. What set these populations apart was their political support for the governing party and the party's leader – then prime minister, now president of the republic. They would publicly and brazenly declare their loyalty to the leader, criticize any and all of his opponents, invest in critical sectors (like the media that would enable him and the party line to dominate the public conversation) and undertake infrastructure projects in Turkey and beyond, which – once completed, are trumpeted as the leader's own success stories. In many ways, their 'scratch my back and I'll scratch yours' relation with the leader and through the leader, with the central authority, was reminiscent of the *mentalité* of government in the *codependent provisioning* food regime. However, in the *codependent provisioning* food regime, the idea of creating a 'national economy' played a crucial role, whereas in this more recent case, there is no such foundational precept. In fact, in contrast to the *codependent provisioning* food regime's racist and xenophobic conceptualization of the nation that treated non-Muslims and non-Sunni Muslims as proto-*enemy* others, the new, post-2010 alliance is open to working with anyone – 'foreigners' or the 'local others' alike. Not only can national assets be privatized and sold to non-citizens, but the central authority might even support its political allies if they want to become shareholders in other nations' public assets.

While this network of relations and transactions may simply be corruption (though I am not sure what can be 'simple' about corruption) or crony capitalism, the redirection of the public resources to political allies-cum-*friends* and the shifting of the *mentalité* in the way in which *friends* and *enemies* are decided are critical here (and, they are not unique to Turkey). Yet, if crony capitalism is not just the sign that the current relationship between the central authority and the political community has broken down, what else is it the sign of? And what if, in the long run, the central authority completely backs away from ensuring the efficient and unhindered functioning of the market? What will displace the market as the new mechanism through which *friends* and *enemies* are defined? Alternatively, if the market is not displaced but sidelined, made to serve these political allies-cum-*friends*, what kind of relationship would come to exist between the central authority and the political community? Is the political community going to be perpetually divided between political allies and opponents? Last but not least, when the whole system becomes unsustainable (due to a financial crisis, climate change, pandemic – take your pick), will we be able to go beyond crude crony capitalism; and if so, what might that look like?

While these questions are worth pondering, I would like to go back to a point I mentioned at the beginning of the book: I had suggested that the public storehouses that enabled the city-states of Machiavelli's era to maintain their independence against sneaky neighbors and powerful emperors alike had disappeared, and gradually with them, the idea that the central authority should protect the members of the political community against hunger and (food) scarcity. Ensuring that one didn't starve became the members' own responsibility and any back-up mechanism, network, or practice, that could protect the members' in case they failed to perform that responsibility, was taken apart by the structural adjustments. I had also suggested that remembering and bringing back the now largely forgotten discussions on the right to subsistence and the right to food might be helpful in battling against and ultimately altering the *necroeconomic* tendencies of the current food regime. What might be worth pointing out, however, is that such a transformation might take time – perhaps as much time as the disappearance of the public storehouses and the shifting of the responsibility took. It wouldn't be surprising, for example, if there were to be a transitory food regime, like *codependent provisioning*, for example, before we could fully move to a food regime in which the central authority once again resumes its duty to protect the *body politic* against hunger, (food) scarcity, and famine.

As I have pointed out in Chapters 3 and 4 – *Unruly Transitions* and *Planned Scarcities* respectively – in the *codependent provisioning* food regime, the central authority intervened into the provisioning apparatus more directly whenever there was a system-wide crisis that threatened the proper functioning of the provisioning apparatus and generated the possibility that the political community might face (food) scarcity, hunger, and/or famine. Thus, while the provisioning apparatus worked through the market mechanism for the most part, both the political community and the provisioning agents could trust that the central authority would step in if there was a major crisis – whether the crisis was due to natural disasters (earthquakes, droughts, etc.) or internal and/or external political-economic events (wars, coups, financial crises, etc.). In other words, as long as the central authority still had a duty to ensure that the members of the political community were protected against hunger and (food) scarcity, it could selectively intervene into the provisioning apparatus. Depending on the event, it could even provision and/or feed the people directly (via rations for example). What was crucial was to (be able to) limit the direct interventions of the central authority (in response) to specific events, and to let the market function at other – normal, so to say – times.

While the internal limitations of the *codependent provisioning* food regime made it intrinsically unstable, its transitory nature can help us think about how we might re-arrange the relationship between the political community and the central authority. For example, rather than only intervening in specific events (emergencies), the central authority may intervene to provide provisioning for specific populations – sort of like a welfare state. Alternatively, it can intervene in specific events, but only for specific populations, which is the kind of response we are seeing in many parts of the world (economic stimulus packages and rent, mortgage, and debt payment postponements) to the COVID-19 pandemic. Finally, it can help establish or maintain alternative economic arrangements for access to provisioning that do not function through the free market or the profit-generation/maximization incentive – again, only for certain populations. As Gibson-Graham (1996) pointed out long ago, these non-capitalist arrangements are in fact already all around us and are intrinsic to the capitalist economy; and vis-à-vis Istanbul's provisioning apparatus, they feature most prominently in the alternative provisioning networks the city's lower-income populations rely on (as discussed in the previous chapter). The central authority can encourage lower-income people to rely on these by formalizing them, but not taxing them, for example, or by offering subsidies to decrease transportation costs, etc. For those who are not yet members of the APN s, it can encourage 'barter markets', where people can collectively exchange whatever they have for whatever they need – whether that be time, labor, tomatoes, or childcare. It is critical, however, that the participants are not left to depend entirely on these alternative economic arrangements either. They should have multiple options and be able to still rely on the market, when and if that is affordable or convenient for them.

A note of caution: Because the duty to protect is so decidedly on the sovereign in the *urban food provisioning* food regime, it might seem appealing, as a form of ordering our relationship with the central authority. However, it is worth remembering that the sovereign of the *urban food provisioning* food regime was a monarch – someone who was, literally and figuratively, the state. And as the state, not only were they only perfunctorily restrained in terms of what they could and could not do vis-à-vis their subjects, but also, there were no effective mechanisms to hold them accountable when they disregarded even those restraints. Hence, the articulation of the right to life and death in what Foucault calls classical sovereignty: The sovereign having the right to put a subject to death or letting them live was the way in which the sovereign displayed, maintained, and re-presented how ultimate his/her power was over the subjects (Foucault 2003). This was also why food scarcity, hunger, and famine, could be so consequential for the sovereign: If the provisioning apparatus malfunctioned and the residents of the city suffered, they made sure that the sovereign suffered as well (by way of rioting, taking his/her opponents' side, or in short, disrupting the always fragile peace at the capital). Thus, the efficient and smooth functioning of the city's provisioning apparatus acted as a mechanism of restraint and accountability on the sovereign. Yet, effective as these mechanisms were, they paled in comparison to the sovereign's right to life and death over his/her subjects. While a citywide riot following food scarcity could topple the sovereign and tarnish the country's and the sovereign's reputation of might and internal peace, the sovereign still maintained his/her absolute right over the life and death of his/her subjects – and regardless of the success or the failure of the riot, s/he was usually not shy about exercising that right, particularly once the riots calmed down (or for that matter, to calm the riots down). In other words, it wasn't a food regime that sought to protect the members' right to subsistence or right to food; such protection happened incrementally, and to a large extent, accidentally. As such, this is a food regime we should neither want to nor try to go back to.

The course of discussion should rather steer towards what I, following Ellen Meiksins Wood, had underlined early on: the "*devaluation* of the political sphere" (Meiksins Wood 2016, 211; emphasis in the original). The rise of capitalism is dependent on the extraction and appropriation of surplus labor purely through economic means, and as such, economic and sovereign power are decoupled from each other; and though economic power rests on sovereign power, the presence of political rights and/or civic status does not necessarily alleviate class inequality. Perhaps this decoupling is exactly what we should target to modify.

One substantive way of doing that could be to challenge and reverse the reliance on the commodity exchange through the market to satisfy basic necessities – most notably, food. After all, laborers labor to earn wages so that they can buy whatever they need. If we can intervene and alleviate the reliance, modify it to an interdependence, perhaps, then we can sever the relation between *necroeconomy* and *necropolitics*. For once basic necessities are communally taken care of, once members of the political community know that they are protected such that they will not be left to die, at least the economic coercions that the sovereign power utilizes to sustain market imperatives will be limited.

On that note, another way of undoing the decoupling between economic and sovereign power would be to constrain extra-economic coercions. As Polanyi suggests, markets cannot live on their own; the state is necessary to both repeal what limits the markets and administer what intervenes with them (2001, 145). Indeed, this administration builds upon what Foucault describes as biopower – the sovereign's right to make live and to let die (Foucault 2003, 241). Perhaps then, what we should work to limit is precisely this capability of the sovereign. Reminding the sovereign that it is constituted and is delegated absolute power so that the members of the political community can live (ibid.), we should push for a *mentalité* of government that cannot let or make some members of the political community die – through neither the penal system nor the food system. Because life as such is the foundation of the sovereign's existence as well as its rights, as Foucault says, it should indeed be outside the contract (ibid.). What we can do, then, is to push for changes in the food regime, such that it recognizes life and its sustenance as a restraint that binds the sovereign and hinders it from exercising its power to let die (and legitimizing it as a component of the sovereign's right).

One final method I can suggest is to un-normalize the economy of death, exposure, and decay, and to break the codependency between *necropolitics* and *necroeconomics*. This would require us to do a lot of consciousness-raising in our political communities. We would have to make people aware that hunger, food scarcity, and malnourishment some of us (*enemies*) are experiencing will not remain contained only to them, that compliance and consent to the food regime – which we hope is enough to keep us in the *friends* category – does not necessarily imply that our lives will be free of such experiences. If enough of us refuse to let ourselves and others be coerced to work under "the penalty of starvation" (Polanyi 2001, 172) and the central authority thus becomes unable to govern through hunger, food scarcity, and malnourishment, perhaps it could be then coerced to change its stance towards the markets. This does not necessarily mean things will improve. As I suggested above, crony capitalism could be one of the outcomes when sovereign power is no longer subjugated to economic power but tries to subsume it. Political privilege might even make a comeback as a method of extracting and appropriating surplus labor.

Perhaps, for now, the right to food is indeed a good place to start "recover[ing] democracy from the formal separation of the 'political' and the 'economic'" (Meiksins Wood 2016, 237). Our priority should be to make sure none of us are left hungry and/or malnourished in our political communities. And we have to do this without relying on the central authority to constantly oversee us – like a Leviathan.

Some Early Sources on Istanbul's *Bağ, Bahçe, and Bostan*

The first source I consider are the *Bostancıbaşı Defterleri* (Bostancıbaşı Books). These refer to records kept by the *Bostancı Ocağı* (Bostancı Guild), a gardening guild that was responsible for maintaining public recreational parks, gardens, orchards, and fields, as well as the woods and waters around Istanbul, along with providing basic security services in the hinterlands and coastal regions of the city (Sakaoğlu 1994a; 1994b; Artan 1994). In addition, they took care of the summer residences and hunting mansions of the (extended) royal family and cultivated the Topkapı Palace gardens (Sakaoğlu 1994b; Artan 1994). From 1790 to 1815, the guild also kept detailed records of the plots and buildings along the shores of the Bosporus and the Golden Horn, including ownership and tenant information, and their demographic breakdown (Sakaoğlu 1994a). Because the *Bostancı*s also recorded the details of the plots and buildings, it is possible to pinpoint where some of the gardens, orchards, and fields in the city were, as well as the usual sizes of Bosporus villages, and the extent of settlement around Istanbul.

Although the Bostancı Guild was operational from the 15th to the 19th century, records are only available for about 25 years (Sakaoğlu 1994b); and as such, the information they provide is limited. Still, the guild itself may provide us with more information about in-city production. Set up as a branch of the Janissary Army, the guild followed the strict hierarchical structure of the army (ibid). *Bostancı*s were divided into three groups, each tasked with specific regions of the city, and within that region, specific types of buildings and plots to maintain (Artan 1994; Sakaoğlu 1994b). The guild master was the *Bostancıbaşı*, who answered directly to the sultan (Sakaoğlu 1994b). He maintained the order and the security of the seashore mansions along the Marmara coastline, as well as the Maiden's Tower and various fortresses and bastions along the Bosporus (ibid). He also managed the docks and harbors through which provisions were received into the city, by controlling the sea traffic along the Bosporus (ibid). Under the *Bostancıbaşı*, *Bostancı*s were organized into three groups; *bostancı hasekileri*, *gılmanan-ı bahçe-i hassa*, and *gılmanan-ı bostaniyan*. The first two were exclusively tasked with maintaining the Palace gardens, hunting areas, and mansions, including those of the (extended) royal family (Artan 1994; Sakaoğlu 1994b). The last group, *gılmanan-ı bostaniyan*, was the most significant for the city's provisioning, since these were the gardeners who were tasked with cultivating the gardens, fields, parks, and orchards of the city (Sakaoğlu 1994b). Produce from these plots, which included various types of vegetables, fruits, and flowers, was used primarily to provision the

Palace (ibid). The surplus was sold in 200 vegetable shops, 17 flower shops, and 30 spinach shops run by the guild around the city (ibid, 307).

Second, various written sources also mention Istanbul's abundant gardens (*bahçes*), orchards (*bağs*) and fields (*tarlas*; *bostans*), and the different types of fruits and vegetables cultivated in the city. Almost 100 years before the *Bostancıbaşı Defterleri*, Eremya Çelebi Kömürciyan, for example, in his *İstanbul Tarihi* (*History of Istanbul*) (~1695; 1952; 1988) describes extensive orchards and vineyards on the Anatolian side, from Üsküdar to Çamlıca and from Kadıköy to Fenerbahçe in 17th century Istanbul (İstanbul 1993a, 533). In the old city quarters, he lists fields around the walls and the gates of the capital – Küçük Langa *bostanı* behind the Davutpaşa gate; Büyük Langa *bostans* in the Yenikapı region; Bayram Paşa *bostans* extending through the Edirne road beginning at the Edirne Gate (İstanbul 1993c, 309). On the northern side of the Golden Horn, especially around Kasımpaşa, where there were famous public gardens and parks, Kömürciyan mentions vineyards, orchards, and fields, in which different types of flowers were cultivated, in addition to fruits and vegetables (ibid). Finally, on both sides of the Bosporus, he cites gardens, orchards, fields, and vineyards owned by the sultan, the (extended) royal family, and laymen alike, with fruits and vegetables unique to specific neighborhoods, such as artichokes of Ortaköy, for example (ibid). Another major source from the same era, Evliya Çelebi's *Seyahatname*, similarly describes Istanbul as a city green with fields, orchards and vineyards adorning the hills looking over the Bosporus and the Golden Horn (Dağlı 2010). Travel documents, from the 17th to 19th century, written by Ottoman subjects and European travelers alike, give accounts comparable to Kömürciyan and Evliya Çelebi.

Thirdly, in paintings depicting the city, parks, gardens, orchards, and fields are easily visible. Based on these, we can assume that there was significant FFV production in and around the city. Alongside the ones imported through the *Yemiş İskelesi* (Fruit Docks), these locally produced FFVs helped Ottoman authorities to keep Istanbul provisioned.

List of Various Foods Provisioned to Istanbul and Their Locations of Production

TABLE 5   List of various foods provisioned to Istanbul and their locations of production
(İnalcık 1994; Ünsal 2010)

General category	Specific category	Item	Locations of production
Me'kulat	Meat (*Et*)	Cattle and pastrami (*pastırma*)	Bucak, Moldavia, Bulgaria (Varna)
		Sheep	Ukraine (Akkerman-Kili/Kilia), Konya, Erzurum
		Chicken	Bursa
	Groceries (*Bakkaliye*)	Olives	Edremit, Erdek
		Onions	Pendik, Kartal, Mudanya
		Raisins and grapes	İzmir, Kuşadası
		Figs	İzmir, Kuşadası, Aydın
		Hazelnuts	Black Sea regions
		Chestnuts	Black Sea regions
		Lemons	Chios
		Oranges	Chios
		Pistachios	Aleppo
		Date	Egypt
Meşrubat (liquids)		Lemon juice (in barrels)	Greece (İstanköy/Cos)
		Grape molasses (*pekmez*)	Gelibolu, Kazdağı
		Wine	Cyprus, Bozcaada
Hububat; Zahire	Grains	Wheat and flour	Crimea, Ukraine (Deşt), Egypt, Romania (Wallachia) and Bulgaria (Dobruca/Dobruja)
		Rice	Egypt (Dimyat/Damietta), Bulgaria (Filibe/ Plovdiv)

TABLE 5   List of various foods provisioned to Istanbul and their locations of production
(İnalcık 1994; Ünsal 2010) (cont.)

General category	Specific category	Item	Locations of production
	Legumes	Beans Lentils Peas Chickpeas (*nohut*) (also consumed dried, as a snack – *leblebi*) Carob (*harnup*)	Anatolia, Egypt
Salt			Crimea, Transylvania, Edremit (Kızılca-Tuzla)
Dairy		Cheese	Bulgaria (Varna), Romania (Eflak/Wallachia), İzmit, Yalova, Eğriboz, Edirne, Thrace and Greece (Crete/ Girit), Italy
Oils and fats		Butter (*sadeyağ*; *tereyağı*)	Crimea (Kefe/ Feodosia), Bulgaria (Varna; Rusçuk/ Ruse)
		Olive oil	Edremit, Gemlik, Greece (Midilli/Lesvos; Crete/Girit)
Pickles			Gelibolu, Kazdağı
Salted fish			Russia (Azak/Azoff), Ukraine (Kili/Kiliya; Kefe/ Feodosia)
Spices		Gum mastic (*Sakız*)	Chios
Sweeteners		Honey	Crimea (Kefe/Feodosia); Anatolia, Greek islands
Stimulants		Coffee	Egypt, Yemen, Ethiopia

Bibliography

5216 Büyükşehir Belediyesi Kanunu. (2004, 07 23). Ankara: Resmi Gazete.

552 Yaş Sebze ve Meyve Ticaretinin Düzenlenmesi ve Toptancı Halleri Hakkında Kanun Hükmünde Kararname (1995, 06 24) Ankara: Resmi Gazete.

28135 Sebze ve Meyve Ticareti İle Hal Kayıt Sistemi Hakkında Tebliğ (2011, 12 07). Ankara: Resmi Gazete.

28489 On Dört İlde Büyükşehir Belediyesi ve Yirmi Yedi İlçe Kurulması ile Bazı Kanun ve Kanun Hükmünde Kararnamelerde Değişiklik Yapılmasına Dair Kanun (2012, 12 06). Ankara: Resmi Gazete.

Akad, Mehmet Tanju. 1994. Balkan Savaşı'nda İstanbul. In *Dünden Bugüne İstanbul Ansiklopedisi*, İlhan Tekeli et al. (eds.), vol. 2, 29–30. İstanbul: Tarih Vakfı Yayınları.

Akçay, Ali Adnan. 1999. Toprak Ağalığından Kapitalist İşletmeciliğe Türkiye Tarımında Büyük Topraklı İşletmeler. In *75 Yılda Köylerden Şehirlere*, Oya Köymen (ed.), 115–131. İstanbul: Tarih Vakfı Yayınları.

Akçura, Gökhan. 1993. Bakkallar. In *Dünden Bugüne İstanbul Ansiklopedisi*, İlhan Tekeli et al. (eds.), vol. 2, 3–5. İstanbul: Tarih Vakfı Yayınları.

Aktüre, Sevgi. 1985. Osmanlı Devleti'nde Taşra Kentlerindeki Değişimler. In *Tanzimat'tan Cumhuriyet'e Türkiye Ansiklopedisi*, Murat Belge et al. (eds.), 891–904. İstanbul: İletişim Yayınları.

Albritton, Robert. 2008. Between Obesity and Hunger: The Capitalist Food Industry. In *Food and Culture: A Reader*, Carole Counihan and Penny van Esterik (eds.), 342–354. New York, NY: Routledge.

Alkon, Alison Hope, and Julian Agyeman. 2011. *Cultivating Food Justice: Race, Class, and Sustainability*. Cambridge, MA: MIT Press.

Alves, Eliseu Roberto de Andrade, and Affonso Celso Pastore. 1978. Import Substitution and Implicit Taxation of Agriculture in Brazil. *American Journal of Agricultural Economics* 60(5): 865–871.

Anguelovski, Isabelle. 2015a. Alternative Food Provision Conflicts in Cities: Contesting Food Privilege, Injustice and Whiteness in Jamaica Plain, Boston. *Geoforum* 58: 184–194.

Anguelovski, Isabelle. 2015b. Healthy Food Stores, Greenlining and Food Gentrification: Contesting New Forms of Privilege, Displacement and Locally Unwanted Land Uses in Racially Mixed Neighborhoods. *International Journal of Urban and Regional Research* 39(6): 1209–1230.

Arı, Kemal. 1999. Türkiye'de Mübadele Dönemi Toprak Mülkiyeti ve Tarımda Değişim. In *75 Yılda Köylerden Şehirlere*, Oya Köymen (ed.), 97–114. İstanbul: Tarih Vakfı Yayınları.

Artan, Tülay. 1994. Bahçeler: Osmanlı Dönemi. In *Dünden Bugüne İstanbul Ansiklopedisi*, İlhan Tekeli et al. (eds.), vol. 1, 543–545. İstanbul: Tarih Vakfı Yayınları.

Atasoy, Yildiz. 2013. Supermarket Expansion in Turkey: Shifting Relations of Food Provisioning. *Journal of Agrarian Change* 13(4): 547–570.

Aydın, Zülküf. 2010. Neo-Liberal Transformation of Turkish Agriculture. *Journal of Agrarian Change* 10(2): 149–187.

Aysu, Abdullah. 2008. *Küreselleşme ve Tarım Politikaları: DTÖ, IMF ve Dünya Bankası'nın Türkiye Tarımına Etkileri*. İstanbul: Su Yayınları.

Baer, Werner, and Isaac Kerstenetzky. 1964. Import Substitution and Industrialization in Brazil. *The American Economic Review* 54(3): 411–425.

Bagchi, Amiya Kumar. 1977. Export-Led Growth and Import-Substituting Industrialization. *Economic and Political Weekly* 12(6/8): 219–224.

Bağımsız Sosyal Bilimciler. 2007. *IMF Gözetiminde On Uzun Yıl: 1998–2002 Farklı Hükümetler Tek Siyaset*. İstanbul: Yordam Kitap.

Balisacan, Arsenio M. 1989. Agriculture in Economic Development Strategies: The Philippines. *ASEAN Economic Bulletin* 6(1): 81–93.

Bargu, Banu. 2014. *Starve and Immolate: The Politics of Human Weapons*. New York, NY: Columbia University Press.

Barndt, Deborah. 2008. On the Move for Food: Three Women Behind the Tomato's Journey. In *Food and Culture: A Reader*, Carole Counihan and Penny van Esterik (eds.), 472–484. New York, NY: Routledge.

Barrett, Hazel R., Brian W. Ilbery, Angela W. Browne, and Tony Binns. 1999. Globalization and the Changing Networks of Food Supply: The Importation of Fresh Horticultural Produce from Kenya into the UK. *Transactions of the Institute of British Geographers* 24: 159–174.

Bartu, Ayfer. 1999. Who Owns the Old Quarters? Rewriting Histories in a Global Era. In *Istanbul: Between the Global and the Local*, Çağlar Keyder (ed.), 31–45. Lanham, MD: Rowman & Littlefield.

Bartu, Ayfer. 2001. Rethinking Heritage Politics in a Global Context: A View from Istanbul. In *Hybrid Urbanism: On the Identity Discourse and the Built Environment*, Nezar AlSayyad (ed.), 131–155. Westport, CT: Praeger.

Benson, Peter, and Edward F. Fischer. 2007. Broccoli and Desire. *Antipode* 39(5): 800–820.

Besky, Sarah. 2015. Agricultural Justice, Abnormal Justice? An Analysis of Fair Trade's Plantation Problem. *Antipode* 47(5): 1141–1160.

Bignebat, Céline, Ahmet Ali Koç, and Sylvaine Lemeilleur. 2009. Small producers, supermarkets, and the role of intermediaries in Turkey's fresh fruit and vegetable market. *Agricultural Economics* 40(1): 807–816.

Biryol, Uğur. 2016. Çayın Tarihsel Yolculuğu, Karadeniz'e Getirilişi ve Şimdiki Ahvali Üzerine. In *Karardı Karadeniz*, Uğur Biryol (ed.), 77–95 Istanbul: İletişim Yayınları.

Blum, Matthias. 2013. War, food rationing and socioeconomic inequality in Germany during the First World War. *The Economic History Review* 66(4): 1063–1083.

Bora, Aksu. 2018. *Kadınların Sınıfı: Ücretli Ev Emeği ve Kadın Öznelliğinin İnşası.* İstanbul: İletişim Yayınları.

Bora, Tanıl. 1997. Türk Sağının İstanbul Rüyaları: Global Şehir, Fatih'in İstanbul'u ve "Yeniden Fetih". *Mediterraneans* 10: 149–157.

Bora, Tanıl. 1999. Istanbul of the Conqueror: The "Alternative Global City" Dreams of Political Islam. In *Istanbul: Between the Global and the Local*, Çağlar Keyder (ed.), 47–58. Lanham, MD: Rowman & Littlefield.

Boratav, Korkut. 1981. *Tarihsel Yapılar ve Kapitalism.* Istanbul: Birikim Yayınları.

Boratav, Korkut. 1995. İktisat Tarihi (1981–1994). In *Türkiye Tarihi 5: Bugünkü Türkiye 1980–1995*, Bülent Tanör, Korkut Boratav, and Sina Akşin (eds.), 161–213. İstanbul: Cem Yayınevi.

Boratav, Korkut. 2007. *Türkiye İktisat Tarihi 1908–2009.* Ankara: İmge Kitapevi.

Boratav, Korkut. 2016. *1980li Yıllarda Türkiye'de Sosyal Sınıflar ve Bölüşüm.* Ankara: İmge Kitapevi.

Botella-Rodriguez, Elisa. 2018. Costa Rica's Outward-Looking Development: From 'Agriculture of Change' to Food Insecurity. *Bulletin of Latin American Research* 37(1): 57–72.

Bradley, Katharine, and Hank Harrera. 2016. Decolonizing Food Justice: Naming, Resisting, and Researching Colonizing Forces in the Movement. *Antipode* 48(1): 97–114.

Brones, Anna. 2018. Food apartheid: the root of the problem with America's groceries. *The Guardian.* Accessed: February 18, 2020. Retrieved from: https://www.theguardian.com/society/2018/may/15/food-apartheid-food-deserts-racism-inequality-america-karen-washington-interview.

Brown, Trent. 2018. *Farmers, Subalterns, and Activists: Social Politics of Sustainable Agriculture in India.* Cambridge: Cambridge University Press.

Brown, Wendy. 2015. *Undoing the Demos: Neoliberalism's Stealth Revolution.* New York, NY: Zone Books.

Bryceson, Deborah F. 2002. The Scramble in Africa: Reorienting Rural Livelihoods. *World Development* 30(5): 725–739.

Budak, Sevim. 1993. Çöp. In *Dünden Bugüne İstanbul Ansiklopedisi*, İlhan Tekeli et al. (eds.), vol. 2, 531–533. İstanbul: Tarih Vakfı Yayınları.

Buğday Ekolojik Yaşamı Destekleme Derneği. 2020. Katılımcı Onay Sistemleri. *Gıda Toplulukları.* Accessed: February 18, 2020. Retrieved from: http://gidatopluluklari.org/?page_id=33.

Burch, David, and Jasper Goss. 1999. Global Sourcing and Retail Chains: Shifting Relationships of Production in Australian Agri-foods. *Rural Sociology* 64(2): 334–350.

Bussolini, Jeffrey. 2010. What is a Dispositif? *Foucault Studies* 10: 85–107.

Byrne, Christine. 2019. It's Great That We Talk About 'Food Deserts' – But It Might Be Time to Stop. *Huffington Post.* Accessed: February 19, 2020. Retrieved from: https://www.huffpost.com/entry/food-desert-problem-access-healthy-options_n_5d1b910ee4b082e55370dee5.

Çakır, Günay, C. Ün, Emin Zeki Başkent, S. Köse, Fatih Sivrikaya, and Sedat Keleş. 2008. Evaluating Urbanization, Fragmentation and Land Use/Land Cover Change Pattern in Istanbul City, Turkey from 1971 to 2002. *Land Degradation and Development* 19: 663–675.

Çakır, Ruşen. 1997. İstanbul İslamcı Bir Şehir mi? *Mediterraneans* 10: 159–166.

Caldwell, Melissa L. 2008. Domesticating the French Fry: McDonald's and Consumerism in Moscow. In *The Cultural Politics of Food and Eating: A Reader*, James L. Watson and Melissa L. Caldwell (eds.), 180–196. Oxford: Blackwell.

Çalışkan, Koray, and Michel Callon. 2009. Economization, Part 1: Shifting Attention from the Economy Towards Processes of Economization. *Economy and Society* 38(3): 369–398.

Çalışkan, Koray, and Michel Callon. 2010. Economization, Part 2: A Research Programme for the Study of Markets. *Economy and Society* 39(1): 1–32.

Canovan, Margaret. 2006. The People. In *The Handbook of Political Theory*, John S. Dryzek, Bonnie Honig, and Anne Phillips (eds.), 349–362. Oxford: Oxford University Press.

Çavuşoğlu, Gülin. 2018. Türkiye'de ve Avrupa'da bulunan Starbucks şubelerinin sayıları hakkındaki iddialar. *Teyit.org.* Accessed: January 20, 2020. Retrieved from: https://teyit.org/turkiyede-ve-avrupada-bulunan-starbucks-subelerinin-sayilari-hakkin-daki-iddialar/.

Chase, Holly. 1994. The Meyhane or McDonald's? Changes in Eating Habits and the Evolution of Fast Food in Istanbul. In *Culinary Cultures of the Middle East*, Sami Zubaida and Richard Tapper (eds.), 73–85. New York, NY: I.B. Tauris Publishers.

Collier, Neil, and Ora DeKornfeld. 2017. How Junk Food Is Transforming Brazil. *The New York Times: International Times Documentaries.* Accessed: January 20, 2020. Retrieved from: https://www.nytimes.com/video/international-home/100000005148449/junk-food-upriver-tbd.html.

Cook, Ian, et al. 2004. Follow the Thing: Papaya. *Antipode* 36(4): 642–664.

Cook, Ian, et al. 2006. Geographies of Food: Following. *Progress in Human Geography* 30(5): 655–666.

Cook, Ian, and Michelle Harrison. 2007. Follow the Thing: "West Indian Hot Pepper Sauce". *Space and Culture* 10(1): 40–63.

Counihan, Carole. 2005. The Border as Barrier and Bridge: Food, Gender, and Ethnicity in the San Luis Valley of Colorado. In *From Betty Crocker to Feminist Food Studies: Critical Perspectives on Women and Food*, Arlene Voski Avakian and Barbara Haber (eds.), 200–220. Amherst, MA: University of Massachusetts Press.

Çubuk, Mehmet. 1993. Boğaziçi. In *Dünden Bugüne İstanbul Ansiklopedisi*, İlhan Tekeli et al. (eds.), vol. 2, 266–281. İstanbul: Tarih Vakfı Yayınları.

Dağlı, Yücel. 2010. Evliya Çelebi'nin İstanbul'u. In *İstanbul Ansiklopedisi*, 362–367. İstanbul: NTV Yayınları.

Davis, Belinda J. 2000a. *Home Fires Burning: Food, Politics, and Everyday Life in World War I Berlin*. Chapel Hill, NC: University of North Carolina Press.

Davis, Mike. 2000b. *Late Victorian Holocausts: El Niño Famines and the Making of the Third World*. New York, NY: Verso.

de Souza, Rebecca. 2019. *Feeding the Other: Whiteness, Privilege and Neoliberal Stigma in Food Pantries*. Cambridge, MA: MIT Press.

Debowicz, Dario, and Paul Segal. 2014. Structural Change in Argentina, 1935–1960: The Role of Import Substitution and Factor Endowments. *The Journal of Economic History* 74(1): 230–258.

Dixon, Jane, and Hugh Campbell. 2009. "Symposium on Food Regime Analysis." *Agriculture and Human Values* 26(4).

Doğan, Aylin. 2018. *"Esir Şehrin" Mutfak Kültürü: Mütareke Dönemi İstanbul Mutfak Kültürü 1918–1922*. İstanbul: Libra Kitapçılık ve Yayıncılık.

Doğancayır, Caner Murat, and Umut Kocagöz. 2018. Kayıtdışı Gıda Temin Kanalları. *beyond.istanbul* 3: 49–53.

Dokuyan, Sabit. 2013. İkinci Dünya Savaşı Sırasında Yaşanan Gıda Sıkıntısı ve Ekmek Karnesi Uygulaması. *Turkish Studies* 8(5): 193–210.

Dölen, Emre. 1993. Askeri Tahiniye Fabrikası. In *Dünden Bugüne İstanbul Ansiklopedisi*, İlhan Tekeli et al. (eds.), vol. 1, 354. İstanbul: Tarih Vakfı Yayınları.

Dutko, Paula, Michele ver Ploeg, and Tracey Farrigan. 2012. *Characteristics and Influential Factors of Food Deserts*. Economic Research Service, USDA, ERR-140.

Dyzenhaus, David. 2001. Hobbes and the Legitimacy of Law. *Law and Philosophy* 20(5): 461–498.

Ekinci, Oktay. 1993. Boğaziçi Yasası. In *Dünden Bugüne İstanbul Ansiklopedisi*, İlhan Tekeli et al. (eds.), vol. 2, 290–292. İstanbul: Tarih Vakfı Yayınları.

Ekinci, Oktay. 2010a. Gecekondulaşma. In *İstanbul Ansiklopedisi*, 411–415. İstanbul: NTV Yayınları.

Ekinci, Oktay. 2010b. Gökdelenler. In *İstanbul Ansiklopedisi*, 426–431. İstanbul: NTV Yayınları.

Ekzen, Nazif. 1984. 1980 Stabilizasyon Paketinin 1958, 1970 ve 1978–1979 Paketleri ile Karşılaştırmalı Analizi. In *Türkiye'de ve Dünyada Yaşanan Ekonomik Bunalım*, İlhan Tekeli (ed.), 165–187. Ankara: Yurt Yayınevi.

Elden, Neyran. 2019. Fatih'te siyanürle öldükleri açıklanan dört kardeş: Bakkaldaki veresiye defterinde 2.260 lira borç. *BBC*. Accessed: February 18, 2020. Retrieved from: https://www.bbc.com/turkce/haberler-dunya-50322797.

Eplett, Layla. 2016. Should the Concept of a Food Desert Be Deserted? *Scientific American*. Accessed: January 10, 2020. Retrieved from: https://blogs.scientificamerican.com/food-matters/should-the-concept-of-a-food-desert-be-deserted/.

Erçakir, Mehmet, and Ali Çevikbaş. 2016. AK Parti İl Başkanı'ndan FETÖ'cülere: Ağaç kökü yesinler. *Hürriyet*. Accessed: May 21, 2019. Retrieved from: http://www.hurriyet.com.tr/gundem/ak-parti-il-baskanindan-fetoculere-agac-koku-yesinler-40242531.

Erder, Sema. 1999. Where Do You Hail From? Localism and Networks in Istanbul. In *Istanbul: Between the Local and the Global*, Çağlar Keyder (ed.), 161–171. Lanham, MD: Rowman & Littlefield.

Erder, Sema. 2010. Göç. In *İstanbul Ansiklopedisi*, 422–425. İstanbul: NTV Yayınları.

Eruzun, Cengiz. 1993. İmar Planları. In *Dünden Bugüne İstanbul Ansiklopedisi*, İlhan Tekeli et al. (eds.), vol. 4, 162–164. İstanbul: Tarih Vakfı Yayınları.

Estabrook, Barry. 2011. *Tomatoland: How Modern Industrial Agriculture Destroyed Our Most Alluring Fruit*. Kansas City, MI: Andrews McMeel Publishing.

Faroqhi, Suraiya. 2009. *Another Mirror for Princes: The Public Image of the Ottoman Sultans and Its Reception*. Piscataway, NJ: Gorgias Press.

Finefrock, Michael M. 1981. Laissez-Faire, the 1923 Izmir Economic Congress and the Early Turkish Developmental Policy in Political Perspective. *Middle Eastern Studies* 17(3): 375–392.

Foucault, Michel. 1990. *The History of Sexuality, Volume I: An Introduction*. Robert Hurley (trans.). New York, NY: Vintage Books.

Foucault, Michel. 1995. *Discipline and Punish: The Birth of the Prison*. Alan Sheridan (trans.). New York, NY: Vintage Books.

Foucault, Michel. 2003. *"Society Must Be Defended": Lectures at the Collège de France 1975–1976*. Arnold I. Davidson (ed.). David Macey (trans.). New York, NY: Picador.

Foucault, Michel. 2007. *Security, Territory, Population: Lectures at the Collège de France 1977–1978*. Arnold I. Davidson (ed.). Graham Burchell (trans.). New York, NY: Palgrave Macmillan.

Foucault, Michel. 2008. *The Birth of Biopolitics: Lectures at the Collège de France 1978–1979*. Arnold I. Davidson (ed.). Graham Burchell (trans.). New York, NY: Palgrave MacMillan.

Frank, Andre Gunder. 1966. The Development of Underdevelopment. *Monthly Review* 18(4): 17–31.

Franz, Martin, Alexandra Appel, and Markus Hassler. 2013. Short Waves of Supermarket Diffusion in Turkey. *Moravian Geographical Reports* 21(4): 50–63.

Friedmann, Harriet, and Philip McMichael. 1989. Agriculture and the State System: The Rise and Decline of National Agricultures, 1870 to the present. *Sociologia Ruralis* 29(2): 93–117.

Gibson-Graham, J. K. 1996. *The End of Capitalism (As We Knew It): A Feminist Critique of Political Economy*. Minneapolis, MN: University of Minnesota Press.

Göktaş, Uğur. 2010. Esnaf ve Loncalar. In *İstanbul Ansiklopedisi*, 359–362. İstanbul: NTV Yayınları.

Goldman, Wendy Z., and Donald Filtzer. 2015. *Hunger and war: food provisioning in the Soviet Union during World War II*. Bloomington, IN: Indiana University Press.

Gönenç, Sertaç, and Erkan Rehber. 2007. Privatization in Agro-Food Sector: The Case of Turkish Dairy Industry. *British Food Journal* 109(9): 661–674.

Goodman, David, Melanie DuPuis, and Michael K. Goodman. 2012. *Alternative Food Networks: Knowledge, Practice, and Politics*. New York, NY: Routledge.

Greenwood, Antony. 1988. *Istanbul's Meat Provisioning: A Study of the Celepkeşan System*. PhD Dissertation, University of Chicago.

Güran, Tevfik. 2004. İstanbul'un İaşesi. In *İstanbul: Şehir ve Medeniyet*, Şevket Kamil Akar (ed.), 319–325. İstanbul: Klasik Yayınları.

Hamsici, Mahmut. 2020. Sibel Ünli: İstanbul Üniversitesi öğrencisi genç kadının ölümü hakkında neler biliniyor? *BBC*. Accessed: February 18, 2020. Retrieved from: https://www.bbc.com/turkce/haberler-turkiye-51002638.

Hann, Chris. 1990. *Tea and the Domestication of the Turkish State*. Huntingdon: Eothen Press.

Harvey, Arnold. D. 2007. *Body Politic: Political Metaphor and Political Violence*. Cambridge: Cambridge Scholars Publishing.

Health and Safety Labour Watch (Turkey). 2020. We resist for life, to defend life! In 2019 at least 1736 workers lost their lives. *ISIG Meclisi*. Accessed: March 31, 2020. Retrieved from: http://isigmeclisi.org/20274-we-resist-for-life-to-defend-life-in-2019-at-least-1736-workers-lost-their-liv.

Hill, Mark, and Warren Montag. 2015. *The Other Adam Smith*. Stanford, CA: Stanford University Press.

Hionidou, Violetta. 2013. Relief and Politics in Occupied Greece, 1941–4. *Journal of Contemporary History* 48(4): 761–783.

Hobbes, Thomas. 1996. *Leviathan*. Richard Tuck (ed.). New York, NY: Cambridge University Press.

Hopewell, Kristen. 2016. The Accidental Agro-Power: Constructing Comparative Advantage in Brazil. *New Political Economy* 21(6): 536–554.

IBB Hal Müdürlüğü. 2020. *Hal Fiyatları*. Accessed: January 20, 2020 Retrieved from: http://gida.ibb.istanbul/hal-mudurlugu/hal-fiyatlari.html.

İçöz, Özge. 2003. *Telekomünikasyon Sektöründe Regülasyon ve Rekabet*. Ankara: Rekabet Kurumu.

IFOAM. 2007. Participatory Guarantee Systems: Shared Vision, Shared Ideals. *IFOAM*. Accessed: February 18, 2020. Retrieved from: https://www.ifoam.bio/sites/default/files/page/files/ifoam_pgs_web.pdf.

İlbaş, Mehmet Hadi. 1999. Türkiye'de Kooperatifçilik ve Köy-Koop Deneyimi. In *75 Yılda Köylerden Şehirlere*, Oya Köymen (ed.), 241–247. İstanbul: Tarih Vakfı Yayınları.

İnalcık, Halil. 1994. İaşe: Osmanlı Dönemi. In *Dünden Bugüne İstanbul Ansiklopedisi*, İlhan Tekeli et al. (eds.), vol. 5, 119–116. İstanbul: Tarih Vakfı Yayınları.

İstanbul Umum Pazarcılar Esnaf Odası. 2020. *Pazarlar Listesi*. İstanbul, Turkey. Accessed: January 20, 2020. Retrieved from: http://www.istanbulpazarcilarodasi. com/istanbulda-kurulan-pazarlar.

İstanbul. 1993a. Bağlar. In *Dünden Bugüne İstanbul Ansiklopedisi*, İlhan Tekeli et al. (eds.), vol. 1, 533. İstanbul: Tarih Vakfı Yayınları.

İstanbul. 1993b. Kent İçi Ulaşım. In *Dünden Bugüne İstanbul Ansiklopedisi*, İlhan Tekeli et al. (eds.), vol. 4, 524–526. İstanbul: Tarih Vakfı Yayınları.

İstanbul. 1993c. Bostanlar. In *Dünden Bugüne İstanbul Ansiklopedisi*, İlhan Tekeli et al. (eds.), vol. 2, 309–310. İstanbul: Tarih Vakfı Yayınları.

İstanbul. 1993d. Kapanlar. In *Dünden Bugüne İstanbul Ansiklopedisi*, İlhan Tekeli et al. (eds.), vol. 4, 430–431. İstanbul: Tarih Vakfı Yayınları.

İstanbul. 1993e. Kıtlıklar. In *Dünden Bugüne İstanbul Ansiklopedisi*, İlhan Tekeli et al. (eds.), vol. 5, 8–10. İstanbul: Tarih Vakfı Yayınları.

Jacobs, Andrew, and Matt Richtel. 2017a. "How Big Business Got Brazil Hooked on Junk Food." *The New York Times*. Accessed: January 20, 2020. Retrieved from: https:// www.nytimes.com/interactive/2017/09/16/health/brazil-obesity-nestle.html.

Jacobs, Andrew, and Matt Richtel. 2017b. "She Took on Colombia's Soda Industry. Then She was Silenced." *The New York Times*. Accessed: January 20, 2020. Retrieved from: https://www.nytimes.com/2017/11/13/health/colombia-soda-tax-obesity.html.

Julier, Alice. 2013. The Political Economy of Obesity: The Fat Pay All. In *Food and Culture: A Reader*, Carole Counihan and Penny van Esterik (eds.), 546–562. New York, NY: Routledge.

Kaldijan, Paul. 2004. Istanbul's Bostans: A Millennium of Market Gardens. *Geographical Review* 94(3): 284–304.

Kandiyoti, Deniz. 2015. *Cariyeler, Bacılar, Yurttaşlar: Kimlikler ve Toplumsal Dönüşümler*. İstanbul: İletişim Yayınları.

Kaplan, Martha. 2007. Fijian Water in Fiji and New York: Local Politics and a Global Commodity. *Cultural Anthropology* 22(4): 685–706.

Karademir, Zafer. 2017. *İmparatorluğun Açlıkla İmtihanı: Osmanlı Toplumunda Kıtlıklar (1560–1660)*. İstanbul: Kitap Yayınevi.

Karaömerlioğlu, M. Asim. 2000. Elite Perceptions of Land Reform in Early Republican Turkey. *The Journal of Peasant Studies* 27(3): 115–141.

Kauffer, François. 1996. Istanbul Planı/Map of Istanbul, 1776, in Antoine-Ignace Melling, Voyage pittoresque de Constantinople et des rives du Bosphore, Paris, 1819. In *Dünya Kenti İstanbul Sergisi/Istanbul a World City Exhibition*, Tarih Vakfı, 110. İstanbul: Yapı Kredi Yayınları.

Kazgan, Gülten. 1999. 1980lerde Türk Tarımında Yapısal Değişme. In *75 Yılda Köylerden Şehirlere*, Oya Köymen (ed.), 31–36. İstanbul: Tarih Vakfı Yayınları.

Kazgan, Gülten. 2002. *Tanzimattan 21. Yüzyıla Türkiye Ekonomisi: Birinci Küreselleşmeden İkinci Küreselleşmeye*. İstanbul: İstanbul Bilgi Üniversitesi Yayınları.

Kazgan, Gülten. 2003. *Tarım ve Gelişme*. İstanbul: İstanbul Bilgi Üniversitesi Yayınları.

Kazgan, Gülten. 2006. Mal ve Sermaye Hareketlerinde Tam Serbestleşme, TL'nin Konvertibilitesi ve Uluslararası Anlaşmalar: 1990lı Yıllar. In *Tanzimattan 21. Yüzyıla Türkiye Ekonomisi: Birinci Küreselleşmeden İkinci Küreselleşmeye*, Gülten Kazgan, 153–188. İstanbul: İstanbul Bilgi Üniversitesi Yayınları.

Kazgan, Gülten. 2013. Devletin Yeni Rolü: Özel Zararların Kamulaştırılması ve Kamusal Yararların Özelleştirilmesi. In *Tanzimat'tan 21.Yüzyıla Türkiye Ekonomisi*, Gülten Kazgan, 225–254. İstanbul: İstanbul Bilgi Üniversitesi Yayınları.

Keyder, Çağlar. 1985. Osmanlı Devleti ve Dünya Ekonomik Sistemi. In *Tanzimat'tan Cumhuriyet'e Türkiye Ansiklopedisi*, Murat Belge et al. (eds.), 642–652. İstanbul: İletişim Yayınları.

Keyder, Çağlar. 1999a. A Tale of Two Neighborhoods. In *Istanbul: Between the Global and the Local*, Çağlar Keyder (ed.), 173–186. Lanham, MD: Rowman & Littlefield.

Keyder, Çağlar. 1999b. The Housing Market from Informal to Global. In *Istanbul: Between the Global and the Local*, Çağlar Keyder (ed.), 143–159. Lanham, MD: Rowman & Littlefield.

Keyder, Çağlar. 1999c. The Setting. In *Istanbul: Between the Global and the Local*, Çağlar Keyder (ed.), 3–28. Lanham, MD: Rowman & Littlefield.

Keyder, Çağlar. 1999d. Türkiye'de Tarımda Küçük Meta Üretimin Oluşumu. In *75 Yılda Köylerden Şehirlere*, Oya Köymen (ed.), 163–172. İstanbul: Tarih Vakfı Yayınları.

Keyder, Çağlar. 2005. Globalization and Social Exclusion in Istanbul. *International Journal of Urban and Regional Research* 29(1): 124–134.

Keyder, Çağlar. 2010. Istanbul into the 21st Century. In *Orienting Istanbul – Cultural Capital of Europe?*, Deniz Göktürk, Levent Soysal, and İpek Türeli (eds.), 25–34. New York, NY: Routledge.

Keyder, Çağlar. 2014. 2000lerde Devlet ve Tarım. In *Bildiğimiz Tarımın Sonu: Küresel İktidar ve Köylülük*, Çağlar Keyder and Zafer Yenal, 191–218. İstanbul: İletişim Yayınları.

Keyder, Çağlar. 2017. *Türkiye'de Devlet ve Sınıflar*. İstanbul: İletişim Yayınları.

Keyder, Çağlar, and Ayşe Öncü. 1993. *Istanbul and the Concept of World Cities*. Istanbul: Friedrich Ebert Foundation.

Keyder, Çağlar, and Ayşe Öncü. 1994. Globalization of a Third-World Metropolis: Istanbul in the 1980's. *Review: A Journal of the Fernand Braudel Center* 17(3): 383–421.

Keyder, Çağlar, and Zafer Yenal. 2014a. Artık Herşey Metalaşıyor: Küreselleşen Türkiye'de Tarımsal Dönüşüm. In *Bildiğimiz Tarımın Sonu: Küresel İktidar ve Köylülük*, Çağlar Keyder and Zafer Yenal, 49–103. İstanbul: İletişim Yayınları.

Keyder, Çağlar, and Zafer Yenal. 2014b. Bir Köy Vardı Uzakta ... In *Bildiğimiz Tarımın Sonu: Küresel İktidar ve Köylülük*, Çağlar Keyder and Zafer Yenal, 13–48. İstanbul: İletişim Yayınları.

Keyder, Çağlar, and Zafer Yenal. 2014c. Değişen Köyler ve Tarım Tartışmaları. In *Bildiğimiz Tarımın Sonu: Küresel İktidar ve Köylülük*, Çağlar Keyder and Zafer Yenal, 169–190. İstanbul: İletişim Yayınları.

Keyder, Çağlar, and Zafer Yenal. 2014d. Tarımsal Dönüşüm ve Proleterleşme Süreçleri: Tarihsel Bir Bakış. In *Bildiğimiz Tarımın Sonu: Küresel İktidar ve Köylülük*, Çağlar Keyder and Zafer Yenal, 137–168. İstanbul: İletişim Yayınları.

Koç, Ahmet Ali, Gulden Boluk, and Sureyya Kovacı. 2009. Concentration in Food Retailing and Anti-Competitive Practices in Turkey. *113th EAAE Seminar "A Resilient European Food Industry and Food Chain in a Challenging World".* Chania, Crete, Greece. Paper Presentation.

Köymen, Oya. 1999. Cumhuriyet Döneminde Tarımsal Yapı ve Tarım Politikaları. In *75 Yılda Köylerden Şehirlere*, Oya Köymen (ed.), 1–31. İstanbul: Tarih Vakfı Yayınları.

Kuban, Doğan. 1994. Kentin Gelişmesi. In *Dünden Bugüne İstanbul Ansiklopedisi*, İlhan Tekeli et al. (eds.), vol. 4, 530–547. İstanbul: Tarih Vakfı Yayınları.

Küçükerman, Önder. 2010. Sanayi. In *İstanbul Ansiklopedisi*, 796–800. İstanbul: NTV Yayınları.

Kurdakul, Necdet. 1985. Ticaret Antlaşmaları. In *Tanzimattan Cumhuriyet'e Türkiye Ansiklopedisi*, Murat Belge et al. (eds.), 666–667. İstanbul: İletişim Yayınları.

La Via Campesina. 2003. Food Sovereignty. *La Via Campesina.* Accessed: February 25, 2020. Retrieved from: https://viacampesina.org/en/food-sovereignty/.

Leitch, Alison. 2013. "Slow Food and the Politics of 'Virtuous Globalization'." In *Food and Culture: A Reader*, Carole Counihan and Penny van Esterik (eds.), 409–425. New York, NY: Routledge.

Lozada, Eriberto P. 2008. Globalized Childhood? Kentucky Fried Chicken in Beijing. In *The Cultural Politics of Food and Eating: A Reader*, James L. Watson, and Melissa L. Caldwell (eds.), 163–179. Oxford: Blackwell.

Luxemburg, Rosa. 2003. *The Accumulation of Capital.* London: Routledge.

Machiavelli, Niccolò. 2016. *The Prince.* Quentin Skinner and Russell Price (eds.). Russell Price (trans.). Cambridge: Cambridge University Press.

Magnan, Andre. 2012. Food Regimes. In *The Oxford Handbook of Food History*, Jeffrey M. Pilcher (ed.), 370–388. Oxford: Oxford University Press.

Mardin, Şerif. 2015a. *Jön Türklerin Siyasi Fikirleri 1895–1908.* İstanbul: İletişim Yayınları.

Mardin, Şerif. 2015b. *Yeni Osmanlı Düşüncesinin Doğuşu.* İstanbul: İletişim Yayınları.

Mardin, Şerif. 2017. *Türk Modernleşmesi.* İstanbul: İletişim Yayınları.

Mbembe, Achille. 2003. Necropolitics. Libby Meintjes (trans.) *Public Culture* 15(1): 11–40.

Meiksins Wood, Ellen. 2005. *Empire of Capital.* New York, NY: Verso.

Meiksins Wood, Ellen. 2016. *Democracy Against Capitalism: Renewing Historical Materialism.* New York, NY: Verso.

Meiksins Wood, Ellen. 2017. *The Origin of Capitalism: A Longer View.* New York, NY: Verso.

Metinsoy, Murat. 2012. İkinci Dünya Savaşı Yıllarında Devlet ve Köylüler: Hububat Alımları, Toprak Mahsulleri Vergisi ve Köylü Direnişi. *Tarih ve Toplum Yeni Yaklaşımlar* 15: 85–125. İletişim Yayınları.

Migros. 2011. Migros: Tarihçe. Accessed: January 20, 2020. Retrieved from: https://www.migroskurumsal.com/Icerik.aspx?IcerikID=43#.

Milli Prodüktivite Merkezi Tarım Şubesi. 1968. *Türkiyede Konserve ve Soğuk Hava Deposu İşletmeciliğinin Mevcut Durumu ve Ekonomik Önemi.* Ankara: Şan Matbaası.

Montag, Warren. 2005. Necro-economics: Adam Smith and Death in the Life of the Universal. *Radical Philosophy* 134: 7–17.

Mouré, Kenneth. 2010. Food Rationing and the Black Market in France (1940–1944). *French History* 24(2): 262–282.

Murphey, Rhoads. 1987. Provisioning Istanbul: The State and Subsistence in the Early Modern Middle East. *Food and Foodways* 2(1): 217–263.

Nabhan, Gary Paul. 2013. Rooting Out the Causes of Disease: Why Diabetes is So Common Among Desert Dwellers. In *Food and Culture: A Reader,* Carole Counihan and Penny van Esterik (eds.), 330–341. New York, NY: Routledge.

Nagan, Winston P., and Aitza M. Haddad. 2012. Sovereignty in Theory and Practice. *San Diego International Law Journal* 13: 429–519.

Öğüt, Şebnem Timur. 2009. Material Culture of Tea in Turkey: Transformations of Design through Tradition, Modernity and Identity. *The Design Journal* 12(3): 339–363.

Öncü, Ayşe. 1993. Understanding Istanbul: The Painless Coexistence of Zekeriyaköy and Sultanbeyli, İlhan Tekeli (ed.) *İstanbul* 1(2): 73–75.

Öncü, Ayşe. 1997. The Myth of the 'Ideal Home' Travels Across Cultural Borders to Istanbul. In *Space, Culture and Power: New Identities in Globalizing Cities,* Ayşe Öncü and Petra Weyland (eds.), 56–72. New Jersey, NJ: Zed Books.

Öncü, Ayşe. 1999. Istanbulites and Others: The Cultural Cosmology of Being Middle Class in the Era of Globalism. In *Istanbul: Between the Global and the Local,* Çağlar Keyder (ed.), 95–119. Lanham, MD: Rowman & Littlefield.

Oral, Necdet. 2015. *Türkiye'de Tarımın Ekonomi Politiği 1923–2013.* Ankara: Nota Bene.

Oshima, Harry T. 1986. The Transition from an Agricultural to an Industrial Economy in East Asia. *Economic Development and Cultural Change* 34(4): 783–809.

Oyan, Oğuz. 2015. Tarımda IMF-DB Gözetiminde 2000li Yıllar. In *Türkiye'de Tarımın Ekonomi-Politiği 1923–2013,* Necdet Oral (ed.), 111–130. Ankara: Nota Bene.

Öz, Özlem, and Mine Eder. 2012. Rendering Istanbul's Periodic Bazaars Invisible: Reflections on Urban Transformation and Contested Space. *International Journal of Urban and Regional Research* 36(2): 297–314.

Özbay, Ferhunde. 2019. *Kadın Emeği: Seçme Yazılar*. İstanbul: İletişim Yayınları.

Özdemir, Biltekin. 2009. *Osmanlı Devleti Dış Borçları: 1854–1954 Yüz Yıl Süren Boyunduruk*. Ankara: Ankara Ticaret Odası.

Öztürk, Murat. 2012. *Agriculture, Peasantry, and Poverty in Turkey in the Neo-liberal Age*. Wageningen: Wageningen Academic Publishers.

Pachirat, Timothy. 2013. *Every Twelve Seconds: Industrialized Slaughter and the Politics of Sight*. New Haven, CT: Yale University Press.

Pamuk, Şevket. 1986. İkinci Dünya Savaşı Yıllarında İaşe Sorunu ve Köylülük. *Tarih ve Toplum* (35): 281–285.

Pamuk, Şevket. 1999. İkinci Dünya Savaşı Yıllarında İaşe Politikası ve Köylülük. In *75 Yılda Köylerden Şehirlere*, Oya Köymen (ed.), 57–66. İstanbul: Tarih Vakfı Yayınları.

Pamuk, Şevket. 2012. *Osmanlıdan Cumhuriyete Küreselleşme, İktisat Politikaları ve Büyüme – Seçme Eserleri II*. İstanbul: Türkiye İş Bankası Kültür Yayınları.

Pamuk, Şevket. 2014. *Osmanlı Ekonomisi ve Kurumları – Seçme Eserleri I*. İstanbul: Türkiye İş Bankası Kültür Yayınları.

Pamuk, Şevket. 2015. *Türkiye'nin 200 Yıllık İktisadi Tarihi: Büyüme, Kurumlar ve Bölüşüm*. İstanbul: Türkiye İş Bankası Kültür Yayınları.

Patel, Raj. 2007. *Stuffed and Starved: The Hidden Battle for the World Food System*. New York, NY: Portobello Books.

Philpott, Daniel. 2016. Sovereignty. The *Stanford Encyclopedia of Philosophy*. Edward N. Zalta (ed.). Accessed: August 8, 2019. Retrieved from: https://plato.stanford.edu/archives/sum2016/entries/sovereignty/.

Pilcher, Jeffrey. M. 2008. Taco Bell, Maseca, and Slow Food: A Postmodern Apocalypse for Mexico's Peasant Cuisine? In *Food and Culture: A Reader*, Carole Counihan, and Penny van Esterik, (eds.), 400–410. New York, NY: Routledge.

Pitkin, Hannah. 1964a. Hobbes's Concept of Representation-I. *The American Political Science Review* 58(2): 328–340.

Pitkin, Hannah. 1964b. Hobbes's Concept of Representation-II. *The American Political Science Review* 58(4): 902–918.

Pitkin, Hannah. 1967. *The Concept of Representation*. Berkeley, CA: University of California Press.

Polanyi, Karl. 2001. *The Great Transformation: The Political and Economic Origins of Our Time*. Boston, MA: Beacon Press.

Poppendieck, Janet. 2013. Want Amid Plenty: From Hunger to Inequality. In *Food and Culture: A Reader*, Carole Counihan and Penny van Esterik (eds.), 563–571. New York, NY: Routledge.

Purdam, Kingsley, Elisabeth A. Garratt, and Aneez Esmail. 2015. Hungry? Food Insecurity, Social Stigma and Embarrassment in the UK. *Sociology* 50(6): 1072–1088.

Robins, Kevin, and Asu Aksoy. 1995. Istanbul Rising: Returning the Repressed to Urban Culture. *European Urban and Regional Studies* 2(3): 223–235.

Robins, Kevin, and Asu Aksoy. 2012. Reshaping, Installing, Pioneering, Spearheading ... Realignment of Istanbul. In *Cities, Cultural Policy and Governance*, Helmut K. Anheier and Yudhisthir Raj Isar (eds.), 184–193. New York, NY: Sage.

Rostow, Walt Whitman. 1960. *The Stages of Economic Growth: A Non-Communist Manifesto*. Cambridge: Cambridge University Press.

Rousseau, Jean Jacques. 1972. *The Social Contract*. New York, NY: Penguin Books.

Sakaoğlu, Necdet. 1994a. Bostancıbaşı Defterleri. In *Dünden Bugüne İstanbul Ansiklopedisi*, İlhan Tekeli et al. (eds.), vol. 2, 308. İstanbul: Tarih Vakfı Yayınları.

Sakaoğlu, Necdet. 1994b. Bostancı Ocağı. In *Dünden Bugüne İstanbul Ansiklopedisi*, İlhan Tekeli et al. (eds.), vol. 2, 305–307. İstanbul: Tarih Vakfı Yayınları.

Sakaoğlu, Necdet. 2007. *20. Yüzyılın Başında Osmanlı Coğrafyası (1907–1908)*. İstanbul: DenizKültür Yayınları.

Sakaoğlu, Necdet, and Nuri Akbayar. 2000. *Osmanlı Dünyasından Yansımalar*. İstanbul: Creative Yayıncılık.

Samancı, Özge. 2009. 1835 Yılına Ait Bir Narh Defterine Göre İstanbul'da Bazı Gıdaların Fiyatları. *Yemek ve Kültür* 17: 56–60.

Schlosser, Eric. 2008. The Chain Never Stops. In *Food and Culture: A Reader*, Carole Counihan and Penny van Esterik (eds.), 441–451. New York, NY: Routledge.

Schmitt, Carl. 1976. *The Concept of the Political*. George Schwab (trans.). New Brunswick, NJ: Rutgers University Press.

Schrock, Thomas S. 1991. The Rights to Punish and Resist Punishment in Hobbes's Leviathan. *The Western Political Quarterly* 44(4): 853–890.

Searcey, Dionne, and Matt Richtel. 2017. Obesity was Rising as Ghana Embraced Fast Food. Then Came KFC. *The New York Times*. Accessed: January 20, 2020. Retrieved from: https://www.nytimes.com/2017/10/02/health/ghana-kfc-obesity.html.

Seidman, Guy. 2008. Unexceptional for once: Austerity and food rationing in Israel, 1939–1959. *Southern California Interdisciplinary Law Journal* 18(1): 95–130.

Sencer, Muzaffer. 1999. Toprak Reformu Çabaları ve Tartışmaları. In *75 Yılda Köylerden Şehirlere*, Oya Köymen (ed.), 22–25. İstanbul: Tarih Vakfı Yayınları.

Sey, Yıldız. 1993. Apartman. In *Dünden Bugüne İstanbul Ansiklopedisi*, İlhan Tekeli et al. (eds.), vol. 1, 281–283. İstanbul: Tarih Vakfı Yayınları.

Sheridan, Patricia. 2011. Resisting the Scaffold: Self-Preservation and Limits of Obligation in Hobbes's Leviathan. *Hobbes Studies* 24(2): 137–157.

Silier, Oya. 1981. *Türkiye'de Tarımsal Yapının Gelişimi (1923–1938)*. İstanbul: Boğaziçi Üniversitesi Yayınları.

Smith, Adam. 1982. *The Wealth of Nations: Books 1–3*. New York, NY: Penguin Classics.

Soyak, Alkan. 1996. *Teknolojik Gelişme ve Özelleştirme: Telekomünikasyon Sektörü Üzerine Bir Uygulama*. İstanbul: Kavram Yayınları.

Sputnik News TR. 2019. AK Partili Akbaşoğlu: Asgari ücretle geçinen 5 kişilik aile 3 öğün çay-simit tüketirse 1120 lira cebinde kalır. *Sputnik News TR*. Accessed: May 21,

2019. Retrieved from: https://tr.sputniknews.com/turkiye/201904171038787026-ak-partili-akbasoglu-asgari-ucretli-gunde-uc-ogun-simit-yerse-1120-lira-cebine-kalir/.

Srinivas, Tulasi. 2008. "As Mother Made It": The Cosmopolitan Indian Family, "Authentic" Food, and the Construction of Cultural Utopia. In *Food and Culture: A Reader*, Carole Counihan and Penny van Esterik (eds.), 355–376. New York, NY: Routledge.

Steinberger, Peter J. 2002. Hobbesian Resistance. *American Journal of Political Science* 46(4): 856–865.

Swonk, Diane, David Rosenberg, Mohamed A. El-Erian, Adam Posen, Eduardo Porter, and Trevor Jackson. 2020. Why are stocks soaring in the middle of a pandemic? *Foreign Policy*. Accessed: May 29, 2020. Retrieved from: https://foreignpolicy.com/2020/05/29/stock-market-rally-coronavirus-pandemic/.

T.C. Ticaret Bakanlığı. 2020. Ürün Fiyat Detayları (Ocak 20 2020). Accessed: January 21, 2020 Retrieved from: T.C. Ticaret Bakanlığı Hal Kayıt Sistemi http://www.hal.gov.tr/Sayfalar/FiyatDetaylari.aspx.

Tabakoğlu, Ahmet. 1987. Osmanlı Ekonomisinde Fiyat Denetimi. *İstanbul Üniversitesi İktisat Fakültesi Mecmuası*, 111–150.

Tabakoğlu, Ahmet. 2014. Osmanlı Döneminde İstanbul'un İaşesi. *Osmanlı İstanbulu Uluslararası Sempozyumu*. İstanbul: İstanbul 29 Mayıs Üniversitesi, 99–168.

Tanielian, Melanie S. 2018. *The Charity of War: Famine, Humanitarian Aid and World War I in the Middle East*. Stanford, CA: Stanford University Press.

Tanyeli, Uğur. 2010. Apartmanlar. In *İstanbul Ansiklopedisi*, 134–137. İstanbul: NTV Yayınları.

Tekeli, İlhan. 1984. Sunuş. In *Türkiye'de ve Dünyada Yaşanan Ekonomik Bunalım*, İlhan Tekeli (ed.), 7–28. Ankara: Yurt Yayınları.

Tekeli, İlhan. 1985. Tanzimat'tan Cumhuriyet'e Kentsel Dönüşüm. In *Tanzimat'tan Cumhuriyet'e Türkiye Ansiklopedisi*, Murat Belge et al. (eds.), 878–890. İstanbul: İletişim Yayınları.

Tekeli, İlhan. 2009. *Modernizm, Modernite ve Türkiye'nin Kent Planlama Tarihi*. İstanbul: Tarih Vakfı Yayınları.

Tekeli, İlhan. 2011. *Kent, Kentli Hakları, Kentleşme ve Kentsel Dönüşüm Yazıları*. İstanbul: Tarih Vakfı Yayınları.

Tekeli, İlhan, and Selim İlkin. 1999. Devletçilik Dönemi Tarım Politikaları (Modernleşme Çabaları). In *75 Yılda Köylerden Şehirlere*, Oya Köymen (ed.), 43–56. İstanbul: Tarih Vakfı Yayınları.

Temel, Mehmet. 1998. Mütareke Döneminde İstanbul'un İaşe Sorunu. *Toplumsal Tarih* 9(52): 40–45.

Tokdemir, Ertuğrul. 1988. *Türkiye'de Tarımsal Yapı (1923–1933)*. İstanbul: İstanbul Teknik Üniversitesi.

Toprak, Zafer. 1978. Cihan Harbi Yıllarında İttihat ve Terakki'nin İaşe Politikası. *Boğaziçi Üniversitesi Dergisi* 6: 211–225.

Toprak, Zafer. 1982. *Türkiye'de Milli İktisat (1908–1918)*. Ankara: Yurt Yayınları.

Toprak, Zafer. 1985. Tanzimat'tan Sonra İktisadi Politika. In *Tanzimat'tan Cumhuriyet'e Türkiye Ansiklopedisi*, Murat Belge et al. (eds.), 668–671. İstanbul: İletişim Yayınları.

Toprak, Zafer. 1994a. Altıncı Daire-i Belediye. In *Dünden Bugüne İstanbul Ansiklopedisi*, İlhan Tekeli et al. (eds.), vol. 1, 220–223. İstanbul: Tarih Vakfı Yayınları.

Toprak, Zafer. 1994b. Birinci Dünya Savaşı'nda İstanbul. In *Dünden Bugüne İstanbul Ansiklopedisi*, İlhan Tekeli et al. (eds.), vol. 2, 239–243. İstanbul: Tarih Vakfı Yayınları.

Türk-İş. 2018. *Asgari Ücret Değerlendirme Raporu*. Ankara: Türkiye İşçi Sendikaları Federasyonu.

Turkish Statistical Institute. (2019, 10). Unemployment. Ankara.

Turkkan, Candan. 2016. What is Being Sustained? Sustainability and Food Exchange Sites in Istanbul. In *Women, Urbanization, Sustainability: Practices of Survival, Adaptation, and Resistance*, Anita Lacey (ed.), 119–154. New York, NY: Palgrave Macmillan.

Turkkan, Candan. 2018. Feeding the global city: urban transformation and urban food supply chain in 21st-century Istanbul. *Journal of Urbanism: International Research on Placemaking and Urban Sustainability* 26(2): 181–202.

TZMOB. 2017. Üretici market fiyatlarında Nisan ayı. Retrieved from Türkiye Ziraat Odaları Birliği. Accessed: January 20, 2020. Retrieved from: https://www.tzob.org.tr/basin-odasi/haberler/uretici-market-fiyatlarinda-nisan-ayi.

TZMOB. 2019. Üretici market fiyatlarında Kasım ayı. Retrieved from Türkiye Ziraat Odaları Birliği. Accessed: January 20, 2020. Retrieved from: https://www.tzob.org.tr/basin-odasi/haberler/uretici-market-fiyatlarinda-kasim-ayi...20191202095645.

Ünsal, Artun. 2010. Semt Pazarları. In *İstanbul Ansiklopedisi*, 815–819. İstanbul: NTV Yayınları.

Uzun, Ahmet. 2006. *İstanbul'un İaşesinde Devletin Rolü: Ondalık Ağnam Uygulaması 1783–1857*. Ankara: Türk Tarih Kurumu Yayınları.

Uzun, Cemile Nil. 2003. The Impact of Urban Renewal and Gentrification on Urban Fabric: Three Cases in Turkey. *Royal Dutch Geographical Society* 94(3): 363–375.

Waever, Matthew. 2018. KFC was warned about switching UK delivery contractor, union says. *The Guardian*. Accessed: February 20, 2018. Retrieved from: https://www.theguardian.com/business/2018/feb/20/kfc-was-warned-about-switching-uk-delivery-contractor-union-says.

Wallerstein, Immanuel. 1974. *The Modern World-System I: Capitalist Agriculture and the Origins of the European World-Economy in the Sixteenth Century*. New York, NY: Academic Press.

Warrender, Howard. 1957. *The Political Philosophy of Hobbes: His Theory of Obligation*. Oxford: Clarendon Press.

Winson, Anthony. 1983. The Formation of Capitalist Agriculture in Latin America and Its Relationship to Political Power and the State. *Comparative Studies in Society and History* 25(1): 83–104.

Wise, Timothy. 2019. *Eating Tomorrow: Agribusiness, Family Farmers and the Battle for the Future of Food.* New York, NY: The New Press.

Wolters, Eugene. 2014. Understanding Jean Baudrillard with Pumpkin Spice Lattes. *Critical Theory.* Accessed: January 19, 2020. Retrieved from: http://www.critical-theory.com/understanding-jean-baudrillard-with-pumpkin-spice-lattes/.

Wright, Thomas C. 1985. The Politics of Urban Provisioning in Latin American History. In *Food, Politics, and Society in Latin America*, Thomas C. Wright and John C. Super (eds.), 24–45. Lincoln, NE: University of Nebraska Press.

Yaltırık, Faik. 1993. Bahçeler. In *Dünden Bugüne İstanbul Ansiklopedisi*, İlhan Tekeli et al. (eds.), vol. 1, 542–548. İstanbul: Tarih Vakfı Yayınları.

Yenal, Zafer. 2014. Tarım ve Gıda Üretiminin Yeniden Yapılanması ve Uluslararasılaşma. In *Bildiğimiz Tarımın Sonu: Küresel İktidar ve Köylülük*, Çağlar Keyder and Zafer Yenal, 103–136. İstanbul: İletişim Yayınları.

Yükseker, Deniz. 2004. Trust and Gender in a Transnational Market: The Public Culture of Laleli, Istanbul. *Public Culture* 16(1): 47–65.

Yurt Ansiklopedisi. 1981. Istanbul. In *Yurt Ansiklopedisi: Türkiye, İl İl: Dünü, Bugünü, Yarını*, Taha Parla et al. (eds.), vols. 5 and 6, 3765–4240. İstanbul: Anadolu Yayıncılık.

Zarka, Yves Charles. 2004. The Political Subject. In *Leviathan after 350 Years*, Tom Sorell and Luc Foisneau (eds.), 167–182. Oxford: Oxford University Press.

Zürcher, Erik Jan. 1997. *Turkey: A Modern History.* New York, NY: St. Martin's Press.

Index

Printed in the United States
by Baker & Taylor Publisher Services